Transfer Pricing Developments Around the World 2020

Transfer Pricing Developments Around the World 2020

Edited by

Michael Lang

Raffaele Petruzzi

Wolters Kluwer

Published by:
Kluwer Law International B.V.
PO Box 316
2400 AH Alphen aan den Rijn
The Netherlands
E-mail: international-sales@wolterskluwer.com
Website: lrus.wolterskluwer.com

Sold and distributed in North, Central and South America by:
Wolters Kluwer Legal & Regulatory U.S.
7201 McKinney Circle
Frederick, MD 21704
United States of America
Email: customer.service@wolterskluwer.com

Sold and distributed in all other countries by:
Air Business Subscriptions
Rockwood House
Haywards Heath
West Sussex
RH16 3DH
United Kingdom
Email: international-customerservice@wolterskluwer.com

ISBN 978-94-035-2392-7

e-Book: ISBN 978-94-035-2393-4
web-PDF: ISBN 978-94-035-2394-1

Editors

Prof. Dr. DDr. h.c. Michael Lang is Head of the Institute for Austrian and International Tax Law of WU (Vienna University of Economics and Business, Austria) and academic director of both the LL.M. Program in International Tax Law and the Doctoral Program in International Business Taxation (DIBT) of this university. He is president of the Austrian Branch of the International Fiscal Association (IFA) and has been a visiting professor at Georgetown University, Washington, DC; New York University, New York; Sorbonne, France; Bocconi, Italy; Peking University (PKU), China; University of New South Wales (Sydney), and at other universities.

Dr. Raffaele Petruzzi is the Managing Director of the WU Transfer Pricing Center at the Institute for Austrian and International Tax Law at WU (Vienna University of Economics and Business) and an international tax advisor specializing in international corporate taxation and transfer pricing at L&P Global (Vienna, Austria) and at Ludovici Piccone & Partners (Milan, Italy).

Since 2007, Raffaele has gained extensive experience in dealing with topics related to international corporate taxation and transfer pricing, both from a professional and an academic perspective. From the professional perspective, he has gained relevant experience in advising clients on specific topics (e.g., international tax issues and transfer pricing issues related to services, permanent establishments, financing, business restructuring, intangibles, and indirect taxes), international tax and transfer pricing risk management and compliance, drafting and reviewing intra-group agreements, optimizing international tax structures, as well as implementing mechanisms of dispute avoidance (e.g., rulings and APAs) and dispute resolution (e.g., MAPs and arbitrations). From the academic perspective, he is a frequent speaker in international conferences and lecturer of numerous courses (in Europe, Asia, and Latin America), as well as author of many publications on international tax and transfer pricing topics. Moreover, he regularly cooperates with professionals in advisory, the business community, governments and international organizations (e.g., OECD, United Nations, World Bank Group, European Commission). *Inter alia*, he has gained experience in providing assistance on tax policy issues, capacity building for tax administrations, and advising governments on projects related to fight against tax evasion. Finally, among others, he is a member of the United Nations Subcommittee on Article 9 (Associated enterprises: Transfer Pricing), of the International Fiscal Association (IFA), and of Transfer Pricing Economists for Development (TPED).

Raffaele holds a Master of Science in Business Administration and Law (major: Corporate Taxation) at Bocconi University (Italy), a Master of Laws (LL.M.) in International Tax Law at WU, and a Ph.D. in International Business Taxation at WU.

Contributors

Markus Baur is Tax Director for Transfer Pricing at IBM, based in Vienna/Austria. He is the Transfer Pricing leader for EMEA and AP. His responsibilities cover global Transfer Pricing advance pricing agreements (APAs) and Controversy. Since joining IBM in 1999, he has held various positions in tax and finance. Before joining IBM he worked for a local law firm and a Big Four firm in Germany. Markus has a Law degree and is specialized in international taxation.

Thomas D. Bettge is a senior associate with KPMG LLP's national Transfer Pricing Dispute Resolution practice, specializing in transfer pricing controversies and related international tax matters. He has co-authored numerous articles on transfer pricing and related topics, and contributes to two treatises published by Warren Gorham & Lamont: Transfer Pricing Strategies and U.S. International Taxation—Practice and Procedure. He obtained a J.D. from the Penn State Dickinson School of Law, where he graduated first in his class.

Svitlana Buriak is a teaching and research associate at the Institute for Austrian and International Tax Law at WU (Vienna University of Economics and Business, Austria) cooperating with the WU Transfer Pricing Center. She received her Law degree from the National Law University in Kharkiv, Ukraine, in 2016 and an LL.M. in International Business Law from the Central European University in Budapest, Hungary, in 2017. Svitlana is pursuing a doctoral degree in Business Law at the WU where she writes her dissertation on the topic of corporate taxation of highly digitalized MNEs. Svitlana has also gained practical experience in corporate taxation and transfer pricing while working in the Tax and Investment Law Department of ILF Law Firm, (Kyiv, Ukraine).

Giammarco Cottani is Director Global Tax Policy at Netflix, where he oversees all direct and indirect tax public policy-related issues the group faces in all the countries in which it operates.

Previously, Mr. Cottani was a partner of the international tax law firm Ludovici Piccone & Partners, where he coordinated the transfer pricing practice with regard to dispute prevention and resolution and complex audit assistance for large multinational enterprises. Before that, he was an adviser to the Italian tax authorities on international tax and transfer pricing issues and was one of the delegates for Italy involved in the Organisation for Economic Co-operation and Development (OECD) BEPS (base erosion and profit shifting) Project. Prior to that, he worked as a transfer pricing adviser in the Transfer Pricing Unit of the OECD, where he was involved in the introduction of the new Chapter IX of the OECD Transfer Pricing Guidelines concerning business restructurings. He has (co-)led over twenty events in the area of transfer pricing for a number of non-OECD countries and has also been involved in a number of technical assistance projects for tax administrations on behalf of international and regional organizations in various parts of the world.

Mr. Cottani has been involved in a number of ongoing technical assistance projects for the tax administrations of three EU Member States, mainly in the areas of transfer pricing, manipulation of profit by using permanent establishments and aggressive tax planning. Furthermore, he regularly lectures at postgraduate courses in International Taxation both in Europe and the Americas.

Stefaan De Baets has been Senior Counsel in the Transfer Pricing team of PwC Belgium since January 1, 2016, where he is responsible for avoiding and settling transfer pricing controversy, further developing the transfer pricing market, and promoting the key presence of PwC on that market as well as delivering contributions to the development of transfer pricing policies. From April 1, 2011 to December 31, 2015, he was Transfer Pricing Advisor at the OECD in Paris, France. Until he joined the OECD, Stefaan worked for the Federal Public Service of Finances in Belgium, mostly on transfer pricing, for more than twenty years. He was a delegate for Belgium to the OECD Working Party 6 (transfer pricing) from March 1996 to March 2011 and to the Joint Transfer Pricing Forum form March 2003 to March 2011. Stefaan is a guest lecturer on international taxation at the University of Lausanne (Switzerland), the Catholic University of Leuven (Belgium), and the Ecole des Mines (France).

Between 2015 and 2018, Giammarco has been involved in a number of technical assistance projects for tax administrations in several LATAM countries on behalf of international and regional organizations: CIAT (Panama); SRI (Ecuador); DIAN (Colombia 2018). Giammarco is a lecturer at Wien University—WU Transfer Pricing Centre and a lecturer at the Advanced LL.M. in International Tax Law, University of Leiden (the Netherlands). He received his degree in Law and Economics from LUISS Rome University in 2003, an LL.M. in European and International Taxation from the European Tax College (Tilburg and Leuven) in 2005, and a Ph.D. in Corporate Taxation from LUISS Rome University in 2009.

Karol Dziwiński received his Law degree from the University of Warsaw, Poland, in 2016 and a first level master's in Italian Law from the University of Catania, Italy, in 2017. Currently, he is a research and teaching associate at the Institute for Austrian and International Tax Law, WU (Vienna University of Economics and Business, Austria) and a team member of the WU Transfer Pricing Center. He also cooperates scientifically in the area of international tax law with Henkel AG & Co. KGaA in Düsseldorf, Germany, focusing on transfer pricing issues. Karol is pursuing a doctoral degree in

Business Law at the WU where he writes his dissertation on the topic of DEMPE functions and intangibles. Previously, he worked in the tax advisory department of KPMG Poland in Warsaw.

Mark J. Horowitz is a Principal in KPMG LLP's national Transfer Pricing Dispute Resolution practice and has fifteen years of experience assisting clients with transfer pricing issues. He primarily represents multinational enterprises in transfer pricing and international tax controversy matters, such as APAs, competent authority cases, examinations, and various other matters. He also has extensive experience regarding the planning, structuring, and documentation of transfer pricing arrangements.

Diana Kabir is an economic analyst in NERA's Transfer Pricing Practice, based in London. Her expertise includes analyzing related-party cross-border transactions and constructing arm's length solutions for clients based on robust economic analysis. Her primary transfer pricing focus is in the financial services arena. Ms. Kabir began her career at the Australian Taxation Office, Australia's tax administration, and spent five years working her way up to become a Transfer Pricing Manager. Since Ms. Kabir joined NERA, she has brought her experience with government transfer pricing audits and APAs to the NERA team.

Ms. Kabir has assisted with building practical and adaptable transfer pricing analysis tools for Eastern European tax authorities and worked on APA guidance with clients. Her current focus is on providing consulting services and necessary documentation for a broad range of financial services sectors, including asset management, real estate, and private and retail banking, among others. She has undertaken analysis on loan pricing, interest rate benchmarking, guarantees, and project finance, to name a few.

Ms. Kabir received a bachelor of Commerce (liberal studies) from the University of NSW, Australia. She also completed her master's in Economics at UNSW with a focus on macroeconomic analysis, econometric measurement, and public policy.

Mark R. Martin is a Principal in KPMG LLP's Washington National Tax practice. He is a former adjunct professor in the Graduate Tax Program at the University of Cincinnati and Attorney-Advisor in the United States Tax Court. With over twenty years of experience, Mark Martin regularly advises clients on complex international tax and transfer pricing restructuring projects. Mark Martin also advises clients on all aspects of tax controversy, including competent authority discussions and APA negotiations covering a wide range of industries, including retail, consumer electronics, energy, chemicals, and financial products. Mark Martin is the author and co-author of numerous articles and other publications on tax issues, including several treatises published by Warren Gorham & Lamont: Transfer Pricing Strategies and U.S. International Taxation—Practice and Procedure. Mark is also a regularly featured speaker on tax issues at conferences, seminars, meetings, and other events. Prior to joining KPMG, Mark Martin led the U.S. and International Tax Practice and the Transfer Pricing Affinity Group at a large global law firm.

Emily Muyaa is the Managing Principal for Sub-Saharan Africa in the IBFD Africa and Middle East Department. In this capacity, she oversees IBFD's product offering in the region. Ms. Muyaa regularly works in an advisory capacity for African governments on international tax (including transfer pricing) and lectures at IBFD international tax training courses. She is a Member of the United Nations Transfer Pricing Subcommittee. Ms. Muyaa is the Project Manager for the IBFD Centre of Studies in African Taxation (CSAT), a think tank devoted to the study and development of African taxation. She is a founding member of the Transfer Pricing Economists for Development (TPED—www.tped.eu), a Paris-based think tank that aims to promote business economics knowledge-sharing in transfer pricing, for emerging economies.

Ms. Muyaa is a visiting lecturer at the University of Cape Town, South Africa and the University of Amsterdam, the Netherlands. Before joining IBFD in 2014, she worked in the Transfer Pricing Division of the Large Taxpayers Office at the Kenya Revenue Authority. She holds a certificate in tax administration from the Kenya Revenue Authority Training Institute (now Kenya School of Revenue Administration), an undergraduate degree in Law from the University of Nairobi, a postgraduate diploma in Law from the Kenya School of Law and an LL.M (Adv.) in International Taxation from the International Tax Center at Leiden University, the Netherlands. During her LL.M studies, Ms. Muyaa also worked at the Transfer Pricing Division of EY Amsterdam. She holds an advanced diploma in accounting and business from the Association of Chartered Certified Accountants (ACCA) and is an advocate of the High Court of Kenya and a member of the Law Society of Kenya.

Wendy Nicholls is joint global head of transfer pricing for the Grant Thornton member firms. She has thirty years of international tax experience and is recognized in the Euromoney Guides to the World's Leading Transfer Pricing Advisers and the World's Leading Woman in Business Law.

She sits on the EU Joint Transfer Pricing Forum where government, tax authority and business representatives work to solve practical transfer pricing issues within Europe, and recently provided particular input on the topic of profit splits.

Wendy advises on transfer pricing planning, dispute resolution, APA, implementation and documentation. She helps clients deal with the BEPS changes. She is a regular speaker and author and has acted as an expert witness in the field. Wendy also has expertise in sectors where intellectual property is important, including technology and brands.

Sid Paruthi has been providing transfer pricing consulting services since 1998. He has extensive experience helping companies evaluate their transfer pricing strategies, preparing economic valuation modeling, and providing support for planning and compliance with local transfer pricing rules.

Sid has a thorough understanding of transactions, including intangible property migration; buy-ins, cost-sharing, and transfers of tangible goods; services and royalties; APA; and competent authority matters.

He has experience with companies in a wide variety of industries, including technology (hardware and software), consumer electronics, life sciences, and manufacturing and distribution.

Prior to joining Moss Adams, Sid spent seven years as the global head of transfer pricing at Apple and Oracle. Earlier in his career, he worked for Big Four firms across Europe and the United States, where his clients included Fortune 100 companies.

Amanda Pletz, an Associate Director in NERA's Transfer Pricing Practice, specializes in cross-border related-party transactional pricing and asset valuation issues with a focus on the financial services sector and financing arrangements. She has also been involved in a range of studies for multinationals across a plethora of sectors. In the financial services sector, Ms. Pletz has carried out a range of transfer pricing studies in private banking, asset management, private equity, real estate, insurance, trading, and retail banking, among others. In financing, she has advised on intercompany capital structure issues; cash pooling; pricing of loans; hybrid instruments; guarantees; captive insurance arrangements; leasing, loan, company, and other asset valuations. Her valuation experience also extends into oil field exploration ventures.

Ms. Pletz provides expert opinion reports in relation to tax audits globally and has assisted clients with economic analysis for advanced pricing agreements with local authorities across Europe. In litigation, she has been involved in cases considering intercompany guarantees, retrospective banking business valuations, financing arrangements, and trade analyses. She has also been involved in dispute cases involving state aid and has provided economic analysis for international arbitration.

Ms. Pletz regularly speaks on the economics of intercompany financing transactions and transfer pricing issues in the financial services sector. She has been recognized by Who's Who Legal in their Consulting and Corporate Tax Experts 2019 directory, where clients recommended her for her "thorough and detailed economic analysis" and praised her "understanding of not just the economics of transfer pricing, but also of how to apply them in a particular business context."

Ms. Pletz lectured on economics and banking for the University of Pretoria, South Africa and on microeconomics for the London School of Hygiene and Tropical Medicine of the University of London. She is also a guest speaker at the University of Lausanne, Switzerland and has been lecturing as part of the university's executive program in transfer pricing on the economics of intercompany financing transactions. Ms. Pletz holds master's, honors, and bachelor's degrees in Economics from the University of Pretoria.

Sam Sim is a member of International Association of Tax Judges, Practice Council of New York University School of Law and of ADIT Committee of UK Chartered Institute of Taxation.

Mr. Sim was Regional Vice-President (Europe, Middle-East, Africa, Asia and Latin America) of TEI. He has led global teams as Deputy Global Head of Transfer Pricing and Transfer Pricing Geo Leader for EMEA and Asia-Pacific in large FTSE 100 and Fortune 100 MNEs.

He is passionate about digital taxation and transfer pricing, holds an appointment as a research fellow at the Center for Artificial Intelligence at SMU and has co-authored IEEE and IBM Research papers on Blockchain. This is in addition to graduate level teaching at the Master of Tax program at Singapore University of Social Science, University of Leiden's Executive Tax Program, Vienna University's Transfer Pricing program and IBFD programs. He practiced as a New York tax attorney and is the author of *The Logic and Practice of Transfer Pricing* (Lexis-Nexis), *Singapore Transfer Pricing Masterguide* 2018/2019 (CCH) and co-editor of *Asia Voices: BEPS and Beyond* (IBFD).

Isabel Verlinden leads PwC's Global Transfer Pricing practice with over 3,000 full-time Transfer Pricing experts. In that capacity, she is a member of PwC's Global Tax Leadership team. She gathered first-hand knowledge of the TP challenges faced by companies operating across the globe based on over twenty years of experience working for PwC (and its legacy Firms) in Brussels and Washington, DC.

For many years, Isabel helps navigating leading global companies in a vast array of industries through the pitfalls stemming from cross-border transactions where domestic rules may lack coherence and consistency not to mention lack of adaptation to the rapidly evolving world market by technological advancement. This is typically an area where direct tax and the growing attention to indirect taxes come together in the analysis. Her work is often accompanied by ensuring upfront certainty through APAs. In the absence of upfront assurance, seeking effective means to alleviate double taxation is part of her day-to-day practice as well. She represents PwC vis-à-vis the OECD in all Transfer Pricing related matters.

She is also PwC's representative at the European Commission's Joint Transfer Pricing Forum.

She is an active writer for international tax and business periodicals. She has (co-)authored over one-hundred articles and books to date. She is often solicited by academia and event organizers to talk about transfer pricing. Isabel has a degree in Applied Economics (University of Louvain, Belgium)—Major International Business Affairs, a degree in Financial Economics (Brussels University, Belgium)—Major in Accountancy and a degree in commercial and Financial Sciences (Brussels University)—Major in Fiscal Sciences.

Summary of Contents

Table of Contents

CHAPTER 1
Global Transfer Pricing Developments

Svitlana Buriak & Karol Dziwiński

1 RECENT DEVELOPMENTS ON THE WORK OF INTERNATIONAL ORGANIZATIONS

1.1 Transfer Pricing Developments at the OECD

1.1.1 Digitalization of the Economy

Addressing the tax challenges of the digitalized economy remained to be a priority in the Organisation for Economic Co-operation and Development's (OECD's) agenda in 2019. In the beginning of the year, the Inclusive Framework issued a Policy Note on Addressing the Tax Challenges of the Digitalisation of the Economy.[1] Under this Policy Note, the Inclusive Framework agreed, on a without prejudice basis, to undertake work on the following two pillars:

- *Pillar 1* addresses the allocation of taxing rights between jurisdictions and describes proposals for new profit allocation and nexus rules based on the concepts of "significant economic presence" as well as the exploitation of "user participation" and "marketing intangibles" in a jurisdiction.
- *Pillar 2* (also referred to as the Global Anti-Base Erosion Proposal (GloBE) proposal) calls for the development of a coordinated set of rules to address ongoing risks from structures that allow multinational enterprises (MNEs) to shift profit to jurisdictions where they are subject to no or very low taxation.

1.1.2 Pillar 1 and the Secretariat's Proposal for a "Unified Approach"

The duration and intensity of the project on updating the current tax treaty model to address the challenges posed by technological developments illustrate the complexity of the issues both from the technical and from political perspectives. The project is of high relevance and importance for all countries around the globe since it will ultimately reshape the current international tax system and will lay down new rules that might affect the international trade, structures of global value chains, and how much value and taxes are captured by different jurisdictions. The work of the OECD on the issue has been continuing full stream even during the outbreak of the coronavirus in spring 2020 which places high pressure on the policy makers and responsibility to deliver the outcomes within the timeframe set by the G20 Ministers of Finance. Hence, the authors are looking forward to a final consensus-based solution that is expected to be adopted already later this year. Let us recall the most relevant milestones of the project made by the OECD and G20/OECD Inclusive Framework on Base erosion and profit shifting (BEPS).

In February 2019, the OECD published a public consultation document on possible solutions to the tax challenges arising from the digitalization of the economy.[1] The Inclusive Framework put forward three proposals based on views of different countries on how those challenges could be tackled, which are the following:[2]

(1) *User participation* (suggested by the United Kingdom (U.K.): this proposal suggested modifying current profit allocation rules to require the allocation of an amount of profit of certain types of highly-digitalized business models to the jurisdiction where those businesses have an "active and participatory" user base.[3]

(2) *Marketing intangibles* (suggested by the United States (U.S.)): the second proposal introduced a concept of marketing intangibles as a profit allocation key building an intrinsic functional link to the market jurisdiction.[4] Such marketing intangibles would include brand and trade name brand, trade name, customer data, and relationships.

(3) *Significant economic presence* (suggested by India): the third proposal was more closely related to the concept of the "source state" and aimed to establish a taxable nexus for MNEs to the jurisdiction where they perform significant economic activities without being physically present there. A significant economic presence could be evidenced by *the existence of a user base and the associated data input; the volume of digital content derived from the jurisdiction; billing and collection in local currency or with a local form of payment; the maintenance of a website in a local language; responsibility for*

1. Public Consultation Document, Addressing the Tax Challenges of the Digitalisation of the Economy, February 13-March 6, 2019, OECD/G20 Base Erosion and Profit Shifting Project, available at https://www.oecd.org/tax/beps/public-consultation-document-addressing-the-tax-challenges-of-the-digitalisation-of-the-economy.pdf, accessed August 28, 2020.
2. OECD, Public Consultation Document, February 13-March 6, 2019, *supra* n 1, section 2.2. *See also*, Capristano Cardoso, Gabriela (2019). Global Transfer Pricing Developments. In: Transfer Pricing Developments Around the World 2019, edited by Lang, Michael, Petruzzi, Raffaele, Storck, Alfred, 1-39. Alphen aan den Rijn: Kluwer Law International.
3. The "user participation" proposal would apply only to highly-digitalized business models like social media platforms, search engines, and online marketplaces since, for such business models, "soliciting the sustained engagement and active participation of users is a critical component of value creation." With respect to the profit allocation mechanics, the proposal put forward an idea to allocate a portion of residual profits of the MNE between all "user jurisdictions" based on a pre-agreed allocation metric (e.g., revenues). OECD, Public Consultation Document, February 13-March 6, 2019, *supra* n 1, paragraphs 18-19, 22.
4. Similar to the "user participation" proposal, a portion of residual profits would be required to be allocated to the market jurisdictions of the MNE.

> *the final delivery of goods to customers or the provision by the enterprise of other support services such as after-sales service or repairs and maintenance; or sustained marketing and sales promotion activities, either online or otherwise, to attract customers.*[5]

A public consultation meeting on the three proposals was held on March 13-14, in Paris where the OECD has received extensive feedback from stakeholders, practitioners, and academics on the strength and weaknesses of each proposal. The user participation proposal received the strongest criticism since it would ring-fence only several types of business models (i.e., social media platforms, search engines, and online marketplaces) and, therefore, would fail to tackle the broader tax challenges of digitalization. The second proposal, while putting forward an interesting idea potentially applicable to any business, did not sufficiently develop a concept of marketing intangibles. Finally, the last proposal was widely supported by many academics, businesses, and practitioners due to its closest alignment with the economic substance of business activities performed in the market jurisdictions. However, the proposal did not specify enough how profits should be allocated to a significant economic presence.

In its further work, the OECD observed that the three alternative proposals contain a number of significant commonalities, which ultimately resulted in releasing a Secretariat Proposal for a "Unified Approach" in October 2019. The Secretariat's Unified Approach suggested creating a new nexus rule allocating taxing rights to the market jurisdiction that is not dependent on physical presence but based on sales revenue.[6] The new nexus does not seem to require, at least not explicitly, any value-creating activities performed in the market state besides sales and, therefore, goes against the concept of "source" under the current OECD Model. In addition, the nexus rule should apply to the enterprises falling within its scope which will cover "automated digital services" and "consumer-facing businesses," the latter being broadly defined as "businesses that generate revenue from supplying consumer products."[7] As of now, these terms do not shed any light on what types of enterprises should be covered and, therefore, the scope of the new taxing right remains unclear.[8]

Concerning the profit allocation rules, the OECD expressed its willingness to make a revolutionary step to adopt the rules of attribution of profits to market jurisdictions that go beyond (and even against) the conventional arm's length principle (hereinafter "ALP"). At the same time, the arm's length profit allocation should still apply in bilateral relations between the source and residence states. Thereby, the

---

5. The OECD proposed a fractional apportionment method in order to allocate the profit to an SEP or a form of withholding tax as a collection mechanism. OECD, Public Consultation Document Addressing the Tax Challenges of the Digitalisation of the Economy, p. 17.
6. OECD, Public Consultation Document: Secretariat Proposal for a "Unified Approach" under Pillar One, October 9, 2019-November 12, 2019 (OECD Secretariat Proposal for a "Unified Approach"), paragraph 17.
7. *Ibid.*, paragraph 20.
8. Buriak, Svitlana (2020). A new taxing right for the market jurisdiction: Where are the limits? Intertax 48(3): pp. 301-316. The new nexus is aimed to be designed as a self-standing treaty provision to avoid any spill-over effect with the existing PE provision. OECD, A Unified Approach, at paragraph 15 and paragraph 22.

proposal creates a so-called three-tier system with different rules of profit allocation that are applicable in relation to the market, source, and residence states.[9] This system, being evidently incoherent, will lead to the intensification of the pricing setting and profit allocation mechanisms. In a nutshell, the three-tier system implies the following profit allocation mechanism:[10]

(1) *Amount A*—a share of deemed residual profit allocated to market jurisdictions using a formulaic approach, i.e., the new taxing right.
(2) *Amount B*—a fixed remuneration for baseline marketing and distribution functions that take place in the market jurisdiction.
(3) *Amount C*—binding and effective dispute prevention and resolution mechanisms relating to all elements of the proposal, including any additional profit for which in-country functions exceed the baseline activity compensated under Amount B.

The proposal made a step toward solving the existing problem of a mismatch between the possibility to remotely conduct economic activities in a jurisdiction and the tax treaties relying on the physical presence to grant jurisdictions a taxing right. However, does the proposal solve more problems than it creates? A tripartite system of profit allocation, multiple layers of taxation potentially resulting in double or triple taxation, a lack of an effective dispute resolution mechanism are the major pitfalls of the current proposal, elimination of which might take additional several years. Moreover, a formulary allocation of profits to the market state which, only based on the sales revenue, is bluntly misaligned with the economic reality of the business activities, differences between business models, and the role of the market in generation of profits. This undermines all of the achievements of the BEPS Project, and Actions 8-10 in particular, the main goal of which was the taxation of profits where value is created.

Chapter 5 of this volume will analyze the issues surrounding the new nexus rule in detail while *Chapter 6* will continue to discuss what could be strengths and weaknesses of the profit allocation mechanism.

1.1.3 Pillar 2: Global Anti-Base Erosion Proposal

The second pillar, also called the GloBE, explores the opportunity of changing the international tax architecture to prevent some risks of shifting profits by MNEs to low-tax jurisdictions. The proposal suggests developing a coordinated set of rules aiming at closing the "tax avoidance gaps" that have not been resolved by the BEPS Project and implementing a minimum taxation of income. The implementation of these rules would require changing domestic law and double tax treaties. The second pillar contains the following four components:[11]

9. Paragraph 15, The Unified Approach.
10. The Unified Approach, at section 15.
11. Public consultation document, Global Anti-Base Erosion Proposal ("GloBE")—Pillar Two, November 8, 2019-December 2, 2019.

(1) *an income inclusion rule* that would provide that the income of a foreign branch or a controlled entity should be subject to tax provided that the income was taxed in the foreign jurisdiction at an effective rate that is below a minimum rate;
(2) *an undertaxed payments rule* providing a denial of a deduction or imposition of source-based taxation (including withholding tax) for a payment in a related-party transaction provided that the payment was not subject to tax at or was taxed below a minimum rate;
(3) *a subject to tax rule* complementing the undertaxed payment rule by subjecting a payment to withholding or other taxes at source and adjusting eligibility for treaty benefits on certain items of income;
(4) *a switch-over rule* would be implemented into tax treaties that would allow a residence state to switch from an exemption to a credit method for which the profits attributable to a permanent establishment (PE) or derived from immovable property (i.e., not part of a PE) are subject to an effective rate below the minimum one.

The main idea behind the proposal is to make profit shifting less attractive and to provide less opportunity for "excessive" tax competition. The economic studies provide some evidence that MNEs shift profits to tax havens and low-tax jurisdictions by means of transfer mispricing[12] and financing structures[13] or by re-allocating IP[14] and risks.[15,16] The advantageous effect of the implementation of minimum tax in that regard would be the improvement of international allocation of capital, shifting the profits across a firm's affiliates to low-tax jurisdictions, and mitigating the impact of tax competition on investment decisions.[17]

At the same time, there are still a number of open issues regarding the policy rationale and the necessity of implementing the GloBE as well as its design. First of all, it is not clear which tax avoidance and profit-shifting schemes are aimed to be tackled by the GloBE proposal and were not addressed by the BEPS Project.[18] Second, the minimum tax would significantly limit the fiscal sovereignty of the states to design their

12. Cristea, Anca; Nguyen, Daniel. (2016). Transfer pricing by multinational firms: New evidence from foreign firm ownerships, American Economic Journal: Economic Policy 8(3): pp. 170-202. Davies, Ronald B.; Martin, Julien; Parenti, Mathieu; Toubal, Farid (2018). Knocking on tax haven's door: multinational firms and transfer pricing, Review of Economics and Statistics, MIT Press, vol. 100(1), 120-134.
13. *See* e.g., Huizinga, Harry; Laeven, Luc; Nicodeme, Gaetan (2008). Capital structure and international debt shifting, Journal of Financial Economics 88(1): 80-118.
14. Griffith, R., H. Miller and M O'Connell (2014). Ownership of intellectual property and corporate taxation, Journal of Public Economics 112: 12-23.
15. *See* Becker, J., N. Johannesen, N. Riedel (2018). Taxation and the Allocation of Risk Inside the Multinational Firm, CESifo Working Paper No. 7033.
16. International effective minimum taxation –the GLOBE proposal, Joachim Englisch and Johannes Becker.
17. *Ibid.*
18. Leopoldo Parada, The GloBE Puzzle: A Debate Way Beyond Use of Financial Accounts, available at https://mnetax.com/the-globe-puzzle-a-debate-way-beyond-use-of-financial-accounts-36669, accessed August 28, 2020.

tax policy. Moreover, there are a number of critical design considerations, e.g., (i) how the effective tax rate (ETR) should be calculated and which rate should be agreed upon; (ii) whether there should be any carve-outs from the rules for different tax incentive policies or will they create new BEPS issues; (iii) what type of blending has to be preferred, i.e., global, per jurisdiction, per entity, etc. Finally, there might be some significant problems of compatibility of the GloBE proposal with tax treaties that have to be resolved.[19]

All in all, while aiming to prevent different tax avoidance schemes, one of the key objectives of the GloBE proposal should be to ensure the simplicity of the system and easiness of administration of taxes for both developed and developing countries. With that purpose, a number of simplification measures have to be considered, e.g., for the calculation of the ETR, establishing an order of the application of the proposed rules and their relationship with other domestic and tax treaty provisions, developing of blacklists, and carve-outs.[20]

1.1.4 OECD Transfer Pricing Guidelines for Financial Transactions

In July 2018, the OECD released a Public Discussion Draft on BEPS Actions 8-10 on Financial Transactions (hereinafter "the Discussion Draft").[21] During 2019, Working Party 6 on the Taxation of Multinational Enterprise held several meetings to resolve the twenty-five areas of disagreements identified in the nonconsensus discussion draft.[22] In February 2020, the OECD/G20 finally published a long-awaited Transfer Pricing Guidance on Financial Transactions (hereinafter "the Final Guidance or the Guidance").[23] This document remarks on a significant development of the transfer pricing guidelines (TPG) that previously did not include any specific regulations on determining the arm's length conditions of intra-group financial transactions. The final guidance aims to help eliminate, to a certain extent, the transfer pricing (TP) disputes, inconsistencies, and unclarities around the pricing of financial arrangements. More specifically, the guidance provides clarifications on the accurate delineation of the actual financial transaction with respect to the characterization of the financing instruments as debt or loan, treasury functions, financial guarantees, captive insurance, and determining risk-free and risk-adjusted rates of return. The major changes of the guidance on the

19. *See*, Leopoldo Parada, The GloBE Puzzle: A Debate Way Beyond Use of Financial Accounts.
20. Englisch and Parada.
21. OECD, Public Discussion Draft, BEPS Actions 8-10, Financial Transactions, July 3-September 7, 2018, available at https://www.oecd.org/tax/transfer-pricing/BEPS-actions-8-10-transfer-pricing-financial-transactions-discussion-draft-2018.pdf, accessed August 28, 2020.
22. Julie Martin, Agreement Reached on OECD Transfer Pricing Guidelines for Financial Transactions, Official Says MNE Tax, June 8, 2019, available at https://mnetax.com/final-financial-transaction-transfer-pricing-guidelines-expected-by-year-end-oecd-official-says-34225, accessed August 28, 2020.
23. *Transfer Pricing Guidance on Financial Transactions: Inclusive Framework on BEPS: Actions 4, 8-10*.

pricing of intra-group loans compared to the discussion draft are the more elaborated clarifications on the use of credit ratings and impact of group membership.[24]

1.1.4.1 Determination of Whether a Purported Loan Should Be Regarded as a Loan

On the issue of characterization of loans, the guidance stipulated that it neither prevents countries from implementing approaches to address debt and equity funding of an entity and interest deductibility under domestic legislation nor does it mandate that the way of the accurate delineation suggested by it is the only one to be respected to characterize the corporate financing instruments.[25] Hence, the guidance leaves a margin of freedom for countries to adopt diverse approaches, which might result in double taxation for MNEs. With respect to introducing the measures to limit the deductibility of interest expenses by different jurisdictions, it remains critically important how these rules can be interpreted in line and co-exist with the ALP rules. Some jurisdictions may adopt the interest limitation rules by means of establishing a fixed debt-to-equity ratio or based on the interest coverage test or other multiple tests that, from one side, might eliminate the compliance burden and increase the predictability of the system. On the other hand, the tests can be far from the economic reality of business transactions and lead to double taxation if different tests are preferred by different states.[26] In this way, interest deductibility rules, as special anti-tax avoidance provisions, might potentially go beyond what is necessary to achieve the legitimate purpose of these rules.[27] In the European Union (EU), for example, such rules in the latter scenario would be considered as being against the fundamental principles of the single market.[28] Nevertheless, the guidance provides a helpful indicative list of factors and economically relevant characteristics that might evidence that a purported loan should be regarded as such to accurately recognize the underlying transaction.[29,30]

24. Monique van Herksen et al., INSIGHT: New OECD Guidance on Transfer Pricing Aspects of Financial Transactions—Part 1, available at https://news.bloombergtax.com/transfer-pricing/insight-36, accessed August 28, 2020.
25. *Ibid.*, paragraph 10.9.
26. WU Transfer Pricing center, Comments on the Public Discussion Draft on BEPS Actions 8-10, Financial Transactions, September 2018, p. 402.
27. *Ibid.*, p. 403.
28. *See*, for example, ThinCap Group Litigation.
29. Those are: the presence or absence of a fixed repayment date; the obligation to pay interest; the right to enforce payment of principal and interest; the status of the funder in comparison to regular corporate creditors; the existence of financial covenants and security; the source of interest payments; the ability of the recipient of the funds to obtain loans from unrelated lending institutions; the extent to which the advance is used to acquire capital assets; and the failure of the purported debtor to repay on the due date or to seek a postponement.
30. At the same time, it seems that the guidance is not very clear in distinguishing two different phases of transfer pricing analysis i.e., the delineation of the actual transaction and the recognition of it. For example, page 14 of the Final Guidelines. *See*, for more details, WU Transfer Pricing center, Comments on the Public Discussion Draft on BEPS Actions 8-10, Financial Transactions, September 2018, p. 401.

1.1.4.2 *The Economically Relevant Characteristics of Actual Financial Transactions*

The rules on the accurate delineation of financial transactions do not differ from the general guidance contained in the 2017 TPG for any other transaction. Delineation of financial transactions should start from the thorough identification of economically relevant characteristics including: (1) an examination of the contractual terms; (2) a functional analysis identifying the functions performed, the assets used, and the risks assumed by the parties; (3) the characteristics of the financial instruments; (4) the wider economic circumstances of the parties and the market; and (5) the business strategies of the parties and the wider group. Although the final guidance did not specifically mention it, the authors are of the opinion that the functional analysis of the transactions at stake should be complemented by the analysis of how those functions contribute to the wider generation of value by the MNE to which the parties belong.

1.1.4.3 *Treasury Functions*

Treasury functions include cash and liquidity management, corporate financial management, raising debt and equity, and managing the relationship with the MNE group's external bankers and independent credit rating agencies.[31] Moreover, the guidance provides specific clarifications on TP issues arising out of intra-group loans, cash pooling, and hedging financial arrangements under the general umbrella of "treasury functions" (although such financial transactions as intra-group loans and cash pooling arrangements could be undertaken by different units of the MNE independently from more or less centralized treasury functions[32]). As a general consideration, the guidance correctly indicates that "when evaluating the transfer pricing issues related to treasury activities, it is important to accurately delineate the actual transaction and to determine exactly what functions an entity is carrying on rather to rely to any extent upon a general description as 'treasury activities'."[33]

However, the critical points stipulated by the guidance are that, first, the treasury function would usually be considered as a support service to the main value-creating operation[34] and, second, that the treasury will usually not be responsible for higher strategic decisions that are rather a result of policy set at a group level.[35] Even though the OECD also mentioned that, in some circumstances, the treasury might perform functions that are more complex that should lead to an appropriate remuneration, the former statements might be misleading and ambiguous in the cases when a treasury

31. Monique van Herksen, Clive Jie-A-Joen, Fan Bai, Insight, Bloomberg Tax, New OECD Guidance on Transfer Pricing Aspects of Financial Transactions—Part I, p. 3. *See*, paragraphs 10.41-10.43.
32. WU Transfer Pricing Comments, p. 404.
33. Paragraph 10.44, The Final Guidance on Financial Transactions.
34. *Ibid.*, paragraph 10.45.
35. *Ibid.*, paragraph 10.49.

department conducts functions that are more complex and adopts high strategic decisions.[36]

1.1.4.4 *Intra-Group Loans*

The final guidance provides clarifications on how the ALP should specifically apply to intra-group loans, cash pooling, and hedging arrangements.

With respect to intra-group loans, the final guidance in comparison to the Discussion Draft elaborated on the use of credit ratings and impact of group membership as well as included additional approaches to the pricing of intra-groups loans, i.e., credit default swaps[37] and economic modeling,[38] the input on which was requested by the Discussion Draft. The key takeaways from the guidance and considerations on the pricing of intra-group loans are the following:

(1) An analysis of the economically relevant characteristics of the transaction should be performed from both the lender's and borrower's perspectives.[39] For lenders, commercial characteristics such as creditworthiness of the borrower, credit rating, and economic circumstances remain valid considerations. Borrowers will seek to optimize their weighted average cost of capital and will consider the potential impact of changes in economic conditions.

(2) Credit ratings is a useful measure of creditworthiness and, therefore, can help to identify a pool of potential comparables.[40] The guidance considers different situations in which credit ratings can be determined for the overall creditworthiness of an MNE or MNE group or for a specific issuance of debt as well as providing considerations on the ways to determine credit ratings by analyzing quantitative and qualitative factors.

The use of credit ratings is not specific to intra-group loans and, therefore, the discussion in the section could be presented more generally as it is also applicable to other types of intra-group financial transactions. On the matter of the determination of credit rating, the authors consider that it would be important to include additional guidance for the nature of data to be used, approaches to parent ceiling and country ceiling, approaches to valuating credit risks (e.g., credit migration approach, option pricing, actuarial approach, discrete time multi-period model) in order to ensure a high accuracy of credit rating analysis.[41]

(3) The guidance recognizes a potential effect of group membership (affiliation) and implicit support (incidental benefits) on the entity's ability to borrow or

36. WU Comments, pp. 404-405, Monique van Herksen et al., *supra* n 31, p. 3.
37. Section C.1.2.4.
38. Section C.1.2.5.
39. Paragraph 10.51 of the Final Guidance.
40. Paragraph 10.62 of the Final Guidance.
41. WU Comments, p. 406.

the interest rate paid on those borrowings, which would not require any payment or comparability adjustment.[42]

The guidance provides important clarifications on what the implicit support means and in what circumstances the existence of implicit support could be judged; however, the specific methodological approaches to determine the nature of passive association and to measure the adjustments in the case of passive associations are still required.[43]

(4) The MNE group credit rating might be used for the purpose of pricing the accurately delineated loan when the separate entity's credit rating results are not reliable.[44]

Since the judgments on whether separate entity credit rating results might be a matter of high controversy and subjectivity, there might be many disputes arising out of such an approach.

(5) There might be different approaches to pricing intra-group loans which are the comparable uncontrolled price (CUP) method, pricing based on loan fees and charges, based on cost of funds, interest rate benchmarking using credit default swaps, bank opinions, or economic modeling.[45]

1.1.4.5 Other Financial Instruments and Structures Covered by the Guidance

The final guidance on financial transactions in Chapter X also provides specific clarifications for cash pooling structures (section C.2), hedging arrangements (section C.3), financial guarantees (section D), and captive insurance (section E).

A key takeaway from the guidance on cash pooling structures is that a cash pool leader is considered to perform only coordination of agency functions to which limited remuneration applies. This approach might not be necessarily sustainable in practice when a cash pool leader performs a more complex role in the cash pooling structure. The arm's length remuneration of cash pool members should be determined based on the arm's length interest rates that apply to their debit and credit positions taking into account the synergy benefits resulting from the cash pool arrangement. Since the information on cash pooling arrangements between unrelated parties is not available, use of the internal or external CUP could be constrained, and a hypothetic CUP could be more suitable. Moreover, different methods for sharing benefits suggested by the guidance[46] might lead to internal arbitrage in using them and, therefore, further guidance would be beneficial.[47]

42. Paragraph 10.77.
43. WU Comments, p. 406.
44. Paragraphs 10.81-10.82 The Final Guidance.
45. Sections C.1.2.1.-C.1.2.6. of the Final Guidance. For the discussion and considerations on the different approaches, *see* WU Comments, *supra* n 26, pp. 406-407.
46. That is, yield approach (section D.2.2.), cost approach (section D.2.3.), valuation of expected loss approach (section D.2.4.), Capital support method (section D.2.5.).
47. WU Comments, p. 407.

The units of an MNE group might not necessarily formally conclude a contract on hedging arrangements, but the group members' risk will be hedged from the perspective of the group as a whole.[48] Nevertheless, the guidance stipulates that intra-group hedging activities can be considered as intra-group services with or without a written contract, having more complex TP issues in the second scenario (also in the case when the positions of the parties to the hedging contract do not match). A thorough analysis of the arrangement and the accurate delineation of the transaction is required to conclude whether an intra-group service was rendered. Nevertheless, the guidance provides very limited guidance on how these services have to be compensated and, therefore, further elaboration is required.[49]

Even though the guidance provides a good overview of financial guarantees and their peculiarities, further guidance on the various types of financial guarantees (i.e., from letter of credit to formal guarantees) and the distinction between downward, upward, and cross-guarantees could be included. Moreover, there is a need to additionally illustrate the issues of when the guarantee would or would not require a remuneration (e.g., implicit support, comfort letter).

With regard to captive insurance arrangements, the guidance provides that, in addition to general guidelines set out in Chapter I of the TPG, the accurate delineation of the captive insurance transactions should take into account the nature of risks assumed by the tested entity and a proper characterization of risk mitigation functions. The guidance provides a list of indicators that have to evidence that the captive insurance undertakes a genuine insurance business and, therefore, the transaction should be recognized as such.[50] Some of these indicators, such as the presence of risk diversification, might lead to controversial outcomes, e.g., when non-diversification of risks might lead to an automatic disregarding of the captive insurance transaction. Therefore, additional guidance with more examples could treat such a consequence.[51]

For more information on *Recent Developments on Transfer Pricing and Intra-Group Financing*, refer to Chapter 7 of this volume.

1.1.5 Country-by-Country Reporting

In November 2019, the OECD released updated guidelines on the implementation of country-by-country reporting (hereinafter "CbCR")[52] and a summary of common errors of MNE groups when preparing these reports.[53] The final report on Action 13 "Transfer Pricing Documentation and Country-by-Country Reporting" was completed

48. Paragraphs 10.150 and 10.151 of the Final Guidance.
49. For more detailed practical insights, *see* WU Comments, p. 408.
50. Paragraph 10.199 Final Guidance.
51. For more detailed practical insights, *see* WU Comments, p. 410.
52. Guidance on the Implementation of Country-by-Country Reporting, BEPS Action 13, available at https://www.oecd.org/ctp/guidance-on-the-implementation-of-country-by-country-reporting-beps-action-13.pdf, accessed August 28, 2020.
53. OECD (2019), Common errors made by MNEs in preparing Country-by-Country reports, November 2019, available at http://www.oecd.org/tax/beps/common-errors-mnes-cbc-reports.pdf, accessed August 28, 2020.

in October 2015. Since that time, the OECD has been continuously issuing additional guidance on the most relevant and critical issues. In the 2019 guidance, the Inclusive Framework on BEPS again clarified some questions of interpretation that have arisen while implementing Action 13 to ensure consistency in the application of the rules by both tax administrations and taxpayers. Moreover, the summary of common errors made by MNEs in preparing CbC reports aims to provide additional help to MNEs to comply with their reporting obligations. In December 2019, the OECD additionally published a summary of CbC reporting notification requirements.

In general, the OECD updated the content of the existing guidance with respect to "treatment of dividends for purposes of 'profit (loss) before income tax'," "income tax accrued (current year)" and "income tax paid (on cash basis)" in Table 1.[54] Several additional questions were added to the sections: "The use of shortened or rounded amounts in preparing Table 1," "deemed listing provision" and "short accounting periods/long accounting periods." Moreover, four new sections complemented the existing guidelines, namely:

(1) Information with respect to the sources of data in Table 3.
(2) Common errors made by MNE groups in preparing CbC reports.
(3) Local filing.
(4) Lodging a unilateral declaration for the purposes of exchanging CbC reports.

1.1.5.1 Treatment of Dividends for Purposes of "Profit (Loss) Before Income Tax"

In Table 1, with respect to the treatment of dividends, the OECD clarifies that the columns "Revenues" and "Profit (Loss) before Income Tax" should not include the amount of payments received from other constituent entities that are treated as dividends in the payer's tax jurisdiction.[55] Regarding the use of shortened or rounded amounts in preparing Table 1, the OECD clarified that MNEs should use the full financial amounts when completing it as shortened amounts are not acceptable.[56]

1.1.5.2 Deemed Listing Provision

Additional clarification has been added to the section "deemed listing provision" addressing the issue on how this provision operates when the ultimate parent entity

54. EY, Global tax Alert, OECD releases additional guidance on Country-by-Country Reporting and a summary of common errors made by MNE Groups in preparing these reports, November 7, 2019.
55. "This does not apply where a Constituent Entity includes in profit before tax for financial reporting purposes an amount representing all or part of the profit of another Constituent Entity that is transparent for tax purposes." OECD (2019), Guidance on the Implementation of Country-by-Country Reporting, fn 3.
56. However, the OECD noted that some jurisdictions might determine a reasonable level of rounding. This guidance may be revisited in the future. *See* KPMG, Country-by-Country Reporting—OECD Updates Guidance, November 12, 2019, available at https://home.kpmg/ca/en/home/insights/2019/11/country-by-country-reporting-oecd-updates-guidance.html, accessed August 28, 2020.

(UPE) of an MNE is tax resident in a jurisdiction that does not have a securities exchange. In that regard, the OECD considers that an entity will be the UPE of an MNE group if it would be required to prepare consolidated financial statements if its equity instruments were traded on a securities exchange upon which equity instruments of entities tax resident in the same jurisdiction are commonly traded.

1.1.5.3 Short Accounting Periods/Long Accounting Periods

A new question "Can a reporting fiscal year be for a period of other than 12 months?" was also added to "short accounting periods/long accounting periods" section. The OECD has clarified that an MNE should prepare a CbC report for the period covered by the consolidated financial statements prepared by the UPE provided that the MNE is not an excluded one.

1.1.5.4 Information with Respect to the Sources of Data in Table 3

As a general guideline set out in BEPS Action 13, an MNE should consistently use the same sources of data from year to year when preparing CbC reporting. The common sources of data for reporting are the MNEs' consolidation reporting packages, separate entity financial statements, regulatory financial statements, or internal management accounts. The OECD guidance clarifies that an MNE, when reporting, has to provide a brief indication in Table 3 of the sources of data to enable an understanding of the sources of each item of information in the CbC report. In addition, the reporting MNE has to explain, in all circumstances, if any information is taken from different sources of data and if those sources change over time.[57]

1.1.5.5 Local Filing

The first issue addressed in the updated guidance on local filing is whether a jurisdiction can require it when the UPE of an MNE is not required to file a CbC report. The OECD clarifies that the local filing is not accepted, and jurisdiction cannot apply local filing rules when the residence state of the UPE of an MNE does not require a CbC report to be filed, and this is in accordance with the BEPS Action 13 minimum standard. The additional guidance encourages jurisdictions to accept a CbC report based on the same information as that filed in the jurisdiction of the UPE thereby having the same outcome as if the report would be obtained under the exchange of information. Finally, the guidelines specify that the jurisdictions with local filing requirements are advised to apply a filing deadline no earlier than twelve months after the end of the reporting fiscal year. Thereby, the deadline in the jurisdictions with local filing will not come earlier than the one of the jurisdiction of the UPE.

57. Guidance on the Implementation of Country-by-Country Reporting, p. 25.

1.2 TP Developments at the EU

1.2.1 Fiscal State Aid and TP

In previous years, the commission investigated several large-scale cases of alleged state aid by means of transfer mispricing that was endorsed by certain Member States in favor of large MNEs.[58] The year 2019 continued to feature heightened activity around investigations into specific countries' TP practices and their compatibility under EU law in relation to the prohibition of state aid. Margrethe Vestager, Commissioner in charge of competition policy, has been continually pointing out when opening each transfer-pricing related investigation that "Member States should not allow companies to set up complex structures [or arrangements] that unduly reduce their taxable profits and give them an unfair advantage over competitors."[59] Thus, in January 2019, the commission opened an in-depth investigation of whether the tax rulings granted by the Netherlands to Nike may have given the company an unfair advantage over its competitors.[60] In March, the same investigation was initiated against Huhtamäki, a Finnish food and drink packaging company, examining whether the tax rulings granted by Luxembourg, that were disclosed as a part of "Luxleaks," are in line with EU state aid rules.[61] In September, thirty-nine Belgian MNEs became a target of the commission in a major investigation of the "excess profits" tax rulings granted to these companies by Belgian tax authorities.[62] This investigation followed the general court's decision from February 2019[63] that annulled the earlier commission's decision concluding that the Belgian "Excess Profit" tax scheme is illegal.[64]

The year 2019 was also remarkable from the perspective of the general court's decisions in state aid. On September 24, 2019, it upheld the European Commission's ruling ordering Luxembourg to recover EUR 23.1 million from Fiat[65] and annulled the

58. The conclusions of this article are based on the analysis of the European Commission's decisions in Apple (SA.38373), Amazon (SA.38944), Fiat (SA.38375), McDonald's (SA.38945), and Starbucks (SA.38374) as well as the letter to the Member State in Ikea (SA.46470).
59. EC: *State aid: Commission opens in-depth investigation into tax treatment of Nike in the Netherlands*, Press release, January 10, 2019, available at https://ec.europa.eu/commission/presscorner/detail/en/IP_19_322, accessed August 28, 2020.
60. *Ibid.*
61. EC: *State aid: Commission opens in-depth investigation into tax treatment of Huhtamäki in Luxembourg*, Press release, March 7, 2019, available at https://ec.europa.eu/commission/presscorner/detail/en/IP_19_1591, accessed August 28, 2020.
62. EC: *State aid: Commission opens in-depth investigations into individual "excess profit" tax rulings granted by Belgium to 39 multinational companies*, September 16, 2019, available at https://ec.europa.eu/commission/presscorner/detail/en/IP_19_5578, accessed August 28, 2020.
63. EC: *State aid: Commission concludes Belgian "Excess Profit" tax scheme illegal; around €700 million to be recovered from 35 multinational companies*, Press release, January 11, 2016, available at https://ec.europa.eu/commission/presscorner/detail/en/ip_16_42, accessed August 28, 2020. Commission Decision (EU) 2016/1699 of January 11, 2016 on the excess profit exemption State aid scheme SA.37667 (2015/C) (ex 2015/NN) implemented by Belgium (OJ 2016 L 260), p. 61.
64. General Court of the European Union, Judgment in Joined Cases T-131/16 *Belgium v. Commission* and T-263/16 *Magnetrol International v. Commission*.
65. Judgment of the General Court, *Grand Duchy of Luxembourg and Fiat Chrysler Finance Europe v. European Commission*, Case T-755/15, ECLI:EU:T:2019:670.

commission's ruling ordering the Netherlands to recover EUR 25.7 million from Starbucks.[66]

A starting point that is addressed in every case is the nature of the ALP in the EU. In several decisions, the commission assumed that the tax base of integrated entities should not be assessed in the same way as stand-alone undertakings (i.e., based on the accounting result) but by means of proxies that indicate a reliable approximation of the market-based outcome in conditions of free competition between independent companies (i.e., the ALP).[67] Moreover, in support of this position, the commission went further in the Starbucks case to argue that the ALP does not necessarily stem from the domestic legislation but "is a general principle of equal treatment in taxation falling within the application of Article 107(1) ... from whose scope the national tax rules are not excluded."[68] For a long time, such an approach as the ALP being a general principle of equal treatment in taxation was strongly criticized by the international tax experts because of the lack of any legal and theoretical foundation for the statement. In this regard, the general court, in principle, denied the existence of any general principle of equal taxation and the ALP as its projection stemming from Article 107 TFEU in Starbucks and Fiat. Nevertheless, the court stressed that, in light of the objective of the general corporate tax system (of Luxembourg and the Netherlands at stake) of treating independent and associated enterprises in a similar manner, there is a need to assess the tax base of integrated entities based on a "reliable approximation of a market-based outcome"[69] while the ALP would then be the correct tool to reach this objective.[70] Furthermore, the court assessed that "the [ALP] principle is a tool for checking that intra-group transactions are remunerated as though they had been negotiated between independent undertakings."[71]

Even though the court has recognized the relevance of the ALP, the commission's and the Court of Justice of the European Union's (CJEU) practice does not give much material substance to that principle apart from requiring that the transactions between integrated and stand-alone companies should be priced alike. The ALP can have a variety of different interpretations that can be evidenced by the ever-increasing number of TP disputes, different approaches to the interpretation of the OECD TPG and the UN TP Manual, and diverse domestic court practice.[72] Therefore, it remains quite questionable whether the commission has the power to dictate to Member States how the ALP has to apply. Therefore, it is not surprising that, in some cases, the commission

66. Judgment of the General Court, *Starbucks and Starbucks Manufacturing EMEA v. Commission*, T-636/16, ECLI:EU:T:2019:669.
67. SA.38373, *Apple*, paragraphs 249-255; Buriak/Lazarov, p. 915.
68. SA.38374, *Starbucks*, paragraph 264; *See*, Wattel, Peter J. (2016). Stateless income, state aid and the (which?) arm's length principle, Intertax 44: 792.
69. *Fiat*, paragraph 176.
70. Jérôme Monsenego (September 28, 2019), Some observations on Starbucks, Fiat, and their potential impact on future amendments to the arm's length principle, Kluwer International Tax Blog, available at http://kluwertaxblog.com/2019/09/28/some-observations-on-starbucks-fiat-and-their-potential-impact-on-future-amendments-to-the-arms-length-principle/, accessed August 28, 2020.
71. *Fiat*, §155.
72. Jérôme Monsenego, *supra* n 70.

attempted to avoid conducting a full-fledged TP analysis but only challenged the state's measures based on the EU state aid law.[73] This approach would be closer in line with the fiscal autonomy of the states to apply its domestic law coherently unless it discriminates against the principles of the single market. However, at the same time, it might lead to outcomes of the cases that are far from the economic reality of intra-group transactions and the most relevant TP practice.

Chapter 2 of this volume will take a closer look at each TP related commission's investigation and the court's decision delivered in 2019 as well as with regard to the practical TP aspects.

1.2.2 The Work of the EU JTPF

In March 2019, the EU Joint Transfer Pricing Forum (JTPF) published a report on the Application of the Profit Split Method (PSM) within the EU.[74] The increased integration of MNEs and the globalization of national economies and markets led to a more frequent reliance on the PSM. Therefore, its clarification was one of the priorities identified in the OECD/G20 BEPS Action Plan. Therefore, the EU JTPF also took the initiative to examine the use of the PSM within the internal market and to work out a common approach to the challenges on its application that were raised by the OECD. Complications of applying the PSM embrace measuring the relevant revenue and costs between all related enterprises parties to the controlled transaction and the difficulties of identifying appropriate profit-splitting factors.

The EU JTPF report provides clarifications on several essential aspects of the application of the PSM addressing the main concepts around the application of the PSM and how to split profits based on the concepts described in the revised OECD guidelines.[75] Unlike the OECD guidelines, though, the report additionally provides clarification on to what extent the activity of an MNE could be considered as highly integrated and to what extent its contribution is unique and valuable.

The OECD TPG and the EU JTPF report consider the use of the PSM appropriate in the following circumstances:[76]

- the existence of a unique and valuable contribution by each party to the controlled transaction; and/or

73. For example, Huhtamaki case.
74. EU Joint Transfer Pricing Forum, The Application of the Profit Split Method within the EU, DOC: JTPF/002/2019/EN, available at https://ec.europa.eu/taxation_customs/sites/taxation/files/report_on_the_application_of_the_profit_split_method_within_the_eu_en.pdf, accessed August 28, 2020.
75. EY, Global Tax Alert, EU Joint Transfer Pricing Forum releases report on application of profit split method within the EU and provides summary of achievements of present mandate, April 12, 2019, available at https://www.ey.com/Publication/vwLUAssets/EU_Joint_Transfer_Pricing_Forum_releases_report_on_application_of_profit_split_method_within_the_EU_and_provides_summary_of_achievements_of_present_mandate/$FILE/2019G_001785-19Gbl_TP_EU%20Joint%20TP%20Forum%20-%20Report%20on%20PSM%20application%20within%20the%20EU.pdf, accessed August 28, 2020.
76. 2017 TP Guidelines.

- a high level of integration regarding business transactions to which the transaction relates; and/or
- the shared assumptions of economically significant risks or separate assumption of economically closely related risks by the parties to the transaction.

One of the three circumstances is sufficient for justifying the application of the PSM. The EU JTPF report provided further guidance on the use of the PSM in the circumstances of the existence of unique and valuable contributions and addressed the following issues:

- How should unique and valuable intangibles be interpreted.
- Is the concept "unique" separate from the concept of "valuable."
- If a potential economic benefit were not realized, should the contribution still be considered "valuable."
- Can a unique and valuable contribution be present and the PSM applied accordingly even if the parties of the transactions do not share the assumption of closely related risks.

The concept of intangibles should be understood within the definition of Chapter VI of the TPG, which is broader and goes beyond legal or accounting definitions in national laws. To be unique and valuable, intangibles must be independently unique, i.e., no comparables are available, and potentially valuable. A unique and valuable contribution should represent a key source of actual or potential economic value in business activities.

Concerning the circumstances of highly integrated business transactions, the report addresses the following issues:

- How to distinguish "highly integrated" and "integrated" business operations.
- Should the criterion of highly integrated business operations stand on its own, or should it be considered in the context of the criterion on unique and valuable contributions.
- Should the presence of a cross-entity and cross-border business unit structure be an indication of highly integrated business operations.

Finally, with regards to the circumstances of shared assumption of economically significant risks and separate assumption of closely related risks, the report explains several issues:

- Should the hallmarks of "shared assumption of economically significant risks" and "separate assumption of closely related risks" be considered in isolation, or are these derivative criteria to the one on "highly integrated business operations."
- What is the meaning of "closely related" risks.

The annexes to the report provide important schematic guidance on when and how to apply the PSM and an indicative list of PSM splitting factors identified by JTPF members based on a survey on the experiences of the members in the practical application of the PSM. The report concludes that the PSM is not used that frequently in current tax practices. Nevertheless, the emergence of the new business models that are heavily relying on intangible property and closely integrated business transactions as well as with the new role of the market in value creation might lead to a higher relevance of the PSM for the allocation of profits of MNEs. For example, the PSM was referred to as appropriate for taxation of "significant digital presence" by the EU Commission's proposal addressing the tax issues of the digital economy. All in all, the illustration of splitting the profits among the MNE group members may seem relatively easy in theory, but the application of the PSM remains highly complex in practice with lots of ambiguities. Therefore, there is a need for exploring further opportunities to simplify the method in practice and for guidance on how to analyze and map the global value chains of MNEs.

1.3 TP Developments at the United Nations

In 2019, the United Nations did not issue any major reports or updates to its already existing works. However, this does not mean that there have been no developments in the area of tax law.

First, the UN kept on working on the tax issues related to the digitalization of economy. In a report released in April 2019,[77] the Drafting Group first analyzed the works done on other international fora (mainly coming from the OECD/G20) and then came up with four questions that also contained TP aspects. With regard to value creation, the Drafting Group indicated that Location Saving Advantages are a topic which could possibly be considered in view of the increasing role of developing countries in the modern world economy. Further, the complexity of the approaches examined by the Inclusive Framework was discussed, indicating the example of marketing intangibles as proving the difficulty of calculating routine and non-routine profits under the above-mentioned approaches. The report did not bring any solutions to the existing issues but rather provided food for thought and encouraged the members of the Committee of Experts to discuss the encountered issues.

Further, the United Nations Handbook on Selected Issues for the Taxation of the Extractive Industries by Developing Countries was issued in February 2019.[78] It contained a number of chapters discussing specific tax considerations of the industry and also covered TP issues. The handbook focused on the analysis of the major stages in the extractive industries value chain and suggested methods and approaches that might be considered in addressing specific issues. Already in the following months of 2019, the updates to the handbook were discussed by the Committee of Experts on

77. Committee of Experts on International Cooperation in Tax Matters, *Tax Issues related to the Digitalization of the Economy: Report*, E/C.18/2019/CRP.12, April 5, 2019, available at https://www.un.org/esa/ffd/wp-content/uploads/2019/04/18STM_CRP12-Work-on-taxation-issues-digitalization.pdf, accessed August 28, 2020.

78. *United Nations Handbook on Selected Issues for Taxation of the Extractive Industries by Developing Countries*, United Nations, 2018, available at https://www.un-ilibrary.org/economic-and-social-development/united-nations-handbook-on-selected-issues-for-taxation-of-the-extractive-industries-by-developing-countries_4632a533-en, published February 24, 2019.

International Cooperation in Tax Matters. In the update issued in April 2019,[79] the committee indicated issues that might be relevant from the point of view of TP such as split contracts, use of proprietary technologies and intangibles, digitalization of economy, and services rendered by affiliates of service providers and subcontractors.

Finally, and perhaps most significantly, the Subcommittee on TP has been working on updating the UN Practical Manual on Transfer Pricing. In the report released in April 2019,[80] the Subcommittee indicated the progress in relation to drafting the new chapter on financial transactions, revising the text on profit splits as well as the text on establishing TP capability, risk assessment, and TP audits. The draft chapter on financial transactions discussed a variety of issues, including the importance of corporate financing decisions, rules and measures against base erosion, common types of intra-group financial transactions, delineation of such a transaction, potentially applicable TP methods, intra-group loans and financial guarantees, cash pooling practices and captive insurance as well as the identification of four steps to determine the arm's length nature of intra-group loans. With reference to the transactional PSM, the draft sought consistency between the UN guidance and the work of the Inclusive Framework on BEPS. Finally, the works on establishing TP capability, risk assessment, and TP audits were done mainly to streamline sequences of presentation and to eliminate the overlaps in the former version of the text.

1.4 Other Organizations

The year 2019 was not a groundbreaking one when it comes to TP developments among international organizations. In addition to the already mentioned works of the OECD, UN and EU, only two other developments can be mentioned.

First, in July 2019, a meeting of the finance ministers of the Group of Seven (G7) took place during which the issues such as taxation of the digital sector and a minimum worldwide tax on large businesses were discussed.[81] The countries agreed to adapt tax rules to tax multinational companies, especially in the digital sector, that create value with little or no physical presence. It was also agreed to put minimum taxation in place in order to end harmful tax competition between states and the aggressive optimization pursued by some businesses.[82] This agreement gave an official foundation for the works of the OECD on the Unified Approach and GloBE proposals.

---

79. Committee of Experts on International Cooperation in Tax Matters, *Update of the Handbook on Selected Issues for Taxation of the Extractive Industries by Developing Countries*, E/C.18/2019/CRP.11, April 8, 2019, available at https://www.un.org/esa/ffd/wp-content/uploads/2019/04/18STM_CRP11-Update-Handbook-Taxation-Extractive-Industries.pdf, accessed August 28, 2020.
80. Committee of Experts on International Cooperation in Tax Matters, *Co-coordinator's Report on Work of the Subcommittee on Transfer Pricing*, E/C.18/2019/CRP.1, April 8, 2019, available at https://www.un.org/esa/ffd/wp-content/uploads/2019/04/18STM_CRP1_Update-UN-Practical-Manual-on-Transfer-Pricing.pdf, accessed August 28, 2020.
81. Available at https://home.kpmg/us/en/home/insights/2019/07/tnf-g7-country-finance-ministers-agreement-on-taxation-of-digital-economy.html, accessed December 19, 2019.
82. Available at https://www.gouvernement.fr/en/g7-finance-major-progress, accessed December 19, 2019.

In 2019, certain progress was also made by the Platform for Collaboration on Tax which, in September, published a draft version of its Practical Toolkit to Support the Successful Implementation by Developing Countries of Effective Transfer Pricing Documentation Requirements.[83] The toolkit was designed to support the successful implementation of effective TP documentation requirements by developing countries and was supposed to consider measures concerning the documentation of all of the stages of a taxpayer's TP analysis that governments could put in place. According to the platform, the toolkit also took into account current international approaches and country practices for transfer-pricing documentation and discussed various policy considerations and options to guide developing countries.

After publishing the draft toolkit, a round of public consultations was launched in order to obtain feedback from the public.[84] The platform looks for publishing the final version of the toolkit in 2020.

2 RECENT DEVELOPMENTS IN COUNTRIES SPECIFIC TP LEGISLATION, GUIDELINES, AND JURISPRUDENCE

2.1 Arm's Length Principle and TP Methods

In 2019, a number of countries worked on the application of arm's length method in their jurisdiction. Perhaps most importantly, three developing countries can be mentioned as the ones that introduced the most significant amendments—Bangladesh, India, and Mongolia.

Bangladesh introduced specific new requirements with regard to related parties' transactions such as obligatory disclosure of such transactions in the income tax returns and taxation of additional income arising from an arm's length TP adjustment performed by a tax authority. In addition, the methodology of arriving at an arm's length price was clarified and the definition of deemed international transaction was revised.[85]

India proposed secondary TP adjustment provisions through which it required taxpayers to repatriate excess funds held outside India that resulted from the difference between the price as agreed between the parties and the adjustment to the respective transaction. Missing timely remission of the funds would result in imputed interest income.[86]

83. Available at http://documents.worldbank.org/curated/en/505481569449944639/Practical-Toolkit-to-Support-the-Successful-Implementation-by-Developing-Countries-of-Effective-Transfer-Pricing-Documentation-Requirements, accessed December 19, 2019.
84. Available at https://www.worldbank.org/en/news/press-release/2019/09/27/the-platform-for-collaboration-on-tax-invites-comments-on-draft-toolkit, accessed December 19, 2019.
85. Available at https://www.ey.com/gl/en/services/tax/international-tax/alert--bangladesh-enacts-2019-20-budget-proposals, accessed January 7, 2020.
86. Available at https://www.ey.com/gl/en/services/tax/international-tax/alert--india-releases-2019-20-union-budget---update-on-corporate-tax-proposals, accessed January 7, 2020.

Mongolia revised its rules on corporate taxation which also included the introduction of dealing at arm's length between related parties.[87] Tax authorities were given the competence to adjust the transaction to a fair market value should the parties have failed to deal at arm's length.

The other national developments were more of a clarifying character and did not introduce any dramatic changes to the local legal system. Canada decided that the adjustments under the TP rules were to apply before any other provision of Canada's tax law.[88] Hong Kong provided guidance on the interpretation of the ALP under the domestic law as well as guidance on pricing and treatment of service and intangible transactions.[89] Poland, within the extensive amendment of its TP laws, introduced a number of conditions regarding adjustments reducing tax liability that had to be fulfilled by the taxpayer if such an adjustment was to be recognized by tax authorities.[90] Finally, Zambia revised certain TP related definitions (like actual conditions, arm's length conditions, and related or associated persons) and proposed providing for a TP adjustment arising from a transaction with a resident (domestic) and non-resident related person.[91]

As far as TP methods are concerned, 2019 was not a groundbreaking year in the domestic legislation all over the world. Only three countries implemented changes worth mentioning. Ireland decided to implement the 2018 OECD Revised Guidance on the Application of the Transactional PSM into its domestic law[92] while Japan added the discounted cash flow to the list of officially recognized TP methodologies.[93] Finally, Paraguay, upon the introduction of the official TP rules, also included a sixth valuation method known as the sixth method.[94]

All in all, general TP developments around the world in 2019 did not prove to be extraordinary; however, the introduction of relevant TP rules in states that so far did not have any respective legislation proved that TP remained an important topic on the agenda of domestic legislators in multiple countries. With the new chapter of the OECD TPG on financial transactions and the ongoing works of the OECD on the Unified Approach, it is certain that TP will not disappear from the list of domestically relevant topics.

87. Available at https://www.ey.com/gl/en/services/tax/international-tax/alert--mongolia-amends-its-transfer-pricing-regulations, accessed January 7, 2020.
88. Available at https://home.kpmg/xx/en/home/insights/2019/03/tnf-canada-transfer-pricing-measures-federal-budget.html, accessed January 7, 2020.
89. Available at https://home.kpmg/us/en/home/insights/2019/07/tnf-hk-guidance-transfer-pricing-documentation-cbc-reports.html, accessed January 7, 2020.
90. Available at https://home.kpmg/xx/en/home/insights/2019/03/tnf-poland-application-of-transfer-pricing-regulations-clarified-for-2018-transactions.html, accessed January 7, 2020.
91. Available at https://home.kpmg/us/en/home/insights/2019/10/tnf-zambia-transfer-pricing-measures-2020-budget.html, accessed January 7, 2020.
92. Available at https://www.ey.com/gl/en/services/tax/international-tax/alert--ireland-publishes-finance-bill-2019---transfer-pricing-updates, accessed December 19, 2019.
93. Available at https://www.ey.com/gl/en/services/tax/international-tax/alert--japan-enacts-2019-tax-reform-bill, accessed August 28, 2020.
94. Available at https://www.ey.com/gl/en/services/tax/international-tax/alert--paraguay-enacts-new-tax-reform, accessed August 28, 2020.

2.2 Taxation of Digital Economy

Just as in previous years, taxation of the digital economy turned out to be a hot topic as much on the international level as it is domestically and has resulted in numerous countries initiating relevant works or even already introducing digital taxes into their legal systems. European jurisdictions seemed to have been the most heavily involved in the introduction of relevant regimes.[95] Apparently, after many years in which the local tax systems were abused by MNEs operating in European markets, countries did not want to put their actions off any longer and preferred to introduce their solutions unilaterally rather than waiting for a multilateral compromise at the OECD or EU level. Thus, 2019 was a year when the final solutions were approved in Austria,[96] Italy,[97] and France.[98]

The solutions applied by these jurisdictions are pretty similar. In France, the tax is imposed at a rate of 3% on the gross revenues derived from digital activities of which French "users" are deemed to play a major role in value creation. The taxpayers are obligated to pay the new tax if they exceeded two thresholds in the previous calendar year, namely, revenues of over EUR 750 million for taxable digital services supplied worldwide and EUR 25 million for taxable digital services supplied in France. What is perhaps most important is that the new tax affects not only digital companies but, in general, digital business models. The above-mentioned thresholds are identical in Austria. Here, however, the applicable tax rate will amount to 5%, and the object of taxation comprises advertising services rendered in Austria. Finally, the Italian solution envisages the tax rate of 3% generated from specific B2B and B2C digital services rendered to Italian customers. The applicable thresholds are total worldwide revenues of not less than EUR 750 million and revenues of not less than EUR 5.5 million obtained in Italy from digital services as defined in the legislation.

Other European countries that worked on the introduction of the digital services tax included Belgium,[99] Czechia,[100] Spain[101] and the U.K.[102] Here, however, discussion

95. Asen, Elke, Announced, proposed, and implemented digital services taxes in Europe, Tax Foundation, July 18, 2019, updated on October 25, 2019; available at https://taxfoundation.org/digital-taxes-europe-2019/, accessed August 28, 2020.
96. Available at https://www.bmf.gv.at/steuern/Abgabenaenderungsgesetz-2020.html, accessed August 28, 2020.
97. Available at https://home.kpmg/us/en/home/insights/2019/10/tnf-italy-digital-services-tax-apply-beginning-1-january-2020.html, accessed December 19, 2019.
98. Available at https://home.kpmg/us/en/home/insights/2019/07/tnf-france-digital-services-tax-enacted.html, accessed December 19, 2019.
99. Available at https://www.bdo.be/en-gb/news/2019/belgium-jumps-on-the-bandwagon-to-tax-online-giants, accessed December 19, 2019.
100. Available at https://home.kpmg/us/en/home/insights/2019/07/tnf-czech-republic-update-on-digital-services-tax.html, accessed December 19, 2019.
101. Available at https://home.kpmg/xx/en/home/insights/2019/02/tnf-spain-digital-services-tax-proposed-in-pending-legislation.html, accessed December 19, 2019.
102. Available at https://home.kpmg/uk/en/home/insights/2019/07/tmd-draft-finance-bill-uk-digital-services-tax.html, accessed December 19, 2019.

on taxes remained in the area of projects as the mentioned countries only introduced first draft bills.

Belgium would like to tax online posting of advertising messages aimed at the users of a platform, the sale of data collected about users, and the offering of digital platforms. Such services would be subject to a tax rate of 3%, and the tax itself would be imposed on companies with a global revenue exceeding EUR 750 million and a total taxable revenue in the EU of at least EUR 50 million. The Digital Service Tax (DST) in Belgium, however, remains just a plan for now due to the political situation and perturbations with creating a new government. Czechia proposed a DST on carrying out targeted advertisement campaigns, use of multi-sided digital interfaces (with more than 200,000 users), and sale of user data, all subject to some specific requirements. Here, the tax rate would amount to 7%, and the applicability thresholds are the total consolidated revenues of the group of at least EUR 750 million and the revenues from taxable digital services from the Czech Republic greater than CZK 50 million (approximately EUR 2 million). Further, the Spanish proposal seems to be sharing the fate of the Belgian proposal as it has not progressed since January 2019 when the first bill for a DST was officially published. Here, the tax at the rate of 3% would be imposed on rendering digital services (including online marketing services and online mediation services) as well as on services that allow third parties to contract and conclude supplies of goods and services or that transfer data. The thresholds for the applicability of DST would be at least EUR 750 million of the total net turnover of the business in the calendar year and at least EUR 3 million of income derived from rendering digital services. Finally, in the U.K., the tax at the rate of 2% should be imposed on services such as social-media platforms, internet search engines, and online market places that derive value from interaction or engagement with U.K. users. The threshold was set at the level of at least GBP 500 million for group's worldwide revenues arising from digital services activity and more than GBP 25 million of these revenues are attributable to U.K. users in an accounting period. The DST should become effective as of April 1, 2020.[103]

It can clearly be seen that the solutions introduced or discussed so far in the EU countries and the U.K. are, at least to a certain extent, similar to the proposal put forward by the EU in March 2018.[104] This is in line with the declared intentions of the Member States concerned which stated that, whenever a final solution is ready, their domestic provisions will be amended in order to comply with the rules envisaged by the EU. However, with the missing agreement by the council[105] and subordination of the further progress of EU works to the developments in the same area at the OECD, it is reasonable to assume that an EU-wide introduction of a digital tax will not happen in

103. Available at https://www.gov.uk/government/publications/introduction-of-the-new-digital-services-tax/introduction-of-the-new-digital-services-tax, accessed December 19, 2019.

104. Proposal for a Council Directive on the common system of a digital services tax on revenues resulting from the provision of certain digital services, COM(2018) 148 final, Council of the European Union, March 22, 2018, available at http://data.consilium.europa.eu/doc/document/ST-7420-2018-INIT/en/pdf, accessed March 11, 2020.

105. Economic and Financial affairs Council, March 12, 2019, available at https://www.consilium.europa.eu/en/meetings/ecofin/2019/03/12/, accessed March 11, 2020.

2020 and, considering the ideas of the OECD, it might prove to be significantly different from what has already been proposed.

Apart from Europe, countries such as Canada, New Zealand, Turkey, Uganda, and Vietnam initiated works on the DST. In Canada, the works resumed after the autumn election[106] with a proposal for a 3% tax on revenues from sales of online advertisements and user data applicable to companies with more than CAD 1 billion (USD 759 million) in worldwide revenue and Canadian revenue of more than CAD 40 million (USD 30 million).[107] New Zealand launched a discussion document with questions about imposing a 3% DST on the gross revenue attributable to New Zealand users of specified digital services and the country's participation in the OECD's search for a multilateral solution.[108] Further, Turkey is perhaps the most advanced among the countries mentioned in this paragraph as the relevant provisions were already enacted in November 2019 and are supposed to take effect from March 2020.[109] The Turkish take on the DST envisages a high (by comparison) rate of 7.5% and taxation of a rather extensive scope of services such as digital advertising services, sales of any audible, visual or digital content as well as services for the provision and operation of a digital platform by which users may interact with each other.[110] Uganda, after the introduction of a controversial "social media tax" in 2018,[111] started to consider taxation of global companies in accordance with the idea that tax is supposed to be paid where income is made.[112] Finally, Vietnam introduced new provisions taxing cross-border payment transactions with non-resident entities and enterprises thus targeting e-commerce and the digital economy.[113]

Clearly, various states around the world are interested in the introduction of some form of DST. So far, however, it seems that not much work has been done and that the proposed solutions tend to significantly vary country-to-country. Therefore, there is much hope in the works conducted by the OECD to come up with a unified solution which could find its application in jurisdictions around the world, preventing possible confusion over completely different concepts in diverse states.

---

106. Soong Johnston, Stephanie. Canadian digital tax likely as Trudeau hangs on to power, Tax Notes, October 22, 2019, available at https://www.taxnotes.com/featured-news/canadian-digital-tax-likely-trudeau-hangs-power/2019/10/22/2b20t, accessed August 28, 2020.
107. Bunn, D., Another digital services tax? Canada adds its proposal to the mix, Tax Foundation, December 12, 2019, available at https://taxfoundation.org/canada-digital-tax-proposal/, accessed August 28, 2020.
108. Available at https://home.kpmg/us/en/home/insights/2019/07/tnf-new-zealand-update-on-digital-services-tax-consultation.html, accessed December 19, 2019.
109. Available at https://home.kpmg/us/en/home/insights/2019/12/tnf-digital-services-tax-enacted-effective-march-2020.html, accessed December 19, 2019.
110. Available at https://home.kpmg/us/en/home/insights/2019/11/tnf-turkey-legislative-proposal-for-digital-services-tax.html, accessed December 19, 2019.
111. Available at https://www.theguardian.com/global-development/2019/feb/27/millions-of-ugandans-quit-internet-after-introduction-of-social-media-tax-free-speech, accessed December 19, 2019.
112. Available at https://news.bloombergtax.com/daily-tax-report-international/uganda-plans-reforms-to-tap-facebook-google-advertising-revenue, accessed December 19, 2019.
113. Available at https://home.kpmg/us/en/home/insights/2019/07/tnf-vietnam-taxation-e-commerce-transactions-remote-digital-sales.html, accessed December 19, 2019.

2.3 Intangibles

After much attention being paid to intangibles in the TP context in recent years, the year 2019 turned out to be definitely calmer. The only country with significant developments in this area was Ireland which adopted the 2017 OECD TP Guidelines as well as some later OECD documents into its law.[114] Thus, the DEMPE concept and updated framework aligning profits with value creation as well as the updated approach to hard-to-value-intangibles and the revised guidance on the application of Transactional Profit Split Method (latter two released in 2018) can now be directly invoked in tax proceedings. The changes effective from January 1, 2020[115] will undoubtedly provide Irish tax authorities with a powerful tool.

Among other countries, Panama established the method for calculating income derived from the transfer or exploitation of IP assets,[116] and Japan clarified the scope of intangibles that are subject to TP rules by appropriately modifying their legal definition.[117] In the U.S., the Court of Appeals dealt with the definition of intangibles in the *Amazon v. Commissioner* case, which will be described later on in this chapter.[118]

2.4 Documentation

The increasing importance of documentation for TP was visible in the activities of various jurisdictions also in 2019. New requirements were introduced around the world both in developing and in developed economies.

With the changes approved in the summer of 2019, Bulgaria joined the group of states officially requiring the submitting of TP documentation.[119] From 2020, both the master file and the local file can be required depending on fulfillment of various conditions (i.e., thresholds of net book value of assets, average number of personnel being part of a multinational group). In the case of non-compliance with the new rules (i.e., missing or incorrect TP documentation), a penalty of up to 0.5% of the volume of the related-party transactions that are required to be documented could be imposed.[120]

114. Available at https://www.ey.com/gl/en/services/tax/international-tax/alert--ireland-publishes-finance-bill-2019---transfer-pricing-updates, accessed December 20, 2019.
115. Available at https://www.matheson.com/news-and-insights/article/irelands-finance-bill-2019-key-international-proposals, accessed December 20, 2019.
116. Available at https://www.ey.com/gl/en/services/tax/international-tax/alert--panama--free-zones--preferential-tax-regimes-and-special-economic-areas-are-now-subject-to-transfer-pricing-regulations, accessed December 20, 2019.
117. Available at https://www.ey.com/gl/en/services/tax/international-tax/alert--japan-enacts-2019-tax-reform-bill, accessed December 20, 2019.
118. Available at https://www.ey.com/gl/en/services/tax/international-tax/alert--united-states-court-of-appeals-affirms-tax-courts-decision-in-amazon-case, accessed December 20, 2019.
119. Available at https://home.kpmg/us/en/home/insights/2019/08/tnf-bulgaria-transfer-pricing-documentation-new-rules-master-local-files.html, accessed December 20, 2019.
120. Available at https://www.ey.com/gl/en/services/tax/international-tax/alert--bulgaria-adopts-mandatory-transfer-pricing-documentation, accessed December 20, 2019.

Denmark was also busy at work in the area of TP documentation which resulted in a draft bill published in September.[121] The three main points of the draft are the obligation to submit the TP documentation to tax authorities along with the corporate tax return, possible imposition of penalties in the case of the missing submission of the above documentation, and the entitlement of tax authorities to assess taxpayers' taxable income on a free basis if the documentation is not submitted by the taxpayer within the requested deadline. Undoubtedly, the latter two points constitute a possible consequence that will motivate the taxpayers to submit the documentation in line with the proposed provisions.

Hong Kong introduced notable changes to its tax ordinance that also focused on TP documentation. The taxpayers operating in Hong Kong are now required to disclose certain related-party information and confirm their compliance with TP documentation requirements in their profits tax return.[122] More importantly, however, the three-tiered TP documentation requirement was officially codified, which also includes submitting CbC reports.[123] In addition, the taxpayers that are not subject to the TP documentation rules are also encouraged by the Hong Kong tax authorities to keep files explaining their TP standing.[124]

Ireland is perhaps the country that revamped its documentation requirements in the most significant way.[125] Among the new provisions, Irish taxpayers can find the requirement to prepare master file and local file documentation, subject to a EUR 250 million and EUR 50 million annual group consolidated revenue threshold, respectively. In addition, the Finance Bill 2019 also introduced a new deadline for preparing TP documentation which is now streamlined with the Irish corporation tax return filing deadline.

Similar to Ireland, Lithuania and Slovakia also decided to align their requirements with the OECD's recommendations. The respective TP documentation requirements of both countries mainly reflect the guidance provided by BEPS Action Plan 13.[126]

Portugal introduced changes effective from October 1, 2019 which clarified and strengthened the TP rules and taxpayer's reporting obligations. Taxpayers classified as "major" are now requested to submit their TP documentation within the deadline for

121. Available at https://home.kpmg/us/en/home/insights/2019/09/tnf-denmark-transfer-pricing-documentation-to-be-filed-with-tax-return-draft-bill.html, accessed December 20, 2019.
122. Available at https://www.ey.com/gl/en/services/tax/international-tax/alert--hong-kong-requires-taxpayers-to-disclose-transfer-pricing-information-in-income-tax-return, accessed December 20, 2019.
123. Available at https://home.kpmg/xx/en/home/insights/2019/03/tnf-hong-kong-review-of-tax-compliance-changes-for-2018-19-year-of-assessment.html, accessed December 20, 2019.
124. Available at https://home.kpmg/us/en/home/insights/2019/07/tnf-hk-guidance-transfer-pricing-documentation-cbc-reports.html, accessed December 20, 2019.
125. Available at https://www.ey.com/gl/en/services/tax/international-tax/alert--ireland-publishes-finance-bill-2019---transfer-pricing-updates, accessed December 20, 2019.
126. Available at https://home.kpmg/xx/en/home/insights/2019/02/tnf-slovakia-guidelines-transfer-pricing-documentation.html; https://home.kpmg/xx/en/home/insights/2019/01/tnf-lithuania-new-transfer-pricing-documentation-requirements-2019.html, accessed December 20, 2019.

submission of the Annual Tax and Accounting Return.[127] In addition, significant penalties were introduced for taxpayers that do not comply with the delivery of the country-by-country (CbC) report, the CbCR notification, or the submission of the TP documentation.[128]

In 2019, Thailand also worked on its first TP documentation requirements which, however, remain at a draft level for now after first being published in June 2019. The draft mainly reflects the recommendations under the 2017 OECD TP Guidelines.[129] In November 2019, Thailand introduced a TP disclosure form that has to be filed by corporate taxpayers having revenues of at least THB 200 million (approximately USD 6.6 million) or more per accounting year.[130] The information reported in the document concerns transactions falling within the scope of Thai TP rules, and failure to report related-party transactions or to provide complete and accurate TP information and disclosures may be subject to a penalty assessment.

On the wave of the recently intensified work on the formalization of international tax rules, both Qatar[131] and United Arab Emirates (UAE)[132] introduced new rules regarding TP documentation. In Qatar, the new legislation prescribes which entities are obliged to file the CbC notifications and CbC reports, the format and deadlines for the respective submission, and possible penalties for non-compliance. In addition, in September 2019, Qatar has also signed the Multilateral Competent Authority Agreement for CbCR for the automatic exchange of information with fifty-six countries. UAE, after Saudi Arabia and Qatar, is the third Gulf Cooperation Council Member State to have adopted the CbCR requirements.[133] Here, the rules are mainly in line with the OECD guidance as far as the format and content of the reports are concerned. The CbC report is required from entities that are tax residents in the UAE and also part of a multinational enterprise (MNE) having consolidated revenues at a certain threshold.

Among other countries, it must be noted that, in Bangladesh, as of July 1, 2019, companies are required to declare in their income tax returns whether they have any international transactions with related parties.[134] Further, Morocco introduced its first documentation requirements with regard to TP policies of taxpayers,[135] Nigeria has

127. Available at https://home.kpmg/us/en/home/insights/2019/11/tnf-portugal-transfer-pricing-documentation-requirements-other-developments.html, accessed December 20, 2019.
128. Available at https://www.ey.com/gl/en/services/tax/international-tax/alert--portugal-amends-transfer-pricing-regulations, accessed August 28, 2020.
129. Available at https://home.kpmg/us/en/home/insights/2019/07/tnf-thailand-draft-regulatory-proposals-transfer-pricing-documentation.html, accessed December 20, 2019.
130. Available at https://home.kpmg/us/en/home/insights/2019/11/tnf-thailand-transfer-pricing-disclosure-form.html, accessed December 20, 2019.
131. Available at https://home.kpmg/us/en/home/insights/2019/09/tnf-qatar-country-by-country-notification-and-reporting-requirements.html, accessed January 9, 2020.
132. Available at https://www.ey.com/gl/en/services/tax/international-tax/alert--uae-introduces-country-by-country-reporting, accessed January 9, 2020.
133. Available at https://home.kpmg/us/en/home/insights/2019/07/tnf-uae-country-by-country-reporting-requirements.html, accessed January 9, 2020.
134. Available at https://www.ey.com/gl/en/services/tax/international-tax/alert--bangladesh-enacts-2019-20-budget-proposals, accessed December 20, 2019.
135. Available at https://www.ey.com/gl/en/services/tax/international-tax/alert--moroccos-2019-finance-bill-introduces-transfer-pricing-documentation-requirement, accessed January 9, 2020.

been working on the electronic system for filing TP documentation (declarations, disclosure forms, CbCR) from 2020,[136] Panama signed the Multilateral Competent Authority Agreement for CbCR,[137] and Peru decided to commit to sending CbC reports to forty-four countries (notably, it received a similar commitment from only one country, i.e., Portugal).[138] Serbia, in the last days of 2019, passed legislation including the requirement of submitting annual CbC report.[139] Finally, Zimbabwe amended its domestic legislation and required taxpayers to submit their TP documents within only seven days of being requested by the tax authorities.[140]

It can be clearly observed that documentation requirements are becoming more and more frequent in various countries around the world. It is to be expected that, over the next years, even more countries will put respective legal provisions in place. This will happen in particular after the 2020 review of CbCR requirements conducted by the OECD (and mandated by BEPS Action 13 Report) will be finalized and new changes to the minimum standard will be agreed on by the Inclusive Framework. The main goals of these works are to come up with a consistent approach to issues when the 2016 guidance turned out to be insufficient and issues that have been raised by jurisdictions or stakeholders and that can only be addressed through a change to the minimum standard.[141] With improved guidance on how to apply the CbCR in practice, more states will undoubtedly be encouraged to introduce their domestic solutions.

2.5 Dispute Resolution

Dispute resolution and dispute prevention remain the areas of interest of tax authorities around the world. The year 2019 proved to be meaningful for the regulations in the area of Advance Pricing Agreements (APAs) as well as the Mutual Agreement Procedure.

Hong Kong concluded its first unilateral APA. This is a significant milestone for the jurisdiction as its local tax authority, i.e., Inland Revenue Department, has previously concluded APAs only with Hong Kong's treaty partners. The year 2019 hence marks the first time a unilateral APA was concluded.[142] The U.S. stressed the

136. Available at https://home.kpmg/us/en/home/insights/2019/10/tnf-nigeria-plans-electronic-filing-transfer-pricing-forms-cbc-reports.html, accessed January 9, 2020.
137. Available at https://www.ey.com/gl/en/services/tax/international-tax/alert--panama-signs-multilateral-competent-authority-agreement-for-country-by-country-reporting, accessed January 9, 2020.
138. Available at https://home.kpmg/xx/en/home/insights/2019/01/tnf-peru-status-cbc-reports-exchanges-under-mcaa-cbc.html, accessed December 20, 2019.
139. Available at https://home.kpmg/us/en/home/insights/2019/12/tnf-serbia-country-by-country-reporting-rules-are-enacted.html, accessed January 9, 2020.
140. Available at https://home.kpmg/us/en/home/insights/2019/11/tnf-zimbabwe-transfer-pricing-documentation-2020-budget-update.html, accessed December 20, 2019.
141. Available at https://www.oecd.org/tax/beps/oecd-releases-consultation-document-on-the-2020-review-of-country-by-country-reporting-beps-action-13-and-invites-public-input.htm, accessed March 11, 2020.
142. Available at https://home.kpmg/xx/en/home/insights/2019/01/tnf-hong-kong-first-unilateral-advance-pricing-arrangement-is-concluded.html, accessed December 18, 2019.

importance of the APA program by publishing relevant statistics for 2018.[143] The 19th annual APA Report showed that the U.S. taxpayers had a constant interest in concluding APAs with 203 filings, which constituted an increase of 101% in comparison to 2017. The highlight of the report was the significant number of pending bilateral APAs with India, a jurisdiction that is well known for its liking of litigation. In addition, the U.S. also introduced an MS-Excel-based tool to facilitate the process of reviewing the APA requests.[144] India, in its 2019-2020 Union Budget, proposed revised secondary adjustment rules. In the case of APAs, a secondary adjustment could be triggered when a TP adjustment results from an APA between taxpayers and tax authorities.[145] Finally, Costa Rica and Portugal have extended the maximum period of validity of an APA from three to five[146] and to four years,[147] respectively.

When it comes to the Mutual Agreement Procedure (MAP), the recent developments in Brazil and in Nigeria can be singled out as both states issued certain guidance regarding the MAP. Brazil clarified the technical rules of submitting a MAP request in the newly updated MAP implementation guidelines[148] while Nigeria issued the first detailed guidance on the MAP for taxpayers who intend to take advantage of this procedure.[149]

2.6 Other Developments

In 2019, specific countries worked intensively on remodeling their TP rules. Among the countries with the most important developments are Botswana, Brazil, Ireland, and Poland.

Botswana introduced its first ever TP regulations that became effective as of July 1, 2019. These regulations are based on the OECD TP Guidelines (even providing legal authority for the interpretation of its domestic rules to the OECD) and, as such, are based on the premise of the ALP. For now, however, the issuance of binding rulings and the conclusion of APAs are not possible.[150]

Brazil, on its way to a full OECD membership, decided to harmonize its TP rules with the OECD TP Guidelines. The project foresees two options to achieve this goal—either immediate alignment of the Brazilian rules with the OECD standards or

143. Available at https://www.ey.com/gl/en/services/tax/international-tax/alert--us-irs-issues-annual-apa-report-for-2018, accessed December 18, 2019.
144. Available at https://home.kpmg/xx/en/home/insights/2019/03/tnf-united-states-functional-cost-diagnostic-model-for-review-of-apa-requests.html, accessed December 18, 2019.
145. Available at https://www.ey.com/gl/en/services/tax/international-tax/alert--india-releases-2019-20-union-budget---update-on-corporate-tax-proposals, accessed December 18, 2019.
146. Available at https://www.ey.com/gl/en/services/tax/international-tax/alert--costa-rica---modifications-to-income-tax-regulations-affect-transfer-pricing, accessed December 18, 2019.
147. Available at https://www.ey.com/gl/en/services/tax/international-tax/alert--portugal-amends-transfer-pricing-regulations, accessed December 18, 2019.
148. Available at https://home.kpmg/xx/en/home/insights/2019/02/tnf-brazil-updated-map-rules-guidelines.html, accessed December 18, 2019.
149. Available at https://www.ey.com/gl/en/services/tax/international-tax/alert--nigeria-issues-guidelines-on-mutual-agreement-procedure, accessed December 18, 2019.
150. Available at https://home.kpmg/us/en/home/insights/2019/07/tnf-botswana-transfer-pricing-regulations-effective-july-2019.html?e, accessed January 8, 2020.

the alignment in stages, allowing a gradual implementation over a longer period of time.[151] Brazil's decision will undoubtedly be welcomed on the international stage as the specific rules that have been binding until now have been a matter of numerous discussions and a reason for conflicts between Brazilian tax authorities and MNEs operating in other states with TP rules based on the OECD standards.

In 2019, Ireland introduced a finance bill (*An Bille Airgeadais, 2019*) that overhauled the entire TP legislation in the country.[152] Apart from the changes that have already been mentioned in the preceding subchapters, other major amendments also include the adoption of the substance over form approach toward related-party transactions. In addition, grandfathering that existed for transactions agreed before July 1, 2010 will be removed, and the Irish Revenue is now allowed to re-characterize the transactions if needed. Finally, TP rules will be applicable to medium-sized enterprises in respect of transactions with consideration payable exceeding EUR 1 million. Such extensive changes to the Irish TP regime will hopefully help align the Irish TP rules with the latest OECD developments. In addition, they are perhaps also an attempt to repair the image of Ireland a bit as a jurisdiction at the forefront of the fight against BEPS.

Further, with the beginning of 2019, Poland has incorporated significant changes to its TP rules both at a substantial level and with regards to the general taxonomy of these rules.[153] Most importantly, the entire TP legislation was inserted into a single chapter of the Corporate Income Tax Act. The main goal of the changes is to reduce the administrative burden by means of increased thresholds for documentation and the introduction of safe harbors. Simultaneously, the amendment vested more power into tax authorities as far as the assessment of related-party transactions is concerned. In addition to the above overhaul, Polish lawmakers were also at work on the drafts regarding areas such as CbC reporting,[154] dispute resolution, and the conclusion of APAs.[155]

Apart from the above five states, 2019 also saw other jurisdictions amending or clarifying their TP rules. Costa Rica modified the definition of related parties and the rules regarding filing of TP returns.[156] In Germany, the end of 2019 saw the publication of the first draft of the Anti-Tax Avoidance Directive Implementation Act[157] which also comprised significant changes to the German interpretation of the ALP, aiming to bring

151. Available at https://home.kpmg/us/en/home/insights/2019/07/tnf-brazil-project-to-align-brazils-transfer-pricing-rules-to-oecd-guidelines.html, accessed January 8, 2020.
152. Available at https://www.ey.com/gl/en/services/tax/international-tax/alert--ireland-publishes-finance-bill-2019---transfer-pricing-updates, accessed January 8, 2020.
153. Available at https://www.ey.com/gl/en/services/tax/international-tax/alert--poland-significantly-revises-transfer-pricing-law-from-1-january-2019, accessed January 8, 2020.
154. Available at https://home.kpmg/xx/en/home/insights/2019/05/tnf-poland-new-rules-relating-cbc-reporting-exchange-information.html, accessed January 8, 2020.
155. Available at https://home.kpmg/xx/en/home/insights/2019/04/tnf-poland-proposals-for-simplified-apa.html, accessed January 8, 2020.
156. Available at https://www.ey.com/gl/en/services/tax/international-tax/alert--costa-rica---modifications-to-income-tax-regulations-affect-transfer-pricing, accessed January 8, 2020.
157. Available at https://www.bundesfinanzministerium.de/Content/DE/Gesetzestexte/Gesetze_Gesetzesvorhaben/Abteilungen/Abteilung_IV/19_Legislaturperiode/Gesetze_Verordnungen/ATADUmsG/0-Gesetz.html, accessed January 9, 2020.

the German TP legislation in line with the OECD developments presented in BEPS Actions 8-10.[158] However, as of January 2020, further works on introducing this new law have been temporarily suspended. New Zealand focused on providing guidance to the BEPS developments of the preceding years, requiring submitting disclosure forms for all tax returns starting in 2020.[159] Portugal clarified and broadened the concept of intra-group transactions, explicitly including categories of transactions such as corporate restructurings and reorganizations.[160] Russia started works on draft legislation concerning TP rules regarding intangibles (i.e., introducing the DEMPE concept to Russian law) and the PSM as well as the MAP.[161] Serbia provided guidance on determining arm's length interest expenses and revenue[162] while Singapore released guidance on commodity marketing and trading activities including hints on how to analyze the economic value of such activities.[163] Finally, Zimbabwe provided clarification concerning the application of the domestic thin cap rules.[164]

Certainly, the local efforts with regard to the implementation of the APA and the MAP have been significant over the last year. It is to be expected, however, that a significant potential exists for an increase in the cross-border tax controversy with the introduction of new domestic rules aimed at combatting tax avoidance as well as with the developments at the international level (works by the OECD or EU). Therefore, APA and MAP legislation should remain an important topic on the agenda of the domestic legislators, and the relevance of these tools will undoubtedly increase.

2.7 Significant Domestic Case Law

In 2019, a few significant domestic cases were issues—*Amazon.Com, Inc. & Subsidiaries v. Commissioner of Internal Revenue,*[165] *Altera Corp. v. Commissioner,*[166] both

158. Available at https://www.ey.com/gl/en/services/tax/international-tax/alert--germany-publishes-draft-atad-implementation-law, accessed January 9, 2020.
159. Available at https://home.kpmg/us/en/home/insights/2019/11/tnf-new-zealand-inland-revenues-focus-on-beps-and-mne-tax-compliance-includes-transfer-pricing.html, accessed January 8, 2020.
160. Available at https://www.ey.com/gl/en/services/tax/international-tax/alert--portugal-amends-transfer-pricing-regulations, accessed January 8, 2020.
161. Available at https://home.kpmg/us/en/home/insights/2019/06/tnf-russia-controlled-transactions-intangibles-profit-split-method-mutual-agreement-procedures.html, accessed January 8, 2020.
162. Available at https://home.kpmg/xx/en/home/insights/2019/03/tnf-serbia-related-party-interest-rates-2019-transfer-pricing-documentation-implications.html, accessed January 8, 2020.
163. Available at https://home.kpmg/us/en/home/insights/2019/06/tnf-singapore-transfer-pricing-guidelines-for-commodity-marketing-and-trading-companies.html, accessed January 8, 2020.
164. Available at https://home.kpmg/us/en/home/insights/2019/07/tnf-zimbabwe-transfer-pricing-rules-clarification-to-thin-capitalisation-measures.html, accessed January 8, 2020.
165. *Amazon.Com, Inc. & Subsidiaries v. Commissioner of Internal Revenue*, 17-72922, Tax Ct. No. 31197-12, available at https://law.justia.com/cases/federal/appellate-courts/ca9/17-72922/17-72922-2019-08-16.html, accessed December 20, 2019.
166. *Altera Corp. v. Commissioner*, No. 16-70496 (9th Cir. 2019), available at https://law.justia.com/cases/federal/appellate-courts/ca9/16-70496/16-70496-2019-06-07.html, accessed January 7, 2020.

decided by the U.S. Court of Appeals and *Glencore Investment Pty Ltd. v. Commissioner of Taxation of the Commonwealth of Australia* that was decided by the Federal Court of Australia.[167]

In *Amazon*, the tax court dealt with the definition of intangibles under the U.S. law provisions binding before the statutory amendment issued with the tax *Cuts and Jobs Act of 2017*. The court concluded that this definition did not include residual business assets such as the value of employees' experience, education and training (known as "workforce in place"), a culture of innovation, going concern value, goodwill, and other unique business attributes and expectancies (which the parties refer to as "growth options"). Thus, the case was solved in favor of Amazon.

The other U.S. case, *Altera*, dealt with the character of stock option costs. The Court of Appeals decided that such costs should be included as costs for TP purposes. It is notable that a similar judgment was withdrawn by the same court in 2018.[168]

The Australian *Glencore* case turned out to be another taxpayer-favorable decision. Here, the case concerned the transfer prices that Glencore used on certain cross-border related-party transactions associated with its copper mining operations. The court stated that it was correct that the taxpayer started the analysis for the actual transaction with its Swiss-based trading entity as similar relations to the case at hand were also present in the practice of independent companies. The decision provided clarity with respect to the use of a hypothetical transaction in considering whether the pricing outcomes were consistent with an independent arm's length outcome and the circumstances when it might be appropriate to adjust the form of the actual transaction entered into by the parties.[169]

Apart from the above cases, the following countries issued decisions that are significant for domestic practice that can also be of interest from an international perspective:[170]

Austria

- *A S.a.r.l.*, determination whether a set-up with a shareholder company located in Luxembourg was abusive, Supreme Administrative Court of March 27, 2019, No. Ro 2018/13/0004.

Brazil

- public ruling on characteristics of Cost Sharing Agreements (Coordination Office of Brazilian Revenue) of September 26, 2019, No. 276.

167. *Glencore Investment Pty Ltd. v. Commissioner of Taxation of the Commonwealth of Australia* [2019] FCA 1432, available at https://www.judgments.fedcourt.gov.au/judgments/Judgments/fca/single/2019/2019fca1432, accessed December 20, 2019.
168. Available at https://news.bloombergtax.com/transfer-pricing/insight-transfer-pricing-cases-of-2019, accessed January 7, 2020.
169. Available at https://home.kpmg/au/en/home/insights/2019/10/price-is-right-glencore-wins-in-the-federal-court-2-october-2019-ti.html, accessed December 20, 2019.
170. Available at https://news.bloombergtax.com/transfer-pricing/insight-transfer-pricing-cases-of-2019, accessed January 7, 2020; *see also*: https://tpcases.com/, accessed August 28, 2020.

Denmark

- *Microsoft*, remuneration for marketing activities, Supreme Court of January 31, 2019, No. 75/2018.
- *MAN Energy Solutions*, adjustment of royalty payments, Supreme Court of September 12, No. BS-4280/2019-HJR.

France

- *Piaggio*, business restructuring, Conseil d'Etat of October 4, 2019, Case No. 418817; *Google*, settlement of the case relating to a PE in France, Court of Appeal in Paris of September 12, 2019, No. PNF-15 162 000 335.

Germany

- *A GmbH*, treatment of a loss coming from waiving the claim from the unsecured clearing account managed for a foreign subsidiary, Federal Fiscal Court of February 27, 2019, No. I R 73/16.

India

- *Aegis Ltd.*, acquisition of preference shares being equivalent to an interest free loan granted to an associated enterprise, High Court of Bombay of January 18, 2019, No. 1248 of 2016.

Israel

- *Broadcom*; business restructuring from a fully-fledged principal to a service provider and transfer of value, Lod District Court of December 2019, No. 26342-01-16.
- *Broadcom*; transfer of value of an Israeli subsidiary, Israeli Supreme Court of August 2019, No. 2454/19.

Italy

- anonymized, treatment of a loss-making Italian group company, Regional Tax Commission of Lombardy of September 2019, No. 928/20/2019.
- *Agusta Holding BV*, challenged corporate structure of a company operating in Italian market via a subsidiary but incorporated in the Netherlands due to the favorable fiscal dividend regime, Supreme Court of Cassation of May 28, 2019, No. 14527/2019.

Luxembourg

- *Lender Societe*, treatment of the interest rate on the shareholder loan, Administrative Court of July 17, 2019, No. 42043C.

Malaysia

- *Shell*, recharacterization of a Cost Contribution Agreement as an intra-group services arrangement, High Court of Malaysia of November 12, 2019, No. BA-25-68-08/2019.

Netherlands

- *Lender BV*, treatment of the interest payment from an affiliated Russian company to the Dutch lender, District Court Noord-Holland of June 5, 2019, No. HAA 17/871.

Norway

- *A/S Norske Shell*, remuneration of R&D works and deductibility of relevant costs, Court of Appeal of September 26, 2019, No. LB-2018-79168-UTV-2019-807.

Portugal

- *Galeria Parque Nascente-Exploração de Espaços Comerciais SA*, deductibility of loan costs for the purchase of shares in the case of a reverse merger, order of the court in response for the request for a preliminary ruling to the CJEU, C-438/18 of July 15, 2019.

Spain

- *ARW Enterprise Computin Solution SA*, deductibility of intra-group management fees, Supreme Court of Justice of September 26, 2019, No. STSJ M 7038/2019.

Sweden

- *Yazaki Europe*, remuneration of a branch with limited functions, Court of Appeal of Göteborg of October 10, 2019, Nos. 2552-2555-17, 2557-2558-17, 3422-18.
- *Technology Partners International Europe Ltd*, the same issue as in the former case, Court of Appeal of Stockholm of October 4, 2019, Nos. 3701-18, 3702-18.

United Kingdom

- *Irish Bank Resolution Corporation Ltd and Irish Nationwide Building Society*, deductibility of notional interest, Upper Tribunal of October 9, 2019, No. UKUT 0277 (TCC).

United States

- *Cavallaro*, valuation of intangibles in relation to a merger, U.S. Tax Court of October 24, 2019, T.C. Memo 2019-144.

- *SIH Partners LLLP, Explorer Partner Corporation, Tax Matters Partner*, inclusion of the controlled foreign company's applicable earnings in own income of a U.S. company under specific conditions, United States Court of Appeals for the Third Circuit of May 7, 2019, No. 18-1862.

Zambia

- *Nestlé Trading Ltd.*, characterization of the entity and the adjustment of the transaction by the tax authorities, Tax Appeals Tribunal of March 28, 2019, No. 2018/TAT/03/DT.

Zimbabwe

- *Delta Beverages Ltd.*, allowing of specific fees such as technical service fees, license of trademarks, technology and know-how, Special Court for Income Tax Appeals of October 11, 2019, No. HH664-19.

2.8 Conclusions

The year 2019 saw significant steps taken on the international level toward the continuation of the fight against tax avoidance and making the contemporary tax rules relevant in the era of increasingly digitalized business models. Intensive works were undertaken by both international organizations and domestic legislators.

Undoubtedly, the most important development in the international taxation also affecting TP was the OECD Secretariat's Proposal on the Unified Approach based on two pillars. Perhaps the most discussed so far was Pillar 1 which has the ambitious goal of determining the rules for the allocation of taxing rights and proposing the new nexus rules. The public discussion on Pillar 1 garnered increased attention of stakeholders from the entire world who presented their opinions during the round of public consultation.[171] At the same time, GloBE (or Pillar 2) turned out to be less relevant for purely TP purposes as its main goal is developing a set of rules addressing MNEs' structures that allow shifting profits to jurisdictions with no or very low taxation. It is expected that a final proposal of new rules for international taxation will be agreed on over the course of 2020. With such significant changes to current rules, it is to be expected that a consensus will require a lot of politically influenced negotiations.

The works on the Unified Approach were not the only ones undertaken by the OECD. In the TP realm, the updated Guidance on the Implementation of CbCR was issued in view of existing practical issues, and the works on the new chapter of the OECD TPG on financial transactions were finalized with the chapter being officially published in February 2020. The latter development can certainly be perceived as being of significant importance to the practice as it was awaited for a longer time. It is to be

171. Available at https://www.oecd.org/tax/beps/public-comments-received-on-the-secretariat-proposal-for-a-unified-approach-under-pillar-one.htm, accessed August 28, 2020.

expected that the chapter might undergo certain modifications in view of the feedback after it has been applied in practice by the national tax administrations or companies.

In the EU, the highlights of the year were the decisions of the CJEU in the high profile cases of *Fiat, Starbucks,* and *Belgian excess profit regime* as well as the investigations and decisions issued by the European Commission. On the other hand, new investigations initiated by the Commission in *Nike* and *Huhtamäki* as well as the resumed investigation of the Belgian excess profit regime prove that the era of intensive state aid investigations in the EU will not end soon. The European Joint Transfer Pricing also remained active in 2019 with the Report on the Application of the PSM within the EU providing a guidance on use cases, methodology, and splitting factors. This work, relying to a considerable extent on concepts provided already by the OECD undoubtedly serves toward creating a common approach to the application of the PSM.

When it comes to developing countries, the United Nations was focusing primarily on updating the Practical Manual on Transfer Pricing with the most significant change being drafting the new chapter on financial transactions. Other changes, although smaller and mainly focusing on the revisions of the already existing content of the manual, serve a further clarification of the most important TP issues. The works on all of the updates should be finalized in 2020 with 2021 scheduled as the issue date of its new version.

In the area of domestic law, a clear trend among many countries was to develop their internal rules for taxation of digital services in the face of slowly progressing works on the international level. So far, these domestic initiatives remain mainly on a drafting level; however, with the first jurisdictions to have introduced the tax in 2019, more may be expected to follow in 2020. This situation raises questions about the compatibility of such solutions with the possible internationally approved concept, and it seems that these questions will have to be answered sooner rather than later. When it comes to general TP legislation, 2019 witnessed, just as in previous years, a number of countries adopting their first TP rules or the ALP into domestic law. More and more countries also require the provisions of detailed TP documentation, and APAs are slowly becoming the most favorite way of preventing potential tax disputes among both tax authorities and tax payers. Finally, TP remained an important subject in litigation. With many significant cases from around the world (including two high profile cases decided in the U.S. and one in Australia), it can be confirmed that TP rules are definitely not crystal clear and still create interpretational issues.

Undoubtedly, after 2019, which turned out to be a year in which significant works toward the new model of taxation were undertaken, 2020 and the following years should be the time when the first tangible solutions crystalize. As the system of global taxation is in urgent need of adaptation to the changed reality relying heavily on digital business models, it seems that all stakeholders will be interested in delivering a final solution as soon as possible. However, with the unclear situation of the global economy in early 2020 that was caused by factors unrelated to business, the question remains of what the most effective system would be and how to manage the situation.

CHAPTER 2

Transfer Pricing Developments in the European Union

Wendy Nicholls & Svitlana Buriak[*]

* Views are the authors' and contributors' own and do not reflect the views of the Grant Thornton International organization, its member firms, or of the employers of the contributors. This chapter was written in early 2020 and may not reflect the latest developments. All internet references were accessed between January 3 and 20, 2020.

1 INTRODUCTION

This chapter considers how transfer pricing (TP) practice has developed in the European Union (EU) over approximately the past year. It is not a jurisdiction-by-jurisdiction review; such summaries are readily available elsewhere. Rather, it touches upon some of the generic similarities and differences, e.g., between "west" and "east," and the "Remainders" versus the "Leavers" (the U.K.) and asks the question: "Is transfer pricing in the EU converging or diverging?" It will mention some instances of when the outgoing European Commission (the Commission) can be said to have succeeded or fallen short of its ambitions in the TP arena and, in practical terms, comments on how useful the Joint Transfer Pricing Forum (JTPF) has been in solving TP problems for businesses and Member States.

The chapter looks at whether the EU acted as a bloc or as a collection of separate entities when adopting the TP guidance of the OECD (Organisation for Economic Co-operation and Development), including the most recent proposals under the Base Erosion and Profit Shifting (BEPS) Project,[1] alongside the G20 (Group of Twenty[2]) and the Inclusive Framework on BEPS (IF on BEPS),[3] which numbers an impressive, albeit potentially unwieldy, 137 jurisdictions.[4]

---

1. OECD, Action Plan on Base Erosion and Profit Shifting, available at https://www.oecd.org/ctp/BEPSActionPlan.pdf, accessed May 28, 2020.
2. The Group of Twenty, or the G20, is the premier forum for international economic cooperation. The G20 brings together leaders of both developed and developing countries from every continent. Collection, G20 members represent around 80% of the world's economic output, two thirds of global population and three-quarters of international trade. Throughout the year, representatives from G20 countries gather to discuss financial socioeconomic issues. The G20 members are Argentina, Australia, Brazil, Canada, China, France, Germany, India, Indonesia, Italy, Japan, Mexico, Russia, Saudi Arabia, Republic of Korea, Turkey, the United Kingdom, the United States, and the European Union, available at https://g20.org.en/about/Pages, accessed May 28, 2020.
3. IF is intended to work on an equal footing to tackle tax avoidance, improve the coherence of international tax rules, and ensure a more transparent tax environment. In particular, the framework:

   - develops standards in respect of remaining BEPS issues;
   - reviews the implementation of agreed minimum standards through an effective monitoring system;
   - monitors BEPS issues, including tax challenges raised by the digital economy; and
   - facilitates the implementation processes of the members by providing further guidance and by supporting development of toolkits to support low-capacity developing countries.

   "Joining the Inclusive Framework offers the opportunity to interested countries and jurisdictions to participate in the BEPS related work on an equal footing with other OECD and G20 countries. Being part of the Inclusive Framework on BEPS will facilitate the implementation, as well as the peer review processes of the Members, by providing them with further guidance and support, including guidance covered by the Platform for Collaboration on Tax established among the IMF, the OECD, the UN and the World Bank Group." (Source, available at http://www.oecd.org/tax/beps/background-brief-inclusive-framework-on-beps.pdf, accessed August 28, 2020).
4. OECD, Members of the OECD/G20Inclusive Framework on BEPS, available at http://www.oecd.org/tax/beps/inclusive-framework-on-beps-composition.pdf, accessed on May 28, 2020.

Looking forward to next year, the chapter also asks: What might the new Commission do in the TP arena, and what should be its priorities? The final question is can and should the EU be a leader or only a, albeit enthusiastic, follower of the OECD and others in the field of TP?

2 PRACTICAL ASSISTANCE: THE EU JTPF

The EU Joint Transfer Pricing Forum (EU JTPF) exists to "assist and advise the European Commission on transfer pricing tax matters."[5] As a reminder, unlike indirect taxes and some areas of direct taxation (like withholding taxes on interest and dividends), TP legislation is not harmonized via directives and is a matter for individual Member State governments. Therefore, the single market and fundamental freedoms must be protected, but Member States still have sovereignty over corporate (and, incidentally, individual) income taxation.

All Member States trying to walk the tightrope in their own way can lead to contortions, complexity, and confusion. An example is the lack of any helpful guidance from the Commission about how to operate the DAC 6 (DAC 6: International Tax Enforcement: disclosable arrangements) on the disclosure of tax avoidance arrangements as discussed later in this chapter (*see* section 5 below) that has resulted in duplication of work and some practitioners proposing to over-disclose for fear of penalties by one or several states.

Noting that TP intra-EU was potentially problematic and would benefit from simplification and clarity, the JTPF was set up in 2002 to help the Commission solve practical TP problems in the EU. Very unusually for such a body, it has both governmental and non-governmental members participating on an equal footing. Wendy Nicholls has been a member of the last mandate under the previous Commission (2015-2019) and, in her view, this composition has made an important contribution to finding pragmatic and helpful solutions and to the understanding that, in many cases, TP is a "zero sum" game, so an overly adversarial approach between taxpayers and tax administrations should be avoided when possible.

The main achievements of the forum over the past two years (the final sub-part of its latest mandate) have been:

- Application of the Profit Split Method (PSM).
- Joint TP audits in the EU.

These are discussed below.

5. Consequently, the EU Commission has initiated a set of coordinated measures, either guidance or recommendations, all subsequently endorsed by the EU Council. They now constitute a recognized congruent and efficient enabling TP framework in the EU. They cover all steps of the TP process from the determination and documentation stage, the TP audit and, finally, the dispute resolution phase, available at https://ec.europa.eu/taxation_customs/business/company-tax/transfer-pricing-eu-context/joint-transfer-pricing-forum_en#heading_1, accessed August 28, 2020.

It is currently unclear whether the forum will be reconstituted under similar terms of reference and similar composition in the future under the new Commission of Ursula von der Leyen. Options may include: a wider forum to include other areas of international taxation, ad hoc working parties consisting of a fluid composition of experts in the area of each topic as it arises rather than a set committee, and/or public consultations on important issues. It would be a pity, in the authors' view, if the advantages of the forum in providing practical and pragmatic guidance no longer existed. The OECD and the IF do great work but comprise a broad range of differing opinions and ideas that definitive guidance from them is almost impossible. The EU JTPF has filled a gap, at least within Europe. Although the wider composition of the latest mandate of the forum (e.g., to include Non-governmental Organization representation on the non-government members' side) has meant a less homogenous group, the diversity of views between representatives has provided constructive challenges and useful debates.

However, the new Commission has already reiterated the wish to move toward "simpler and fairer" tax systems, which has support from the populace at large. Could and should "simpler" morph into "the same"? This seems unlikely in the short term. While attempts to homogenize direct taxation in the EU under a common (consolidated) corporate tax base have been made many times, they have had many problems attached to them and have not yet been adopted. In the meantime, additional practical help and guidance around TP can only be welcomed.

Especially in view of the European fundamental freedoms and the single market, many feel it is disappointing that the EU does not align itself more closely together on TP. On the one hand, Europe should act together on the international stage to assert European and not just national interests provided that the European idea is taken seriously. The economic power of the individual states is too insignificant for that in the international context. On the other hand, the single market should not be made more difficult by tax regulations and certainly not by TP. TP policy must be European and, within the EU, there should be agreement on more practical approaches. The number of mutual agreement procedures (MAPs) unfortunately shows that a considerable proportion of the world's MAPs are intra-European. This completely undermines the single market. Against this background, a TP body is necessary to establish and apply a fair and effective tax system within the EU.

2.1 The Application of the PSM Within the EU (March 2019)

In March 2019, the JTPF agreed on a report on the application of the PSM within the EU.[6]

Sometime previously, the JTPF had considered four potential areas for further work on the PSM:

6. EU Joint Transfer Pricing Forum, The Application of the Profit Split Method in the EU, March 2019, DOC: JTPF/002/2019/EN, available at https://ec.europa.eu/taxation_customs/sites/taxation/files/report_on_the_application_of_the_profit_split_method_within_the_eu_en.pdf, accessed on May 28, 2020.

(1) When to use the PSM?
(2) How to split the profit?
(3) Is there a need for simplification?
(4) How to simplify the application of the PSM?

During the latest mandate, and in view of the shortage of time left, forum members reached consensus on a two stage process whereby, in the first stage, the focus should be on clarifying certain concepts related to the PSM and eventually, in a second later stage, on exploring ways for simplification.

The Commission stressed that "For the avoidance of doubt this Report should be regarded as complementary to, and supportive of, the text of the OECD Revised Guidelines on the application of the Transactional Profit Split Method issued in June 2018."[7] The forum's mandate did not allow for the departure from OECD guidance, and the general (albeit not universal) view of forum members was that clarification and practical assistance on the OECD guidance in this area was the right way forward. The aim of the JTPF exercise, therefore, was to take stock of how the PSM is applied within the EU and work toward a common approach of addressing the relevant challenges arising under the current OECD framework. One of the reasons was that "greater clarification and standardisation, where possible, of the PSM could have significant benefits for both tax authorities and taxpayers as it would reduce compliance costs."[8]

The report recognized that:

> there is a tension between these desirable objectives and the need, as stressed in the Guidelines, for a method that is appropriate for the individual taxpayer. Indeed, there were two different views:
>
> - that it should be possible to simplify the process by standardising the application of the PSM for common business models as the aim is not complete precision but achieving a reasonable estimate in line with the arm's length principle and
> - that it is essential to emphasise the importance of the relevant facts and circumstances in each and every situation when applying the method, i.e. total standardisation was inappropriate as each case should be assessed individually regardless of the resultant complexities.[9]

In order to take stock and gather useful information on the application of the PSM, it was decided to carry out a survey on the experiences of the JTPF members in the practical application of the PSM. Based on the survey, the lack of a common methodology in determining profit splitting factors was recognized as a factor that exacerbates the challenges and could undermine the prospects for applying the PSM even in circumstances when this may be the most appropriate method.

Section 2 of the report provides a description of the PSM, and section 3 aims to clarify its application, i.e., to further clarify the OECD Guidelines (also through

7. *Ibid.*
8. *Ibid.*
9. *Ibid.*

additional examples) regarding the meaning of the "unique and valuable" contribution of the parties to the transaction. In addition, it aims to clarify the difference between integrated business operations (common to all of the transactions involving multinational enterprises (MNEs)) and highly integrated business operations. Section 4 describes a number of potential splitting factors that are listed in the Annex of the report.

2.1.1 When to Use the PSM

The forum noted that:

> In practical terms, the operations would be "highly integrated" when two or more legal entities share and/or combine functions, assets and risks, while jointly achieve a common objective (e.g. a project whereby the parties jointly contribute to each part of the process towards a common outcome). "Highly integrated" does not necessarily mean using the same resources or service provider. Rather, there needs to exist a common objective and a combination of joint contributions. Additionally, it should be sustained that it would not be possible to materialise such a jointly achieved objective without the participation of the other party in the transaction.[10]

In addition, considering the examples provided in the OECD Guidelines, the report reached the conclusion that "taking these examples together, it is clear that where the criterion of highly integrated business operations is satisfied the PSM is likely to be applicable regardless of whether both parties also make unique and valuable contributions."[11] In practice, this often means that, for the application of the PSM, the criteria of high integration should be considered first.

Further points of clarification on the application of the PSM according to the report are:

- The presence of a cross-entity and cross-border business unit structure should not per se be an indication of a highly integrated business operation for the purpose of applying the PSM.
- The OECD Guidelines point out in paragraph 2.126 that the hallmarks of shared assumption of economically significant risks and a separate assumption of closely related risks are not mutually exclusive with the one on highly integrated business operations; each concept should be considered and analyzed on its own.

At the JTPF meeting on October 24, 2018, it was decided that a non-prescriptive list of splitting factors with a brief analysis of the pros and cons of each splitting factor, circumstances, and value drivers would be of benefit to both taxpayers and tax administrations in Member States. The splitting factors were grouped into the following broad categories:

10. *Ibid.*
11. *Ibid.*

- people-based factors;
- sales/volume-based factors;
- asset-based factors;
- cost-based factors; and
- other factors.

Annex 2 of the report contains a flow chart/decision tree that shows, in a simplified way, a number of steps to be considered when assessing when and how to apply the PSM. Annex 3 of the report contains a chart and a table to help identify the key value drivers for the splitting factors that are listed, a description of the circumstances when they may be useful, and the pros and cons for each factor. Informal feedback is that the charts have been found to be very useful by taxpayers and advisers in practical terms.

Nevertheless, even more guidance would be welcomed to help determine how to split profit and potentially how to simplify the application of the PSM. Further work could be done to give indications, for example, about the weight to attribute in the case of using more than one splitting factor. Considering simplification, as an example, in the application of the residual PSM, it could be useful using a standardized benchmark analysis for routine functions (differentiated per industry/sector or also for the kind of activities: production, distribution activities, or services).[12]

2.2 Coordinated Approach to TP Controls Within the EU (October 2018)

Following some successful pilots[13] (e.g., between Germany and Italy, countries in which tax administrations have taken very different paths on audits in the past[14]), it was agreed that there was a need for tax administrations to strengthen their cooperation and be open to experimenting with new forms of collaboration that deepen the exchange of information.

A coordinated approach to TP audits can contribute to better functioning of the internal market on two fronts. It should offer tax administrations a transparent and efficient tool to facilitate the allocation of taxing rights and also prevent the occurrence of double taxation and double non-taxation.[15] The report's aim was to establish best practices, issue recommendations, and encourage closer tax audit cooperation. The

12. In this regard, there is a part of an ongoing OECD project that has established a focus group on the use of benchmarks to increase tax certainty with the aim of enabling wider use of pre-set benchmarks in APA and MAP cases but also in risk assessment and audit to improve the avoidance of disputes and resolution.
13. Braun/Eisgruber/Greil/Schmitz, Joint audits: The German experience, Winter, International Tax Review, 2020, pp. 23-24.
14. The success of the pilot joint audits was also favored by the common language used as Italy selected German speaking tax auditors (living in an Italian Region where German is an official language together with Italian), according to Ms Gianfrate.
15. EU Joint Transfer Pricing Forum, A Coordinated Approach to Transfer Pricing Controls within the EU, October 2018, available at https://ec.europa.eu/taxation_customs/sites/taxation/files/jtpf_report_on_a_coordinated_approach_to_transfer_pricing_controls_within_the_eu_en.pdf, accessed on May 28, 2020.

JTPF encouraged Member States to amend their internal legal framework to allow for effective joint TP audits. The report also provided generic guidelines in the context of coordinated TP audits: organizational matters, taxpayer's rights and obligations, and the various phases within a joint TP audit.

Because TP "is potentially more subjective than other areas of direct and indirect taxation ... [it is particularly] sensitive to disputes,"[16] the guidance noted the importance of developing administrative cooperation on two levels:

(1) between the relevant tax administrations; and
(2) between tax administrations and taxpayers.

The coordinated approach during tax audits and an agreed outcome should also assist the procedures regarding the MAP and bilateral or multilateral advance pricing agreements (APA)s within the EU. The first part of the report provides a number of recommendations to tax authorities of the EU Member States in relation to this cooperation:

- Exchange of information and cooperation between tax administrations should be used when they are expected to assist in the identification of TP risks and to contribute to an efficient audit.
- It is preferable to take a cooperative approach based on dialogue and trust. A cooperative approach is *inter alia* characterized by communication between tax administrations and taxpayers.
- Member States are encouraged to implement legislation that permits the active presence of visiting foreign officials in accordance with Article 11 of the Directive 2011/16/EU (the Directive).
- Member States are encouraged to swiftly lay down the legal framework that would allow them to perform corresponding downward adjustments as a result of a common understanding of the facts and circumstances and of the application of the arm's length principle (ALP).
- Member States should use, in appropriate cases, the possibilities under the Directive on a real-time basis for the purpose of achieving a high degree of coordination, smooth communication, and exchange of information during a TP audit.

The second part of the report provides a set of best practices for a coordinated approach to TP audits. The recommendations made were:

- Member States should ensure that stakeholders are aware of the possibilities and functioning of the available tools for taking a coordinated approach to TP audits. In order to facilitate the communication between stakeholders, tax administrations are encouraged to establish a contact point(s) and publish a functional e-mail box to contact in matters related to coordinated TP audits. To

16. *Ibid.*

enable a cooperative approach, Member States are encouraged, to the extent possible, to be flexible regarding the choice of the audit periods, the timing, and the way the audit is performed.
- Member States participate in coordinated TP audits unless their refusal is based on a reasonable explanation (or local law constraints).
- All must agree and sign an audit plan for each coordinated TP audit.
- Member States must agree to a Memorandum of Understanding if and when they wish to establish a sustained coordinated TP audits program.
- Finally, each coordinated TP audit should finish with a concluding report.

Annex 1 of the report provides a summary table and a list of Member States' national provisions that implement the Directive, including whether national law currently allows the active and/or passive presence of visiting foreign officials and the possibility of performing a downward adjustment as a result of a coordinated TP audit.

2.2.1 Implementation: A Mixed Picture

The European Commission has published a summary regarding the implementation by Member States of Directive 2011/16/EU[17] especially regarding the extent that national law currently allows the active and/or passive presence of visiting foreign officials and the possibility to perform a downward adjustment as a result of a coordinated TP audit.

Most of the Member States currently allow the presence (passive presence) of foreign officials (from other Member States) in their administrative offices and during inquiries (an exception is made by Luxemburg and Romania—the latter only regarding the presence during inquiries). Concerning active participation of foreign officials in the examination of records and interviews of individuals (active participation), there are different opinions. Many of the Member States (including the U.K.) do not allow such active presence while countries like Austria, Germany, Bulgaria, Denmark, France, Finland, Italy, etc. now do allow such active participation.

Regarding the implementation of the legal provisions to allow downward adjustments resulting from coordinated TP audits, Member States also have a mixed approach. Again, countries like Austria, Belgium, Bulgaria, Denmark, Greece, Italy, etc. have introduced such provisions, and some countries, like Spain, allow this under specific circumstances while other countries (including Cyprus, Czech Republic, Finland, France, Ireland, and the U.K.) do not have such provisions.

It is too early to say whether such audits will become more commonplace, but the authors expect not in light of the very high level of resources that are required in the same way as the cooperative compliance programs like ICAP (the International Compliance Assurance Programme; "a voluntary programme for a multilateral co-operative risk assessment and assurance process"[18]).

---

17. *Ibid.*
18. OECD International Compliance Assurance Programme (ICAP), available at http://www.oecd.org/tax/forum-on-tax-administration/international-compliance-assurance-programme.htm, accessed on May 28, 2020.

2.3 East Versus West

Although there does not seem to be a particular east-west distinction in relation to the issue covered above in section 2.2, it is often observed that TP is different between Western and Eastern Europe. In some cases, the rules and documentation requirements are more prescriptive or onerous in some CEE[19] countries (e.g., Hungary requires a file for each transaction, and Poland allows only seven days for a company to produce TP reports when requested). However, the authors have discussed this issue with counterparts in other European countries, and the main difference observed anecdotally seems to be in the area of TP audits. Some Eastern European countries can appear more assertive or aggressive in an audit, but their tax administrations may argue that this is caused by their relative lack of experience. If so, it would be expected that any differences in approach would reduce over time.

Clients in all industries (from financial services to services to consumer and industrial products) often indicate that it is time consuming and duplicative to deal with "similar but different" TP questions in several countries even when several of those countries are in the EU. Joint audits, as noted in section 2.2 above, can be helpful but, as noted above, only when governments agree to give up some "sovereignty." Even then, resource requirements mean that these will apply in a tiny minority of cases and, so far, only bilaterally but not multilaterally. Could the EU not make it easier for taxpayers to deal with intra-EU TP audits? The answer, based on the principle of tax sovereignty and the lack of a single market in direct taxation, as discussed above, appears to be "no." At the moment, this idea is clearly a "bridge too far."

2.4 Remainders Versus Leavers

As the U.K. is scheduled to be in its transition period by the time of the conference (having "left" the EU on January 31), there should be little change for the remainder of 2020. However, what about after that? Many paths are possible, but the main ones are (a) continued very close alignment with the rest of the EU and (b) divergence from the EU.

The new U.K. Government has indicated that it does not wish to extend the transition period beyond the end of 2020, and some believe that London wants to be "Singapore-on-Thames" and distance itself from the EU on free-market terms. However, an extreme U.K. position seems unlikely, and the previously trailed reduction of the U.K. corporate tax rate down to 17% has now been shelved, reinforcing the

19. Central and Eastern Europe. "Central and Eastern European Countries (CEECs) is an OECD term for the group of countries comprising Albania, Bulgaria, Croatia, the Czech Republic, Hungary, Poland, Romania, the Slovak Republic, Slovenia, and the three Baltic States: Estonia, Latvia and Lithuania," available at https://stats.oecd.org/glossary/detail.asp?ID=303, accessed August 28, 2020.

impression that the U.K. has no ambition to become a "pirate state" or tax haven. The U.K. corporate tax rate remains at 19%.[20]

Additionally, in the field of TP, divergence far from the consensus seems unlikely. The main reason for that is because TP is one of the few areas of taxation where global consensus has had some success, notably in the ALP, and, furthermore, the U.K. has played a leading role in supporting the OECD in its TP initiatives to date and sees no reason why that should change.

The U.K. has not held back from introducing anti-avoidance provisions. The Diverted Profits Tax was brought in from April 2015 and subject to potential deferral beyond the budget in March 2020, and the Digital Services Tax that came in from April 1, 2020 at 2% of certain revenues from digital businesses.

It is possible that the post-Brexit, U.K. may decide not to adopt some of the more onerous provisions for business such as DAC 6 (*see* section 5 below) especially given that it already has a successful Disclosure of Tax Avoidance Schemes[21] regime; however, in the event that the Withdrawal Agreement is ratified and there is a "deal" Brexit, then the DAC 6 rules will at least be adopted within the transitional period.[22]

Another area for potential divergence in the future could be public country-by-country reporting (CbCR), if and when this becomes a requirement across the EU.

3 TRANSPARENCY AND DISCLOSURES

Transparency and disclosures are arguably the main areas where the EU as a bloc has the most opportunity to standardize and potentially go further than the OECD/IF.

3.1 DAC 6 and TP

The EU Directive known as "DAC 6"[23] requires the reporting of cross-border arrangements meeting certain hallmarks to allow countries "to react promptly against harmful tax practices and to close loopholes by enacting legislation or by undertaking adequate risk assessments and carrying out tax audits." One of the hallmarks, category E, relates specifically to TP, including hard-to value intangibles and business restructurings:

20. UK HMRC, Overview of Tax Legislation and Rates, March 11, 2020, available at https://assets.publishing.service.gov.uk/government/uploads/system/uploads/attachment_data/file/872040/Budget_2020_overview_of_tax_legislation_and_rates__OOTLAR.pdf, accessed on May 28, 2020.
21. UK, Disclosure of Tax Avoidance Schemes, available at https://www.gov.uk/guidance/disclosure-of-tax-avoidance-schemes-overview, accessed on May 28, 2020.
22. UK HMRC, International Tax Enforcement: Disclosable Agreements, Report on how the powers in section 84 of the Finance Act 2019 will be used in different EU Exit scenarios, presented to the House of Commons pursuant to section 84(8) of Finance Act 2019, January 2020, available at https://assets.publishing.service.gov.uk/government/uploads/system/uploads/attachment_data/file/856709/International_Tax_Enforcement_-_Parliamentary_Report_PDF.pdf, accessed on May 29, 2020.
23. Council Directive 2018/822/EU of May 25, 2018, available at https://ec.europa.eu/taxation_customs/sites/taxation/files/dac-6-council-directive-2018_en.pdf, accessed on May 28, 2020.

(1) An arrangement which involves the use of unilateral safe harbor rules.
(2) An arrangement involving the transfer of hard-to-value intangibles. The term "hard-to-value intangibles" covers intangibles or rights on intangibles for which, at the time of their transfer between associated enterprises no reliable comparables exist; and at the time the transaction was entered into, the projections of future cash flows or income expected to be derived from the transferred intangible, or the assumptions used in valuing the intangible are highly uncertain, making it difficult to predict the level of ultimate success of the intangible at the time of the transfer.
(3) An arrangement involving an intra-group cross-border transfer of functions and/or risks and/or assets if the projected annual earnings before interest and taxes (EBIT) during the three-year period after the transfer of the transferor or transferors are less than 50% of the projected annual EBIT of such transferor or transferors if the transfer had not been made.

However, given that the Directive entered into force in 2018, with reporting required from July 2020, it is very disappointing to note the lack of clarity in the guidance and the lack of consistency between countries about what they are expecting to see. This means that taxpayers operating across the EU are having to consider different reports for each market; a missed opportunity perhaps.

The impact of DAC 6 could be threefold. First, it should mean that tax administrations are in a position to assess potential risk areas and take timely decisions to protect tax revenue. Second, it should provide tax administrations with the required information to timely address aggressive tax planning schemes; it is expected that this will result in an increase in tax audits. Third, the reporting requirement is expected to be a deterrent to implementing aggressive tax planning schemes.

Unlike the Common Reporting Standard, the mandatory disclosure rules could vary in design and implementation across the European Member States. A major problem deriving from this choice is that no guidelines exist, and there is a risk of differing interpretations among the Member States. Tax authorities need to ensure as much harmony as possible, but there is no guarantee of the exact same standards applied among the Member States.

3.2 Public CbCR

The EU proposed a directive back in 2016 to require the expansion of CbCR into the public domain. These additional transparency requirements (similar to those for extractives) would apply to *any* multinational company—whether European or not—that:

- is currently active in the EU single market;
- has a permanent presence in the EU;

- has global revenues exceeding EUR 750,000,000 a year.[24]

So far, the measure has not been approved by the Council of Ministers.[25] Some countries strongly oppose publication and would like this issue to be treated as a tax measure (currently, that would require unanimity) instead of a competition measure.

However, it is likely to keep coming back onto the agenda under the new Commission, and this does not appear to be the last time it is discussed given the public pressure that the EU and Member State governments are under on perceived tax avoidance by multinationals.

4 EU STATE AID AND TP

4.1 The State Aid Battle in 2019

Several TP related state aid cases have been decided by the General Court in 2019. Among them are the decisions regarding a Belgian "excess profit" alleged state aid scheme and the decisions in *Commission v. The Netherlands* (*Starbucks* case) and *Commission v. Luxembourg* (*Fiat* case). The general court annulled the Commission's decision in the cases against the Netherlands and Belgium and confirmed the one against Luxembourg ordering Luxembourg to recover EUR 23.1 million from Fiat.

Meanwhile, the European Commission continued investigating whether some Member States granted an unfair tax advantage to MNEs by means of "transfer mispricing" and lowering their taxable base. In particular, the Commission initiated formal investigation procedures in two new cases of alleged state aid in favor of *Nike*[26] in the Netherlands and *Huhtamäki*[27] in Luxembourg. In September 2019, the Commission also announced that it would conduct individual investigations of thirty-nine multinational companies to assess an existence of the "excess profit" state aid scheme in the administrative tax practice of Belgium.[28] This action was taken following the decision of the general court that annulled the Commission's earlier decision that the tax rulings granted to such multinationals formed part of a Belgian illegal state aid scheme. The following section will more closely examine the decisions of the general court and then into the newly initiated state aid investigations by the European Commission.

24. European Commission, Public country-by-country reporting, available at https://ec.europa.eu /info/business-economy-euro/company-reporting-and-auditing/company-reporting/public-country-country-reporting_en, accessed on May 28, 2020.
25. Danish Mehboob, Public CbCR fails to move forward in EU Council, ITR, November 29, 2019, available at https://www.internationaltaxreview.com/article/b1j7hkz9m2y67b/public-cbcr-fails-to-move-forward-in-eu-council, accessed on May 28, 2020.
26. SA.51284 (2018/NN)—Netherlands—Possible State aid in favor of Nike.
27. SA.50400 (2019/NN-2)—Luxembourg—Possible State aid in favor of Huhtamäki.
28. EC, Press release, State aid: Commission opens in-depth investigations into individual "excess profit" tax rulings granted by Belgium to thirty-nine multinational companies, September 16, 2019, available at https://ec.europa.eu/commission/presscorner/detail/en/IP_19_5578, accessed on March 5, 2020.

4.2 The Decisions of the General Court

4.2.1 Belgium v. Commission

The decision by the general court in *Commission v. Belgium*[29] deals with the Belgian legislation that provides an exemption from corporate income taxation of profits that are beyond arm's length (excess profits). The Belgian Income Tax Code provided that MNEs in Belgium may reduce their tax liability in Belgium if the amount of profits received from the activities in Belgium is higher than that they would receive under arm's length market conditions and is gained due to the advantage of being part of a multinational group (e.g., synergies, economies of scale, reputation, client and supplier networks, or access to new markets).[30]

The Belgian excess profit rulings granted to Belgian companies endorsed the calculation of profits in the way that the profits that went beyond arm's length were not included in their tax base disregarding whether the income had been included in the tax base of a group entity in another jurisdiction.[31] Since Belgium did not tax all accounting profits of multinational groups but used the ALP to determine the amount of profits attributable to their jurisdiction, multinational groups were able to arrange their activities in a way that shifted all of the residual profits to their Belgian entities.

The Commission alleged that the legislation leading to such an exemption is a state aid scheme. In the Commission's view, by deducting "excess profit" from the companies' tax base without a corresponding upward adjustment in the state of the contracting party, the Belgium tax administration selectively misapplied the Belgian income tax code when issuing the tax rulings in question. In particular, the Commission considered that the legal conditions for the application of the excess profit tax regime were not fulfilled by the MNEs that received these disputed tax rulings.

On February 14, 2019, the general court annulled the Commission Decision 2016/1699 of January 11, 2016 on the excess profit exemption state aid scheme implemented by Belgium on the basis that the Commission failed to prove the existence of an aid scheme due to the material discretion left with the tax authorities when issuing the rulings.[32] Therefore, unfortunately, the decision of the general court is not very informative on the material substance of the compatibility of the Belgian excess profit tax with the state aid rules. Belgium argued that it would have no fiscal jurisdiction to tax profits exceeding an arm's length amount as they cannot be attributed to a Belgian entity. This argument would be valid in light of the Court of Justice of the European Union (CJEU) case law in *Hornbach-Baumarkt*[33] in which the court considered that the ALP rule under the German law would not go beyond what is necessary to achieve the objectives perused "relating to the need to maintain the balanced allocation of the power to tax between the Member States and to prevent tax

29. Case T-131/16, *Commission v. Belgium*, EU:T:2019:91.
30. Article 185 §2, b of the "Code des Impôts sur les Revenus/Wetboek Inkomstenbelastingen."
31. Buriak/Lazarov, Between State aid and the fundamental freedoms: The arm's length principle and EU law, 56(4) Common Market Law Review, 2019, pp. 905-948, at p. 923.
32. Buriak, Lazarov, *supra* n 31, at p. 923.
33. Case C-382/16, *Hornbach-Baumarkt AG v. Finanzamt Landau*, EU:C:2018:366.

avoidance" if the corrective adjustment, where required, is "confined to the part which exceeds what would have been agreed between the companies in question under market conditions."[34] Hence, the legitimate objective of balanced allocation of taxing powers between Member States that justify imposing the ALP rules applicable to cross-border transactions against the fundamental freedoms requires Member States to tax only that income that is attributable to their fiscal jurisdiction. In *Belgium v. Commission*, the general court briefly dismissed the point of the Belgian authorities but only as far as the argument is to be understood as challenging the Commission's competence to examine the measures in question.

Following the annulment of the Commission's decision on incompatibility of the Belgian "excess profit" tax scheme with EU state aid rules by the general court, in September 2019, the Commission initiated an in-depth investigation of whether "excess profit" tax rulings endorsed by Belgium in favor of thirty-nine Belgium based MNEs gave those companies an unfair advantage over their competitors. Since the general court did not give an answer on whether the excess profit tax exemption gave rise to illegal state aid but rather considered that the Commission had failed to prove the existence of the scheme, the Commission started an assessment of individual tax treatment of each company that could have received an undue tax advantage. Hence, the discussion on the compatibility of the Belgian "excess profit" legislation with the state aid rules is to be continued.

4.2.2 Luxembourg v. Commission

One of the awaited decisions in the area of fiscal state aid was the decision of the general court in *Luxembourg v. Commission* concerning the tax treatment of *Fiat*.[35]

Fiat Finance and Trade (FFT) was based in Luxembourg and performed financial and treasury activities for Fiat group companies based in Europe (excluding Italy).[36] The FFT's main functions included raising money from the financial markets, consolidating the liquidity of the group, and providing intra-group loans. FFT concluded an APA with the authorities in Luxembourg that endorsed the transactional net margin method (TNMM) for the calculation of annual profits of FFT and a return on the regulatory equity as a profit level indicator. Therefore, the amount of the profit of the company was calculated by an approximation and without going into a transaction-by-transaction analysis.[37] Moreover, for the purposes of applying the profit level indicator, the APA endorsed a hypothetical amount of regulatory equity which allegedly would have been required to cover the risks of similar financial activities of a financial regulated institution. Interestingly enough, when calculating that hypothetical amount, FFT considered that all of their intra-group loans had zero risks and,

34. Case C-382/16, *Hornbach-Baumarkt*, paragraph 49.
35. LU: ECJ, General Court, September 24, 2019, Joined Cases T-755/15 and T-759/15, *Luxembourg v. Commission*, EU:T:2019:670.
36. Lazarov/Buriak, Is Fiat's tank half-full or half empty? The general court's decision in Luxembourg v. Commission (T-755/15), 27(1) International Transfer Pricing Journal, 2020.
37. *Ibid.*, at p. 71.

therefore, should not have been remunerated. Consequently, the APA technically provided the method for calculation of annual profits of FFT for its activities with third parties while all the intra-group loans were not taken into account for determining a tax base.

As an initial point that is relevant for all TP related state aid cases, the general court in *Fiat* upheld the EU Commission's approach in endorsing the ALP as indirectly stemming from Article 107 of the TFEU. The court considered the ALP to be "a tool to check whether a taxable profit of an integrated undertaking ... corresponds to pricing under market conditions" for the purposes of determining the existence of an advantage under Article 107(1) of the TFEU.[38]

On the factual merits of the case, the general court approving the Commission's position accepted that the accounting and not the regulatory equity is an appropriate profit level indicator when return on equity (RoE) is applied for the calculation of the tax base of an entity that performs financing activities. This outcome of the decision might be problematic in light that RoE, if applied to an accounting equity, highly depends on the business capital requirements under the company law and specifics of every jurisdiction. Moreover, a debt/equity arbitrage in the capital structure of MNEs would be an obstacle for an accurate comparability analysis and establishing a reliable benchmark for the calculation of profits based on the TNMM.[39]

On December 4, 2019, Fiat lodged an appeal against the court's order to Luxembourg to recover EUR 30 million of illegal state aid from the company.[40]

4.2.3 The Netherlands v. Commission

The general court's decision in the *Netherlands v. Commission* concerning the tax treatment of Starbucks in the advance pricing rulings issued in its favor resulted in a victory for the multinational group.

In *Starbucks,* the Commission contested the APA (2008) that determined the remuneration agreed for the functions performed by SMBV located in the Netherlands and responsible for Europe, the Middle East and Africa (EMEA) region. SMBV is a Starbucks' roasting facility and intermediary distribution entity for a variety of non-coffee items.[41] SMBV was responsible for executing roasting forecasts provided by Starbucks U.S. and ensuring that the roasting outcome meets the quality standards of Starbucks U.S. With that purpose, SMBV licensed a set of intellectual property (IP) rights from the U.K. based limited partnership (Alki LP) consisting, in particular, of roasting curves dictating the temperature and the length of time required to complete the roasting process.[42] In its turn, Alki LP held all of the IP rights necessary for Starbuck's operations in EMEA region pursuant to the cost sharing agreement with

38. *Luxembourg v. Commission* (T-755/15 and T-759/15), at paragraphs 143, 144 and 151.
39. Lazarov, Buriak, *supra* n 36, at p. 74.
40. Case C-885/19, *Fiat Chrysler Finance Europe v. Commission.*
41. *Starbucks* case, paragraphs 49-50.
42. *Starbucks* case, paragraph 50.

Starbucks U.S.[43] Starbucks also had a subsidiary in Switzerland (SCTC) that acted as the only designated supplier of coffee beans to SMBV. The contested APA considered that the remuneration of the functions performed by SMBV, as a less complex tested party, should be based on TNMM, applying a mark-up only to the costs where SMBV added value. All of the profits in excess of the profits determined pursuant to the applied methodology, in fact, were transferred as royalty payments to Alki LP. The Commission challenged that methodology based on arguments that the contested APA failed to determine an appropriate arm's length price for licensed IP which, in the Commission's opinion, again should be less valuable and amount to "zero" and an arm's length price for the purchase of coffee beans from SCTC starting from 2011.

On September 24, 2019, the general court overturned the Commission's decision that Starbucks had benefited from the illegal state aid granted by the Netherlands.[44] Regarding the issue of whether the Commission was entitled to analyze the tax ruling at stake in light of the ALP, the court decided that Article 107(1) TFEU entitled the Commission to compare the fiscal burden of an integrated entity with comparable transactions of unrelated entities carrying on their activities under market conditions. In that regard, the court notes that the ALP is not a principle of EU law stemming from Article 107 TFEU but is a tool that allows it to check that intra-group transactions are treated equally to those of independent companies when national tax law does not make a distinction between group and stand-alone entities for the purpose of their corporate tax liability.[45]

On the merits of the case, the court dismissed the argument of the Commission that choosing the TNMM method instead of the comparable uncontrolled price method can per se lead to a tax advantage. The court considered that there is no hierarchy between different TP methods and each of them can be equally applied. Regarding the amount of royalty, the court considered that the Commission failed to demonstrate that the level of the royalty should have been zero or that it resulted in an advantage. Hence, the court concluded that the Commission did not demonstrate that the various errors in the application of the TNMM conferred an advantage on SMBV. The Commission did not appeal to the general court's judgment.[46]

4.3 EU Commission State Aid Investigations

4.3.1 Alleged State Aid to Nike

During the course of 2019, the Commission investigated the tax treatment of two Netherlands-based Nike group companies, namely, Nike European Operations

43. *Starbucks* case, paragraphs 104-119.
44. General Court, Cases T-760/15 and T-636/16.
45. Press Release No. 119/19, judgment in Cases T-760/15 *Netherlands v. Commission* and T-636/16 *Starbucks and Starbucks Manufacturing EMEA v. Commission*.
46. *See*, Dmitrios Kyriazis, Why the EU Commission won't appeal the Starbucks judgment, MNE Tax, December 10, 2019, available at https://mnetax.com/why-the-eu-commission-wont-appeal-the-starbucks-judgment-37043, accessed August 28, 2020.

Netherlands (NEON) BV and Converse Netherlands BV,[47] that are responsible for developing, marketing, and recording the sales of Nike and Converse products in the EMEA region. For their operations, the companies obtained licenses to use the IP rights of Nike and Converse products respectively in the region in consideration for a tax-deductible royalty payment.

The method for the calculation of the amount of royalty that NEON and Converse Netherlands (CN BV) should pay for the use of the relevant IP was endorsed by the Dutch tax authorities in several tax rulings in the period from 2006 to 2015. The Commission alleged that the calculation of royalty payments based on a limited operating sales margin does not reflect economic reality and is not in accordance with the ALP. On July 1, 2019, the Commission published a letter to the Netherlands informing the Member State of the initiation of the infringement procedure under Article 108(2) TFEU.[48]

The essence of the dispute is that there is no clear guidance on how to differentiate between core and routine functions under the functional analysis of the MNE. The NEON, according to the Commission, was involved in the development, management, and exploitation of the non-U.S. IP of Nike while the legal and economic ownership over the intangibles that belonged to the company registered in Bermuda in during 2006-2015 and to the fiscally transparent entity in the Netherlands after 2015. The activities and IP relations of CN BV were organized in the same way. The Commission challenged the identification of NEON and CN BV as less complex entities performing only routine wholesaler functions and, accordingly, the application of the TNMM method.

Bearing in mind that all of the contested tax rulings were approved in the pre-BEPS era when the Development, Enhancement, Maintenance, Protection and Exploitation analysis was not developed to the current level and no marketing intangibles and PSM were pushed by tax authorities during TP audits,[49] it is hardly foreseeable that the Commission will succeed in proving the existence of state aid in this case.

4.3.2 *Alleged State Aid to Huhtamäki*

The Commission's formal investigation here concerns three tax rulings granted by Luxembourg (in 2009, 2012, and 2013) to the Luxembourg-based company Huhtalux S.à.r.l., which is part of the Huhtamäki group.

Huhtalux performs intra-group financing activities. The company received interest-free loans from another group entity based in Ireland. Huhtalux used these loans to finance other group entities in the U.S. through interest-bearing loans. In the

47. The two Nike Group entities at stake are tax-transparent under the law of the Netherlands.
48. Article 108(2), Treaty of Functioning of the European Union, *Official Journal C 326, 26/10/2012 P. 0001-0390.*
49. William Byrnes, Nike State aid comments, Kluwer International Tax Blog, July 8, 2019, available at http://kluwertaxblog.com/2019/07/08/nike-state-aid-comments/?doing_wp_cron=1590678042.1692390441894531250000, accessed May 28, 2020.

tax rulings, the tax authorities in Luxembourg endorsed the unilateral deduction of fictitious interest payments for the interest-free loans that the company received from the Irish group entity. A reason for the approval of the deduction was that Huhtalux would be required to pay an arm's length amount of interest for the loans received under the TP rules of Luxembourg.

The Commission was concerned that a unilateral downward adjustment of Huhtalux's taxable base granted by Luxembourg may have led to a selective advantage for the Huhtamäki group. On May 3, 2019, the Commission published a letter to the Netherlands informing the Member State on the initiation of the infringement procedure under Article 108(2) TFEU.[50]

In its analysis, the Commission considered that the contested tax rulings derogated from the reference framework which, before 2015, allowed the Luxembourg tax authorities to reassess the operating result of a company if "a transfer of profit is made possible" due to special economic links between related companies, one being subject to tax in Luxembourg and one being a foreign entity.[51] Moreover, the legislation contained hidden profit distribution rules that the Luxembourg tax authorities interpreted as being equal to the current ALP, namely, that the intra-group transaction prices should correspond to the prices that would have been charged and agreed by independent parties.[52]

The position of Luxembourg fairly points out that the purpose of the provisions is "to tally company's taxable income with its income truly generated in Luxembourg."[53] This position would be in line with the CJEU practice on balanced allocation of taxing powers between the Member States. In this regard, in the authors' view and without a recourse to the EU state aid rules, the core of the problem of the fiscal benefit to a Huhtamäki group comes from Ireland which allowed an interest-free loan from the Irish entity of the Huhtamäki group while the TP analysis in Luxembourg seems to be in good order from a theoretical perspective. Nevertheless, the Commission again, likewise in the Belgian excess profit tax case, claimed that the profits of Huhtalux had to be assessed based on the accounting profits and not on the market-based outcome as in the majority of state aid cases. Thus, the Commission considered that stand-alone companies would not have a possibility to receive a downward adjustment for their accounted profit, "forgetting" that the stand-alone companies would also not be able to receive an interest-free loan.

At the same time, the Commission's analysis of the selectivity fairly stipulates that the Luxembourg legislation did not provide any criterion for a downward adjustment and, therefore, there are high chances that the court will also consider the application of such a provision to be a priori selective to its discretionary measure.[54] Moreover, at the justification level, the Commission rightly points out that the Luxembourg tax authorities did not pursue a legitimate objective of tax avoidance since

50. Article 108(2), Treaty of Functioning of the European Union. State Aid SA.50400 (2019/NN-2), Luxembourg, Possible State aid in favor of Huhtamäki, C(2019) 1615 Final.
51. Paragraph 47, Letter to the Member State, *Huhtamäki* case.
52. *Ibid.*, paragraph 49.
53. *Ibid.*, paragraph 62.
54. *Ibid.*, paragraph 83.

the downward adjustment did not correspond to any upward adjustment of the tax base of the Irish entity.

Nevertheless, Luxembourg also put forward another objective of their legislation at issue being to ensure that the taxable profits of the taxpayer in Luxembourg, having contractual relationships with companies not subject to tax in Luxembourg, "corresponds to the profit truly attributable to the territory of Luxembourg." In response to this point, the Commission claimed the following:

> The need to tax only at arm's length profits and not more ... cannot be considered an objective intrinsic to the tax system as such. The application of the arm's length principle is merely a tool applied specifically to achieve other objectives, such as to prevent companies belonging to corporate groups from being treated better than standalone companies or to avoid double taxation.

It is very interesting how this position co-exists with numerous TP related state aid cases for which the Commission stipulated that an intrinsic objective of the corporate tax system of the Member States is to ensure taxation being in line with the market-based outcome for which the ALP is an appropriate indicator (even if the legislation of the Member State lacks the ALP rule).[55] However, when the market-based outcome seems to go against the interests of the Commission, this rationale is changed. Finally, it is not clear why the treatment of the group entities cannot be better than stand-alone, but it does not seem to be a problem if the taxation leads to worse outcomes for the group entities compared to those that are stand-alone.

All in all, even though the Commission's analysis leads to some very controversial conclusions in some TP related parts, it stands in the major points, i.e., on the existence of the selectivity and, therefore, the authors expect that the Commission will prove the existence of state aid in this case.

5 DIGITAL TAXATION

5.1 OECD Progress

The tax challenges of the digitalization of the economy were identified as one of the main areas of focus of the OECD/G20 BEPS Project, leading to the 2015 BEPS Action 1 Report (the Action 1 Report). The Action 1 Report found that the whole economy was digitalizing and, as a result, it would be difficult, if not impossible, to ring-fence the digital economy.

It was felt that, if the IF does not deliver a comprehensive consensus-based solution within the agreed G20 timeframe, there is a risk that more jurisdictions will adopt uncoordinated unilateral tax measures. A growing number of jurisdictions and public commentators are not content with the taxation outcomes produced by the current international tax system and are seeking to impose new measures to reallocate taxing rights. Those moves risk significantly increasing compliance burdens, double taxation, and uncertainty hence the need to act quickly to try to reach a consensus.

55. *Apple, Amazon, Starbucks, Fiat* cases.

One of the focal points of dissatisfaction related to how the existing profit allocation and nexus rules take into account the increasing ability of businesses in certain situations in order to participate in the economic life of a jurisdiction without an associated or meaningful physical presence. An unparalleled reliance on intangibles and the rising share of services in cross-border trade are among the causes typically identified. This dissatisfaction has created a political imperative to act in a significant number of jurisdictions. Cognizant that predictability and stability are fundamental building blocks of global economic growth, the IF, therefore, was concerned that a proliferation of uncoordinated and unilateral actions would not only undermine the relevance and sustainability of the international framework for the taxation of cross-border business activities but could also more broadly adversely impact global investments and growth.

In 2019, the OECD published a program of work (PoW) to develop a Consensus Solution to the Tax Challenges arising from the Digitalisation of Economy.[56] The PoW adopted by the IF on BEPS at its meeting of May 28-29, 2019, and approved by the G20 Finance Ministers and Leaders at their respective meetings in Japan in June 2019 provided for two pillars to be developed, on a without prejudice basis, with a consensus solution to be agreed by the end of 2020. On November 12, 2019, a Unified Approach to "Pillar 1" that would potentially allocate extra tax to markets was proposed[57] and a public consultation was held. However, at the time of this writing, there are many open questions including which industries should be exempted (e.g., potentially, financial services), whether the new taxing rights should apply only to "B2C" or also "B2B" electronic transactions and, of utmost importance, how the dispute resolution mechanisms will work to reduce double taxation and disputes that will inevitably arise.[58]

Many TP experts have expressed concern about mandatory departures from the ALP, including the authors. Can consensus be achieved?

5.1.1 U.S. Reaction

The view of many U.S. businesses has been that the backdrop to this issue is anti-American. However, the U.S. has so far participated in the process and has been

56. OECD/G20 Inclusive Framework on BEPS, Programme of Work to Develop a Consensus Solution to the Tax Challenges Arising from the Digitalization of the Economy, 2019, available at https://www.oecd.org/tax/beps/programme-of-work-to-develop-a-consensus-solution-to-the-tax-challenges-arising-from-the-digitalisation-of-the-economy.pdf, accessed on May 28, 2020.
57. OECD, Public Consultation Document, Secretariat Proposal for a "Unified Approach" under Pillar One, October 9, 2019-November 12, 2019, available at https://www.oecd.org/tax/beps/public-consultation-document-secretariat-proposal-unified-approach-pillar-one.pdf, accessed on May 28, 2020.
58. *See*, Greil/Müller/Olbert, Transfer pricing for digital business models: Early evidence on challenges and options for reform, 4 World Tax Journal, 2019, pp. 557-588; Greil/Wargowske, The taxation of the digital economy and reallocation of taxing rights: Entering in a new world order, 73(10) Bulletin for International Taxation, 2019; Förster/Greil/Hilse, Taxing the digital economy: The OECD secretariat's new transfer pricing A-B-C and alternative courses of action, 27(1) International Transfer Pricing Journal, 2020.

instrumental in shaping the proposals. Then, in early December 2019, Treasury Secretary Steven Mnuchin wrote to the OECD suggesting that the Pillar 1 proposals be made elective (a safe harbor approach) only.[59] In response, the OECD said:

> We have already held two public consultations attended by stakeholders from around the world and like you, while noting broad support for existing rules, clearly identified the need for greater tax certainty and administrability. This is why the OECD proposal on a "Unified Approach" contains a very strong tax certainty dimension. Without it, there would be no conditions for achieving a consensus.[60]

5.2 EU Response

Attempts led by Germany, France, and Italy to gain agreement on an EU-wide digital tax last year stalled.[61]

Since then, a number of countries, several in Europe, have decided to "go it alone" and pre-empt the OECD solution by imposing their own digital taxes. For example, France has already introduced law. The U.K. has introduced a digital services tax at 2% of turnover to take effect from April 1, 2020.[62] This is narrowly targeted toward U.K. end users of certain online services, and there are *de minimis* limits, so fewer than one hundred businesses should have to pay it. It is still unclear whether the U.K., like France and Spain, may seek to defer collection until it sees whether the OECD can come up with a consensus view on their wider "Pillar 1" plans.

These moves could be seen as an attempt to try to force the OECD to speed up toward consensus or simply as an attempt to regain tax revenues lost to the digital giants as they "reach in" to markets and avoid permanent establishments. Why does the EU not take a combined position here—all Member States would have the same goal here, and concerted action would surely be more powerful? In reality, not all Member States have the same goal. Some smaller economies like Ireland, and even Scandinavia, have gained from the current rules (e.g., Ireland has been a major beneficiary of tech sector jobs, and the Irish Finance Minister, Paschal Donohoe, has estimated Irish corporation tax receipts will fall by about EUR 500 million as a result of BEPS).[63] These different winners and losers can help explain why the EU digital tax proposal mentioned above has not (yet) succeeded.

59. Available at https://aboutbtax.com/NgX accessed via Bloomberg, accessed August 28, 2020.
60. A letter of Secretary of the Treasury of the United States to OECD Secretary General, December 4, 2019, available at https://www.oecd.org/newsroom/Letter-from-OECD-Secretary-General-Angel-Gurria-for-the-attention-of-The-Honorable-Steven-T-Mnuchin-Secretary-of-the-Treasury-United-States.pdf, accessed on May 28, 2020.
61. Franco-German joint declaration on the taxation of digital companies and minimum taxation, available at https://www.consilium.europa.eu/media/37276/fr-de-joint-declaration-on-the-taxation-of-digital-companies-final.pdf, accessed on May 28, 2020.
62. UK HMRC, Overview of Tax Legislation and Rates, *supra* n 20.
63. Christina Finn, Ireland's corporation tax receipts set to take a hit under new rules and fall by up to €2bn, January 9, 2020, available at https://www.thejournal.ie/corporation-tax-ireland-2-4960036-Jan2020/, accessed on May 28, 2020.

In a further recent twist, and if an OECD-wide solution is not reached by the end of 2020 as originally hoped, the European Parliament resolved in December 2019 to work toward an EU plan for a bloc-wide digital tax.[64] This is in line with the signposts set put very early by the new Commission (*see*, for example, the mission letter sent by Commissioner von der Leyen to Paolo Gentiloni as then Commissioner-Designate for the Economy back in September 2019: "You should lead international efforts to find an agreed approach on digital taxation, working with our partners in the Organisation for Economic Co-operation and Development and the G20. If no consensus emerges by the end of 2020, you should lead on the proposal for a fair European digital tax.")[65]

Additionally, at the time of this writing, the position is still fluid. It has been reported that France will defer its digital tax pending the OECD work, until November 2020,[66] which would put more pressure on the U.K. to follow suit. Notwithstanding, it appears that at least some EU-wide digital service tax might yet be applicable within the next few years. It will be important to keep up-to-date with the rapid evolution of the changes in the future

6 CONCLUSION

There is little concrete evidence of the EU acting as a bloc in the area of TP. Nevertheless, the EU JTPF has made a valuable contribution in providing practical help and interpretation/implementation guidance. In general, this additional support for tax administrations and taxpayers follows the OECD debate and guidance but also helps to inform it. It is unclear whether the new Commission will set up something similar in the future, but it is hoped that there will be a route for comments and helpful practical guidance within the EU going forward.

The OECD and IF, and potentially the UN, are the main stages for developing TP guidance and, given that few truly international businesses operate *only* in the EU, this is probably as it should be. TP Guidance needs to be global and, when possible, involve consensus.

Even in areas touching upon TP where the EU *has* issued directives (like DAC 6), the interpretation is left to individual Member States. While this can be frustrating for taxpayers, it is unavoidable, to an extent, given that direct tax is not a harmonized tax in the way that value-added tax is, and so each Member State government has sovereignty.

The new Commission under Ms. Von der Leyen sees the EU setting out on a new chapter post-Brexit. It remains to be seen how the balance of power might shift

64. European Parliament resolution of December 18, 2019 on fair taxation in a digitalized and globalized economy: BEPS 2.0 (2019/2901(RSP)), available at http://www.europarl.europa.eu/doceo/document/TA-9-2019-0102_EN.html, accessed August 28, 2020.
65. Mission Letter from Ursula von der Leyen to Paolo Gentiloni, available at https://ec.europa.eu/commission/sites/beta-political/files/mission-letter-paolo-gentiloni_en.pdf, accessed on May 28, 2020.
66. Available at https://www.washingtonpost.com/world/europe/the-latest/2020/01/22/5dbde6c4-3d06-11ea-afe2-090eb37b60b1_story.html, accessed August 28, 2020.

between the more centralist states and the more independently minded ones. However, one thing is already clear, the new Commissioner sees international tax as being an important policy tool and multinational businesses may expect further changes and challenges around TP in the years ahead.

CHAPTER 3

Transfer Pricing Developments in the United States*

Mark R. Martin, Mark J. Horowitz & Thomas D. Bettge

Transfer pricing remains an important area in the United States (U.S.) as evidenced by both the number of high profile court cases in recent years and the attention that the

* The information in this chapter is not intended to be "written advice concerning one or more federal tax matters" subject to the requirements of section 10.37(a)(2) of Treasury Department Circular 230 because the content is issued for general informational purposes only. The information contained in this chapter is of a general nature and based on authorities that are subject to change. Applicability of the information to specific situations should be determined through consultation with your tax adviser. This chapter represents the views of the author or authors only and does not necessarily represent the views or professional advice of the KPMG LLP.

Internal Revenue Service (IRS) has devoted during the same period to revamping its approach to transfer pricing audits. Consistent with traditional patterns, transfer pricing litigation continues to prove difficult for the IRS, notwithstanding some recent key victories. Yet the IRS' new approach to transfer pricing enforcement, which is meant to conserve resources while focusing on high-risk areas, may ultimately reverse that trend. This chapter addresses both the recent case law highlights and the administrative developments and considers what they mean for the U.S. transfer pricing environment going forward.

1 CASE LAW MILESTONES

Recent U.S. transfer pricing litigation has run the gamut from regulatory challenges based on administrative law's first principles to intensely factual skirmishes over the selection and application of transfer pricing methods (TPMs). While taxpayers continue to prevail in many cases, the IRS has also won significant victories, most notably in *Altera*.

1.1 *Altera Corp. v. Commissioner* (2015, 2019)

The roots of the *Altera* saga[1] reach back to *Xilinx v. Commissioner*[2] in which the U.S. Tax Court (Tax Court) held (and the Ninth Circuit, after initially reversing, ultimately changed course and agreed) that a regulation requiring parties to a cost sharing arrangement (CSA) to share "all of the costs" they incurred could not require the sharing of stock-based compensation (SBC) costs given the lack of evidence that unrelated parties share them. In the meantime, the U.S. Treasury (Treasury) doubled down on its position and revised the regulation to explicitly require sharing of SBC costs, and Altera, now a subsidiary of Intel, brought suit.

The Tax Court, in a reviewed opinion with the unanimous agreement of fifteen judges, agreed with the taxpayer and held that the regulation was arbitrary and capricious under the Administrative Procedure Act. Specifically, the Tax Court took issue with the fact that the government, when promulgating the new regulation through the mandated notice and comment process, failed to respond to significant public comments noting that unrelated parties did not share SBC costs.

The case then took a tortuous path through the Ninth Circuit with an initial opinion withdrawn due to the death of one of the judges on the panel.[3] In a second opinion, the Ninth Circuit reversed, accepting the government's contention that the regulation was justified on the basis of a broad reading of the arm's length standard that permitted the IRS to dispense with a comparables-based analysis, thus rendering the lack of evidence that third parties share SBC costs irrelevant. One judge dissented,

1. Altera Corp. v. Comm'r, 926 F.3d 1061 (9th Cir. 2019), *rev'ing* 145 TC. 91 (2015).
2. Xilinx v. Comm'r, 598 F.3d 1191 (9th Cir. 2010), *superseding* 567 F.3d 482 (9th Cir. 2009), *aff'ing* 125 T.C. 37 (2005).
3. The original opinion, 2018 WL 3542989 (Nos. 16-70496, 16-70497) (9th Cir. July 24, 2018), was withdrawn in August 2018. Altera Corp. v. Comm'r, 898 F.3d 1266 (9th Cir. 2018).

as did three more upon the court's denial of rehearing en banc.[4] On February 10, Altera filed a petition for a writ of certiorari with the Supreme Court, but it will be several months before the court decides whether to take up the case.

1.2 *Amazon.com v. Commissioner* (2017, 2019)

Amazon,[5] like *Altera*, hearkens back to an earlier case, *Veritas v. Commissioner*,[6] which grappled with the scope and valuation of a foreign subsidiary's buy-in to a CSA. Amazon transferred intangible property to a Luxembourg affiliate as a platform contribution transaction (PCT) in connection with a CSA. Amazon valued the PCT at about USD 250 million; the IRS claimed it was worth about USD 3.5 billion. The dispute involved both the methodology used to value the intangibles and the scope of such intangibles; according to the IRS, residual business assets such as goodwill, going concern value, workforce in place and Amazon's culture of innovation were required to be captured in the valuation.

The Tax Court held that the then current definition of intangibles in section 936(h)(3)(B), which was referenced by section 482, did not cover the residual business assets that the IRS sought to include. Moreover, the Tax Court determined that the aggregate valuation approach did not provide a reasonable means of valuing the PCT.

On appeal, the Ninth Circuit affirmed, agreeing that the applicable definition of intangibles covered only independently transferable assets rather than amorphous residual business assets such as goodwill or a culture of innovation. However, prior to the issuance of the Ninth Circuit opinion, the Tax Cuts and Jobs Act expanded the applicable definition of intangibles (now contained in section 367(d)(4)) to cover goodwill, going concern value, workforce in place, and any "other item the value or potential value of which is not attributable to tangible property or the services of any individual." This broad formulation followed the expansion of the regulatory definition in 2009 after the years at issue in *Amazon*.

Despite handing a clear victory to the taxpayer, the Ninth Circuit chose to comment on these developments in dicta, noting that "[i]f this case were governed by the 2009 regulations or by the 2017 statutory amendment, there is no doubt the Commissioner's position would be correct."[7] The regulatory and legislative developments clearly bolster the IRS' position on the scope of intangibles includible in a PCT, but the underlying methodology and use of aggregate valuation depend on the reliability of the approach, and it is thus far from clear that the IRS would necessarily prevail under the new definitions in a similar dispute.

4. Altera Corp. v. Comm'r, 941 F.3d 1200 (9th Cir. 2019) (denying rehearing en banc).
5. Amazon.com, Inc. v. Comm'r, 934 F.3d 976 (9th Cir. 2019), *aff'ing* 148 T.C. 108 (2017).
6. Veritas Software Corp. v. Comm'r, 133 T.C. 297 (2009), *nonacq.*, 2010-49 I.R.B (2010), *action on dec.*, 2010-05 (November 12, 2010).
7. *Amazon*, 934 F.3d at 979 n.1.

1.3 *Eaton v. Commissioner* (2013, 2017, 2019)

Eaton challenged the IRS' decision to set aside two advance pricing agreements (APAs) on the basis of Eaton's inadvertent failure to disclose certain information and commission of computational errors that affected its compliance with the APAs.[8] During the APA period, Eaton discovered that it had committed several errors, all of which it corrected and reported to the IRS in its APA annual reports, including in amended APA annual reports and amended tax returns for certain years. In response, the IRS canceled both APAs, citing misrepresentation, mistakes as to material facts, the failure of APA critical assumptions, and lack of good faith compliance with the APAs. The IRS then proceeded to make transfer pricing adjustments for the APA years.

The initial salvo came in 2013 when the Tax Court determined that the cancellation of the APAs should be reviewed using the abuse of discretion standard rather than the stricter contract law principles urged by the taxpayer.[9] Notwithstanding this setback, the taxpayer went on to prevail in the Tax Court, which concluded in 2017 that the taxpayer's inadvertent errors were not "material," and that the taxpayer's presentation of data based on its own viewpoint was not false or misleading and thus not a "misrepresentation" under the applicable revenue procedure. Accordingly, the court held that the IRS has abused its discretion in canceling the APAs.

The IRS advanced an alternative argument under section 367(d). If the court did not agree with the cancellation of the APAs and the transfer pricing adjustments, the IRS asserted that it had to conclude that intangibles had been transferred to the foreign affiliates as they could not have earned the returns they did absent such a transfer. The court made short shrift of this argument, noting the IRS' failure to specify any intangible that had been transferred. However, given the expanded definition of intangibles now found in section 367(d)(4), it is possible that the IRS will continue to make broad, unspecific claims that value was transferred subject to section 367(d) in future cases.

Eaton resurfaced in 2019 with a supplemental opinion on the issue of penalties.[10] The court had directed the parties to compute the amounts due subject to Tax Court Rule 155, and the IRS included a 40% increase in net transfer pricing adjustment penalty in its computations. The Tax Court disagreed, holding that the APAs remained in effect for the years at issue and, therefore, the increase in the taxpayer's income did not result from a section 482 adjustment. As a result, there could be no net transfer pricing adjustment penalty.

1.4 *Medtronic* (2016, 2018)

In *Medtronic*,[11] the IRS tackled the taxpayer's use of a Puerto Rican subsidiary (Medtronic Puerto Rico Operations Co. or MPROC) to manufacture sophisticated

8. Eaton Corp. v. Comm'r, T.C. Memo. 2017-147.
9. Eaton Corp. v. Comm'r, 140 T.C. 410 (2013).
10. Eaton Corp. v. Comm'r, 153 T.C. No. 6 (2019).
11. Medtronic Comm'r, 900 F.3d 610 (8th Cir. 2018), *vacating and remanding* T.C. Memo. 2016-112.

medical devices and leads which it sold to a U.S. affiliate for distribution to customers. The royalties paid by MPROC had been adjusted in an earlier year in connection with a memorandum of understanding (MOU) with the IRS.

The IRS subsequently repudiated the MOU, asserting deficiencies of more than USD 1.3 billion for the two years at issue. The IRS relied on a comparable profits method (CPM) analysis while the taxpayer had employed the comparable uncontrolled transaction (CUT) method to value the royalties. The proposed CPM analysis treated MPROC as a routine contract manufacturer, ignoring the substantial quality and product liability risks that it bore.

The Tax Court rejected the IRS' blunt approach to pricing the transaction. However, it also disagreed with the aspects of the taxpayer's analysis. Unable to fully endorse either option before it, the court took the taxpayer's CUT approach as its basis and made additional adjustments based on information in the record in order to arrive at its best approximation of a correct result. The court also rebuffed the IRS' vague section 367(d) argument (similar to the one advanced in *Eaton*) and dismissed the IRS' suggestion that the commensurate with income standard under section 482 requires the use of the CPM in cases involving intangibles.

The Eighth Circuit vacated and remanded, finding that the lack of certain factual findings prevented it from evaluating whether the CUT was the best method and whether proper adjustments were made. As a result, a new Tax Court trial must be held.

Despite the setback, the Eighth Circuit opinion is more favorable to the taxpayer than it appears at first glance. Most importantly, the Eighth Circuit did not take issue with the lower court's determination that the IRS' CPM-backed adjustments were arbitrary and capricious. If the appellate court had felt there was merit to the IRS' arguments, it would almost certainly have said so rather than remanding the Tax Court to further develop an analysis that was only necessary because the IRS' adjustments had been rejected. Similarly, the taxpayer's victories on the commensurate with income and section 367(d) arguments remain undisturbed.

1.5 Ongoing Matters

Among the transfer pricing cases working their way through the courts, the most noteworthy is the *Coca-Cola* case. Coke is embroiled in a multi-billion dollar dispute concerning the profitability of its foreign subsidiaries with the IRS taking the position that the subsidiaries are comparable to independent bottlers and should earn significantly less profit. The case resembles *Medtronic* in pitting the taxpayer's CUT analysis against the IRS' CPM. A trial was held in spring 2018, but the Tax Court has not yet issued an opinion.

A separate issue in the Coke case did lead to a Tax Court opinion in 2017 that granted summary judgment in favor of the taxpayer.[12] At issue was the creditability of taxes paid in Mexico, which the IRS contended were ineligible for a foreign tax credit

12. Coca-Cola Co. v. Comm'r, 149 T.C. 446 (2017).

because Coke had failed to reasonably interpret Mexican law and failed to exhaust its Mexican remedies, making the taxes paid noncompulsory. Finding that the taxpayer had relied in good faith on advice from a competent Mexican tax advisor, the court dismissed the government's claim that its interpretation of Mexican law was unreasonable. As for the exhaustion of remedies argument, the court took exception to the IRS' argument, noting that the only effective and practical remedy then available to the taxpayer was a competent authority proceeding, which the IRS had unilaterally foreclosed by designating the matter for litigation. While the outcome of the primary transfer pricing dispute remains to be seen, this opinion indicates that determinations of foreign tax creditability should be reasonable and should not impose undue burdens on taxpayers.

2 DEVELOPMENTS IN IRS TRANSFER PRICING ENFORCEMENT

While prominent cases have taken much of the limelight directed at transfer pricing controversy, administrative developments in how the IRS approaches transfer pricing cases may have more immediate significance for some taxpayers. Developments over the past few years show changes in how the IRS' Large Business and International Division (LB&I) is approaching transfer pricing enforcement, taking a tack that focuses its limited resources in areas where compliance risks are higher.

In August 2018, LB&I introduced new guidelines for transfer pricing examinations, the Transfer Pricing Examination Process (TPEP) which illustrates the IRS' shift to a risk-based approach. The TPEP replaced the prior Transfer Pricing Audit Roadmap that was released in 2014. While TPEP is similar to the prior roadmap, it shows the increased importance of risk considerations for examinations involving transfer pricing.[13]

Subsequently, in February 2019, the LB&I released a memorandum requiring LB&I exam teams to consult with the IRS' Advance Pricing and Mutual Agreement program (APMA) in transfer pricing cases that may lead to adjustments involving countries that are U.S. treaty partners.[14] The underlying intention of the memorandum appears to be to increase the viability and sustainability of IRS transfer pricing adjustments that may be challenged in competent authority proceedings.

More specifically, a group of January 2018 directives regarding transfer pricing examinations shows how LB&I is modifying its enforcement approach in order to conserve resources and hone in on riskier issues while reducing the time spent addressing routine reviews and examinations.[15] These directives, which are discussed

13. TPEP is available at https://www.irs.gov/businesses/corporations/transfer-pricing-examination-process, accessed August 28, 2020.
14. LB&I-04-0219-001. Available at https://www.irs.gov/pub/foia/ig/spder/lbi-04-0219-001.pdf, accessed August 28, 2020.
15. Directive LB&I-04-0118-001 (January 12, 2018); Directive LB&I-04-0118-003 (January 12, 2018); Directive LB&I-04-0118-004 (January 12, 2018), *withdrawn by* Directive LB&I-04-0519-005 (May 21, 2019); Directive LB&I-04-0118-005 (January 12, 2018), *withdrawn by* Directive

below, addressed topics such as routine requests for transfer pricing documentation,[16] challenges to taxpayers' selection of a TPM,[17] and the application of penalties.[18] Additional directives that are no longer in force brought about temporary halts to examinations involving issues on which substantial uncertainty existed for the IRS: one directive decreed a pause in examinations involving CSAs that used multiple reasonable anticipated benefit (RAB) shares until an IRS-wide position could be developed,[19] whereas another paused CSA examinations involving SBC costs pending the Ninth Circuit's decision in *Altera*.[20] Following up on the penalties directive, a set of frequently asked questions (FAQs) released in April 2020 provides guidance on transfer pricing documentation and indicates the LB&I's continuing commitment to a risk-focused approach.[21]

These developments can be situated within a broader context of risk sensitivity in the LB&I. This is particularly evident in its adoption of campaign-based examinations in 2017. The campaign-based approach involves examinations that focus on specified compliance issues rather than general audits and thus represents a realignment of constrained budgetary and personnel resources to achieve strategic aims.[22] Consistent with this approach and with its specific efforts to improve the application of transfer pricing penalties, the LB&I also aims to improve its application of accuracy-related penalties in general, as prompted by a report on penalties from the Treasury Inspector General for Tax Administration (TIGTA).[23]

These developments indicate that the LB&I is moving toward an increasingly risk-focused approach intended to address key issues while reducing the time and resources spent on issues that either pose insignificant risks or will be unlikely to yield adjustments that can be sustained in subsequent proceedings, such as IRS Appeals or competent authority. This should yield some benefits for taxpayers who may benefit from reduced time spent addressing non-issues. However, the LB&I has had issues

LB&I-04-0719-008 (July 31, 2019); Directive LB&I-04-0118-006 (January 29, 2018). LB&I Directives are available at https://www.irs.gov/businesses/corporations/large-business-and-international-lbi-industry-director-guidance, accessed August 28, 2020.

16. Directive LB&I-04-0118-001 (January 12, 2018).
17. Directive LB&I-04-0118-006 (January 29, 2018).
18. Directive LB&I-04-0118-003 (January 12, 2018).
19. Directive LB&I-04-0118-004 (January 12, 2018), *withdrawn by* Directive LB&I-04-0519-005 (May 21, 2019).
20. Directive LB&I-04-0118-005 (January 12, 2018), *withdrawn by* Directive LB&I-04-0719-008 (July 31, 2019).
21. LB&I, Transfer Pricing Documentation Frequently Asked Questions (FAQs) (April 14, 2020), available at https://www.irs.gov/businesses/international-businesses/transfer-pricing-documentation-frequently-asked-questions-faqs, accessed August 28, 2020 (hereinafter "Documentation FAQs").
22. *See*, e.g., Treasury Inspector General for Tax Administration, "Initial Compliance Results Warrant a More Data-Driven Approach to Campaign Issue Selection," 2019-30-066, September 27, 2019, available at https://www.treasury.gov/tigta/auditreports/2019reports/201930066fr.pdf, accessed August 28, 2020 (hereinafter "TIGTA Campaigns Report").
23. Published as "IRS LB&I Rarely Imposing Accuracy-Related Penalties, TIGTA Says," *Tax Notes Today*, June 5, 2019, 2019 TNT 108-30 (hereinafter "TIGTA Penalties Report").

implementing this new approach. As discussed below, successfully resolving these problems will be key to ensuring that the benefits of a risk-centered strategy materialize.

2.1 LB&I Framework for Transfer Pricing Audits

In 2014, the LB&I released a Transfer Pricing Audit Roadmap (Roadmap) that was meant to assist both IRS employees and tax practitioners in planning, executing, and resolving transfer pricing examinations. The Roadmap offered techniques for audits and case development as well as best practice recommendations centered around a suggested twenty-four month exam timeline. In August 2018, the Roadmap was replaced by the TPEP, which is likewise meant to assist the IRS and practitioners in approaching and dealing with transfer pricing exams.[24] While the TPEP attempts to cover the most important issues implicated in transfer pricing audits, it is not meant as a one-size-fits-all template for all examinations. However, the general timelines and framework laid out in the TPEP serve to provide guidance on key issues that may improve the audit process.

One key difference from the Roadmap is the introduction in the TPEP of alternate twenty-four month and thirty-six month timelines, reflecting the LB&I's recognition that, in reality, many transfer pricing exams take longer to complete than was envisioned in the Roadmap. Which timeline is appropriate depends on the complexity of the case and how much fact-finding will be needed, and the TPEP recognizes that actual timelines will vary by case. The TPEP timelines are organized around three phases: planning, execution, and resolution.

Another key difference is that the TPEP places greater emphasis on the importance of risk in transfer pricing examinations, requiring an initial risk assessment and a subsequent reassessment. In keeping with the requirement that exam teams discuss adjustments that may be subject to competent authority relief with the APMA, the initial risk assessment must involve consultation with the APMA if the relevant intercompany transactions involve a U.S. treaty partner.[25] As discussed in more detail below, the goal is to increase the quality of the LB&I's transfer pricing adjustments. Aggressive and inadequately substantiated adjustments have often been reduced or eliminated in competent authority proceedings, resulting in a waste of time and resources.

Both the planning phase and the initial risk assessment contemplated by the TPEP involve review of materials available to the IRS from prior audits as well as the taxpayer's income tax returns. The latter review will focus on subpart F and permanent establishment issues in addition to transfer pricing. The exam team will also examine the taxpayer's country-by-country report, calculate key financial ratios, and benchmark them against industry norms. The initial review also covers Forms 10-K, taxpayer

24. The TPEP is available at https://www.irs.gov/businesses/corporations/transfer-pricing-examination-process, accessed August 28, 2020.
25. *See* TPEP para. 11.10.

websites, and other publicly available information on a taxpayer's operations and will culminate in the development of a preliminary working hypothesis.

In the execution phase, the TPEP contemplates that examiners will engage in further risk assessment, including a review of the taxpayer's transfer pricing documentation. The examination team will request meetings for orientations on the financial statement and transfer pricing and supply chain matters which will further inform its risk assessment, and it will continue to reassess risk throughout the execution phase. The TPEP suggests that examiners should prepare a formal mid-cycle risk analysis to reflect changes in the risk assessment and discuss this analysis with the taxpayer, though it stresses that risk assessment should be a continuous process and should not be confined to the more formal initial and mid-cycle reviews.

Like the Roadmap, the TPEP requires the exam team to develop and use a working hypothesis throughout the examination. As part of the risk reassessment during the exam, the working hypothesis is reviewed, revised and, when necessary, discarded based on the development and documentation of new factual information. The TPEP encourages exam teams to keep an open mind and to practice strategic abandonment. That is, when information that is inconsistent with the working hypothesis comes to the examiners' attention, the team should either adjust its hypothesis or conclude the theory should not be pursued.

By offering a more guided examination approach in TPEP, the IRS hopes to increase efficiency and address taxpayer concerns about "fishing expeditions" (i.e., theories in search of fact) while offering "a good foundation for organizing and formulating a complete analysis at the end of the examination process." However, in the authors' experience, adherence to the generally helpful principles and recommendations of the TPEP (and the Roadmap before it) is inconsistent among exam teams.

2.2 APMA-Exam Consultations for Potential Competent Authority Issues

On February 19, 2019, the LB&I released a memorandum announcing mandatory consultations between IRS exam issue teams and APMA personnel. The new procedure is motivated by concerns of efficiency and effective use of specialized resources and applies to LB&I examinations in which a potential transfer pricing adjustment would involve a U.S. treaty partner. Importantly, the procedure applies whether or not the APMA currently has an effective mutual agreement procedure (MAP) relationship with the country in question.

Consultations with APMA personnel must cover both procedural and substantive issues and will enable the APMA to provide an opinion on whether contemplated adjustments are justifiable under the applicable treaty. While it is the issue teams rather than the APMA that have the final say on whether to pursue transfer pricing issues and, ultimately, adjustments, the consultation procedure should facilitate effective coordination and reduce inefficiency. Presumably, the policy's goal is to reduce the amount of poorly developed IRS transfer pricing adjustments that the APMA must deal with in competent authority, which has led to a high level of unilateral elimination or reduction of adjustments by the APMA.[26] In addition to preventing the waste of IRS and taxpayer resources contesting adjustments that will not ultimately be sustained, this policy may also help to reduce burdens on the APMA's MAP inventory by freeing up resources to spend on meritorious cases.

2.3 Directive on Mandatory Documentation Requests

The January 2018 directive titled "Interim Instructions on Issuance of Mandatory Transfer Pricing Information Document Request (IDR) in LB&I Examinations" eliminates the requirement that exam teams issue an information document request (IDR) requesting transfer pricing documentation in most cases.[27] However, an IDR requesting the taxpayer's documentation must still be issued in two circumstances, and the directive does nothing to curtail IRS examiners' ability to issue an IDR requesting transfer pricing documentation when the examiner believes this is warranted.

Under prior guidance, specifically, the "Langdon Directive"[28] and the 2014 Transfer Pricing Audit Roadmap,[29] IRS personnel were instructed to issue a mandatory IDR seeking § 6662(e) documentation at the commencement of all examinations involving cross-border transactions between related parties. The IDR, which was typically sent alongside or shortly after the initial examination contact letter, triggered a statutory thirty-day response period for the taxpayer and requested, among other things, the principal documentation described in Treasury Regulation § 1.6662-6(d) accompanied by an index of the background documentation.

The directive removes the mandatory IDR requirement for many audits. Under the directive, an IDR requesting transfer pricing documentation must be issued in only two instances: (1) examinations that fall under an LB&I Campaign which calls for the issuance of a mandatory transfer pricing documentation IDR and (2) examinations when Transfer Pricing Practice (TPP) and/or Cross Border Activities (CBA) Practice Area personnel have been assigned either as consultants or as team members and have determined that an IDR is needed. These procedures reflect an attempt by the IRS to "manage transfer pricing issues under examination and related resources in the most efficient and effective manner possible."

Presumably, the directive will result in fewer IDRs being issued for transfer pricing documentation, at least for low-risk taxpayers with a low volume of related party transactions. TPP and CBA personnel should generally only be involved in cases in which the IRS believes there is an appreciable transfer pricing risk. Currently, the only campaigns focused on transfer pricing issues address inbound distributors and

26. *See* U.S. Government Accountability Office, Opportunities Exist to Improve IRS's Management of International Tax Dispute Resolution, GAO-19-81 (March 2019) (indicating that a large number of MAP cases are conceded by APMA).
27. Directive LB&I-04-0118-001 (January 12, 2018).
28. So called after Larry Langdon, then Commissioner of the IRS's Large and Mid-Size Business Division (now LB&I), who issued the directive titled "Transfer Pricing Compliance Directive," on January 22, 2003.
29. As discussed above, the Roadmap has been replaced by the TPEP which does not have a mandatory IDR requirement.

captive service providers, though other campaigns may tangentially implicate transfer pricing matters, and the LB&I plans to announce more campaigns in the future.[30]

It appears from the directive that the LB&I intended to coordinate transfer pricing inquiries with its campaign-based examination strategy. However, a recent TIGTA report concluded that the LB&I has been slow to implement its campaign-based strategy with only 15% of exams generated by campaigns as of February 2019.[31] The TIGTA found that issues were often selected as the basis for campaigns based on employee suggestions or available training materials and that the LB&I did not use data regarding past compliance results and projected compliance impacts to design campaigns. That is, campaigns may cover areas that do not present significant risk while neglecting areas of greater concern. While the LB&I agreed with the TIGTA's recommendations and stated that it will endeavor to improve the campaign process, it remains to be seen how the use and effectiveness of campaigns will develop.[32]

Because mandatory IDRs will be issued under the directive only in these limited circumstances, taxpayers will have an early indication of whether the IRS believes their circumstances pose a significant transfer pricing risk and may be able to anticipate whether an IDR will be issued. Note, however, that exam teams do not always follow these directives precisely. Thus, when TPP or CBA personnel are consulting on a case, it would not be surprising to see mandatory IDRs issued by the international examiner (bearing an IE prefix) or economist (bearing an EC prefix), notwithstanding the directive's indication that the TPP or CBA personnel should issue the IDR. Taxpayers should consider challenging mandatory IDRs that do not follow the rules set forth in this directive. However, the directive is not a source of formal authority, and thus taxpayers have limited ability to make exam teams follow the directive. Nevertheless, in appropriate cases, taxpayers may be successful addressing these issues with IRS management personnel who tend to be more concerned that exam teams are following internal directives.

Of course, examiners retain the authority to issue IDRs requesting transfer pricing documentation after developing the factual context of a case. Therefore, while the number of transfer pricing documentation IDRs will presumably decrease, it remains to be seen how significant this shift will be. In theory, this development should allow the IRS exam to better focus its resources on cases in which there are significant related party transactions and, therefore, any reduction in IDRs may only be for taxpayers that should not have received transfer pricing scrutiny in the first place. In any event, the clear objective is to prioritize the review of transfer pricing documentation in higher-risk cases over broad coverage and review of all LB&I taxpayers' documentation.

Still, the fact that many taxpayers' transfer pricing documentation may go unrequested and unexamined under this new approach does not mean that taxpayers should forego preparing documentation, especially given the heightened standards laid

30. LB&I, Large Business and International Active Campaigns, available at https://www.irs.gov/businesses/corporations/lbi-active-campaigns, accessed August 28, 2020. Examples of other existing campaigns are the Micro-Captive Insurance Campaign and the Related Party Transactions Campaign, both of which are run by the Enterprise Activities practice area.
31. TIGTA Campaigns Report.
32. *See Id.*

out in the transfer pricing penalty directive discussed below. Taxpayers with *de minimis* or low-risk related party transactions may decide that the expense that is inherent in preparing documentation is no longer justifiable absent the mandatory IDR requirement, but such conclusions should be based on a cost benefit analysis after careful consideration.

2.4 Directive on Application of Transfer Pricing Penalties

The directive titled "Instructions for Examiners on Transfer Pricing Issue Examination Scope—Appropriate Application of IRC §6662(e) Penalties" instructs IRS exam personnel to apply a heightened level of scrutiny to taxpayers' § 6662(e) transfer pricing documentation.[33] However, the directive does nothing to change the current state of the law under § 6662 and the applicable regulations and merely reflects a change in IRS scrutiny. The IRS' objective is to ensure that it is "properly using a legislative tool intended to encourage taxpayer compliance" and to increase the "incentive for taxpayers to initially provide adequate and timely documentation."

Under § 6662, transfer pricing adjustments that exceed specified thresholds will generally result in the application of a 20% penalty which is applied to the underpayment of tax resulting from the non-arm's length transfer pricing. In certain more extreme cases, the penalty is increased to 40%. However, taxpayers may guard against the imposition of penalties by preparing transfer pricing documentation that meets the requirements laid out in Treasury Regulation § 1.6662-6(d). This directive clarifies that transfer pricing penalties under § 6662 should apply when an adjustment is made, and the taxpayer: (1) failed to create documentation contemporaneously;[34] (2) failed to provide the documentation within thirty days of an IRS request for it; and/or (3) furnished documentation that was "unreasonable or inadequate."

The directive clarifies that § 6662(e) documentation must be both timely (i.e., contemporaneously prepared and timely provided to the IRS) and adequate (i.e., sufficient to show that the taxpayer reasonably concluded its selection and application of a TPM provided the most reliable measure of an arm's length result) in order to provide protection against transfer pricing penalties. Historically, the penalties were rarely asserted when some material level of documentation had been contemporaneously produced and timely provided. In fact, practitioner experience has been that penalties were rarely applied even in the absence of contemporaneous documentation. Therefore, while this directive is in line with the statute, regulations, and congressional intent, this higher standard marks a significant shift in the practical enforcement of the § 6662(e) documentation rules.

The directive explains that § 6662(e) documentation is, by definition, limited to documentation that was prepared before filing the return and provided to the IRS within thirty days of a request. Taxpayers may not defend against penalties by supplementing § 6662(e) documentation with documents that were either prepared

33. Directive LB&I-04-0118-003 (January 12, 2018).
34. To be effective, documentation must be contemporaneous, i.e., it must be in existence as of the filing of the taxpayer's return. Treas. Reg. § 6662(e)(3)(B)(ii).

after the filing of the return or not provided to the IRS within thirty days of a request, although such supplemental materials may be helpful in defending against proposed adjustments. Therefore, taxpayers should take care to ensure their § 6662(e) documentation is both timely created and provided. In particular, taxpayers and their advisors should ensure that the documentation is complete and should retain evidence of its completion prior to the return filing date.

Of course, timeliness is not enough; the documentation must also be adequate in order to effectively protect against a proposed penalty. As the directive notes, Treasury Regulations § 1.6662-6(d)(2)(ii)(A)(1) through (7) provide factors that examiners should consider in evaluating the adequacy of § 6662(e) documentation. The directive does not supplement those factors or alter the legal framework but rather marks a shift in focus and sufficiency.

For example, the directive remarks that § 6662(e) documentation should include an explicit analysis and conclusion that the method used is the best method.[35] Documentation that lacks these features is deemed inadequate and thus failure to include such an analysis and conclusion will result in imposition of transfer pricing penalties if the applicable thresholds are met. This directive echoes the best method directive that is discussed below by noting that examiners' analysis should start with the taxpayer's selection of the best method, assuming this is supported by timely and adequate § 6662(e) documentation.

The directive instructs examiners to consider sources of information beyond the § 6662(e) documentation to determine if the documentation is adequate. For example, examiners should consider what information was or should have been available to the taxpayer in assessing whether the taxpayer adequately incorporated and addressed such data in the analyses contained in its § 6662(e) documentation. To address this, taxpayers and their advisors may wish to consider whether more information that is typically included in background documentation should be referenced in or included as part of the primary § 6662(e) documentation.

While the directives address the role of transfer pricing documentation in penalty application and method selection, such documentation also plays an important role in a formal risk assessment process as the TPEP instructs examiners to look at such documentation with an eye to identifying and pursuing risk. Moreover, a recent set of FAQs and responses relating to transfer pricing documentation, which is discussed below, stresses the role that high quality documentation can play in facilitating an effective examination, including by leading to the deselection of issues that pose little risk and thus do not require an audit.[36]

The heightened importance of transfer pricing documentation, both in terms of defending against penalties and in terms of persuading the IRS that the taxpayer's transfer pricing is at arm's length, has significant implications for both taxpayers and advisors who should ensure that robust, well-reasoned, and detailed documentation is produced in a timely fashion. Without changing the letter of the law, the IRS has raised

35. Cf. §§ 1.6662-6(d)(2)(ii)(A), 1.6662-6(d)(2)(iii)(A).
36. Documentation FAQs.

the bar for § 6662(e) documentation, and taxpayers and advisors would be well advised to meet this new standard.

2.5 Directive on Best Method Challenges

The directive titled "Instructions for LB&I on Transfer Pricing Selection and Scope of Analysis—Best Method Selection" sets out new approval processes for exam and APA teams to follow before challenging a taxpayer's selection of a TPM, though these processes only apply if certain conditions are met.[37] Specifically, if the taxpayer's contemporaneous transfer pricing documentation or APA submission contains an adequate best method analysis and selection, then exam and APA teams must obtain approval from the Treaty and Transfer Pricing Operations (TTPO) Transfer Pricing Review Panel prior to challenging the taxpayer's TPM selection.

The best method rule of Treasury Regulation § 1.482-1(c) governs the TPM selection under § 482, requiring that the taxpayer apply the method that "provides the most reliable measure of an arm's length result." Because method selection, therefore, comes down to a judgment call about what, given the circumstances of the taxpayer's case, most accurately reflects an arm's length price, there exists substantial space for disagreement. Even the flawless application of a selected TPM will not shield a taxpayer from a transfer pricing adjustment if the IRS determines that the method applied was not the best method. This directive does not alter that basic principle, but it does make it harder for the IRS to determine that the taxpayer's selected method is not the best one.

The directive's review applies to two sets of taxpayers: LB&I taxpayers that have assets of at least USD 10 million and that are required to file Forms 5471 or 5472 with their annual tax returns;[38] and all taxpayers in the APA program. The directive applies to TPP examinations, examinations involving CBA personnel, and examinations by Geographic Practice Area agents without TPP participation.

For the new approval requirement to apply, the directive states that the taxpayer under examination must provide a report that clearly identifies the taxpayer's selection of a method, concludes that the method selected is the best method, and provides an analysis supporting that conclusion as part of its § 6662(e) documentation or APA submission. The directive states that § 6662 documentation will only suffice for this purpose if it is contemporaneous, timely provided to the IRS on request, and adequate as described above with respect to the transfer pricing penalty directive.

In the examination context, when the taxpayer falls into one of the covered categories and has provided adequate supporting documentation, the directive requires the exam team to consult with the TTPO and obtain approval prior to contesting the taxpayer's TPM selection. While the directive notes that the use of unspecified methods may be subject to increased scrutiny at the exam stage, the TTPO's approval is still required before an unspecified method can be challenged. The decision to

37. Directive LB&I-04-0118-006 (January 29, 2018).
38. Treas. Reg. § 1.6046-1 lays out the requirements for who must file Form 5471 and Treas. Reg. § 1.6038A-2 gives the requirements for Form 5472.

remove the best method determination from the sole discretion of the examination team is not grounded in any notion of deference to taxpayers' analyses. Rather, it is motivated by the recognition that the LB&I possesses "limited transfer pricing resources" that are "divert[ed]" by ignoring the taxpayer's analysis and "start[ing] the best method selection analysis from scratch."

Exam teams, therefore, are directed to begin with the taxpayer's method selection rather than make their own best method determinations de novo. The directive instructs them to thoroughly analyze the taxpayer's method application and develop and document any changes to that application at an early date. Importantly, approval is not required for changes to the taxpayer's application of the selected TPM. When exam teams do consider recommending a method change, the directive suggests that they consult the examples of best method selection in Treasury Regulation § 1.482-8.

In the APA context, the directive indicates that the APA team must follow the same approval process in order to change a taxpayer's appropriately substantiated TPM selection.[39] However, when formal competent authority negotiations between the APMA and a treaty partner for a bilateral APA have begun, the directive provides that the competent authorities may change the method selection without consulting with or securing approval from the TTPO.

To secure TTPO approval, the exam or APA team must elevate the recommendation for a method change through the applicable management chain until it reaches a Director of Field Operations who is responsible for referring it to the national TTPO Transfer Pricing Review Panel. The panel consists of the TPP Director (or, if the issue arises in the context of an APA, the APMA Director); a Senior Advisor to the TTPO Director; and the Income Shifting Practice Network Manager. The panel will examine "(1) Why the taxpayer's method is unreliable, (2) Whether the taxpayer's method can be adjusted to make it more reliable, and (3) If not, what method is more reliable, and why." To facilitate this process, the directive indicates that the exam or APA team's initial recommendation must address these questions and include an analysis supporting the alternative method selection. However, IRS personnel have suggested that an application to the panel does not require a formal presentation or the submission of specific documentation and instead can be based on materials developed as part of normal case development.[40]

The restraints that this directive imposes on the IRS' ability to dispute method selection clearly benefit taxpayers. The LB&I's reluctance to continue expending limited resources in contentious method selection battles should mean that more taxpayers will survive examination or APA negotiations with their desired TPM intact.

39. In the bilateral APA context, the test is not which method is the "best method" but, rather, which is the "most appropriate method" under the OECD's transfer pricing guidelines. Organisation for Economic Co-operation and Development, OECD Transfer Pricing Guidelines for Multinational Enterprises and Tax Administrations 2017. Paragraph 2.2 of the OECD guidelines provides that "[t]he selection of a transfer pricing method always aims at finding the most appropriate method for a particular case."
40. Ryan Finley, "IRS Best Method Review Panel Focused on Internal Quality Control," 2020 TNTI 40-6 (February 28, 2020) (quoting remarks of LB&I TTPO Director Jennifer Best).

Yet the directive does not mean that the LB&I is uninterested in or agnostic with respect to method selection issues. In early 2019, the APMA released a functional cost diagnostic model (FCD Model) which applies a cost-based residual profit split analysis for use in certain APA cases. Thus far, the FCD Model has been used primarily in inbound U.S. automotive cases, and IRS personnel have indicated that the model may also be appropriate for use by the exam.[41] A request that the taxpayers complete the FCD Model is not meant to suggest that the profit split is the best method; rather, the tool is conceived of as a means to evaluate the taxpayer's method selection and, when requested from a taxpayer, indicates that the APMA is at least considering challenging the proposed method.

Moreover, taxpayers must take care under the new regime. As this and other developments show, § 6662(e) documentation has become even more critical to reducing controversy exposure. Taxpayers who lack documentation or who have documentation that lacks a clear analysis and conclusion on the method selection will find their TPM open to challenge without the need for TTPO approval. Further, the directive may result not so much in a decrease in transfer pricing controversy as in a shift in focus: while fewer method selection challenges are to be expected, the directive's guidance may lead to more disputes over method application.

Then, too, there always remains the possibility of changes to a taxpayer's best method determination with TTPO approval and, in theory, such changes should be well substantiated and thus potentially harder for taxpayers to overcome than past method selection disputes. LB&I leadership has indicated that the review process is meant to provide a "friendly second set of eyes" and should not be burdensome for exam and APA teams while also acknowledging that deference is due to the taxpayer's TPM selection.[42]

In short, this directive should limit the number of IRS challenges to taxpayers' method selection, but taxpayers must take care that their method application is proper and that their documentation sufficiently addresses the method selection. Moreover, since the directive "is not an official pronouncement of law and cannot be used, cited or relied upon as such," a taxpayer would not be able to make any formal challenge in the event that an exam or APA team deviated from the directive and made an unapproved method change, although involving IRS management personnel could be helpful in such situations. Taxpayers should not rely on the directive to shield against challenges to unreasonable or poorly documented stances on method selection but may benefit from the procedures it requires, which should reduce controversy with respect to defensible method selections that are properly applied and documented.

41. *See* Advance Pricing and Mutual Agreement Program, Functional Cost Diagnostic Model (February 15, 2019), *published as* "IRS Explains Functional Cost Diagnostic Transfer Pricing Model," 2019 WTD 42-20 (March 4, 2019); Ryan Finley, "IRS Examiners May Use APMA Diagnostic Tool in Some Cases," 94 Tax Notes Int'l 198 (April 8, 2019).
42. Ryan Finley, "IRS Best Method Review Panel Focused on Internal Quality Control," 2020 TNTI 40-6 (February 28, 2020) (quoting remarks of LB&I TTPO Director Jennifer Best).

2.6 Withdrawn Directives

The directive entitled "Instructions for Examiners on Transfer Pricing Selection—Reasonably Anticipated Benefits in Cost Sharing Arrangements" instructed LB&I examiners to stop making adjustments to CSAs by changing a taxpayer's multiple RAB shares to a single one when subsequent PCTs are added to an existing CSA until an IRS-wide position on the issue could be finalized.[43] The IRS issued the initial directive because some examination teams had taken the position that the section 1.482-7 regulations required the use of a single RAB share when subsequent PCTs occur.

On July 26, 2018, the IRS Office of Chief Counsel finalized the IRS' position, releasing a memorandum that concluded that multiple RAB shares may be used in a single CSA but only if this is the most reliable approach.[44] This rendered the RAB share directive effectively moot, and the issuance of the June 2019 directive formalized its withdrawal in light of the Chief Counsel memorandum, thus ending the saga.[45] The 2019 directive instructs exam teams to "continue with the application of the most reliable method depending on the facts and circumstances of each case to determine the appropriateness of using single or multiple RAB shares with respect to a single CSA" and to consult with the TPP network and IRS Chief Counsel when needed.

The directive entitled "Instructions for Examiners on Transfer Pricing Selection—Cost-Sharing Arrangement Stock Based Compensation" directed examiners to temporarily stop opening issues related to the SBC included in CSA intangible development costs until the Ninth Circuit issues an opinion in *Altera* on appeal.[46] After the release of the 2019 Ninth Circuit opinion but before that opinion became final,[47] the IRS issued a second directive formally withdrawing the SBC directive after considering the June 7 opinion.[48]

Although no longer in effect, these directives displayed a valuable awareness that resources should not be squandered in developing cases based on inconsistent positions or in pursuing contentious adjustments before the IRS' approach has received the sanction of a court in a test case.

43. Directive LB&I-04-0118-004 (dated January 12, 2018), *withdrawn by* Directive LB&I-04-0519-005 (dated May 21, 2019).
44. AM 2018-003. The memorandum states that "[t]his advice may not be used or cited as precedent." *See also* section 6110(k)(3) ("Unless the Secretary otherwise establishes by regulations, a written determination may not be used or cited as precedent."). However, as a practical matter, it appears that it would be difficult for the IRS to disavow the position taken in the Chief Counsel memorandum. Unless otherwise indicated, section references are to the Internal Revenue Code of 1986, as amended (the Code) or the applicable regulations promulgated pursuant to the Code (the regulations).
45. Directive LB&I-04-0519-005 (dated May 21, 2019).
46. Directive LB&I-04-0118-005 (January 12, 2018), *withdrawn by* Directive LB&I-04-0719-008 (July 31, 2019).
47. The opinion became final with the issuance of the Ninth Circuit's mandate on November 20, 2019 notwithstanding that a petition for a writ of certiorari was filed on February 10, 2020.
48. Directive LB&I-04-0719-008 (July 31, 2019).

2.7 Improving Penalty Application: TIGTA's Penalty Report

The message of the penalties directive is echoed in a May 31, 2019 report from the TIGTA,[49] the title of which succinctly summarizes its message: "Few Accuracy-Related Penalties Are Proposed in Large Business Examinations, and They Are Generally Not Sustained on Appeal." Accuracy-related penalties are governed by § 6662 and include transfer pricing penalties as well as penalties for negligence or disregard of regulations, substantial understatement of tax, transactions lacking economic substance, and other issues.[50]

The TIGTA identified 519 LB&I cases (out of 6,709 reviewed returns) in which § 6662 penalties were proposed from 2015 to 2017. Of these 519 cases, 308 were appealed and, as of December 2018, 195 had been resolved in Appeals, resulting in the elimination or reduction of penalties in 183 cases, or 94%, for a total reduction of USD 765 million. In the great majority of these Appeals cases, the penalty was eliminated entirely; for the remainder, aggregate penalties of USD 26.7 million were reduced to USD 2.5 million following Appeals.

As presented by the TIGTA, these numbers suggest a clear narrative: the LB&I is proposing too few penalties, and too many are being discarded in Appeals. Yet, this is not necessarily the correct narrative. The report drew criticism for "viewing penalties as a revenue raising tool rather than a compliance tool" and for suggesting that the LB&I should impose penalties with comparable frequency to the IRS' Small Business/Self-Employed Division that generally deals with taxpayers with fewer compliance resources.[51] Indeed, based on the rate at which proposed penalties are abandoned or significantly reduced on appeal, it would be possible to argue that LB&I exam teams are proposing too many accuracy-related penalties.

Nonetheless, the TIGTA report on penalties sends an important message, and its procedural discoveries may be more important than its statistical findings. The TIGTA found that, in contravention of IRS policy, LB&I examiners "are not always considering penalties, not always supporting their decisions for non-proposal of accuracy-related civil penalties, and not always involving supervisors in penalty development and approval as required."[52] Under § 6751(b)(1), penalties may not be assessed without written supervisory approval of the initial penalty determination. If the IRS cannot prove compliance with this requirement, a penalty assessment may be reversed.[53] The TIGTA also found shortcomings in internal quality review processes and case file retention.

The LB&I agreed with the TIGTA's recommendations to train examiners to consider § 6662 penalties whenever applicable, follow proper procedures to document penalty development, and obtain requisite approvals. It also expressed agreement with recommendations to improve internal resources, quality review systems, and record

49. TIGTA Penalties Report.
50. *See* § 6662(a).
51. Eric Yauch, "Practitioners Poke Holes in TIGTA Report's Penalty Theories," *Tax Notes Today*, June 6, 2019, 2019 TNT 109-5.
52. TIGTA Penalties Report at 9-10.
53. *See*, e.g., Chai v. Comm'r, 851 F.3d 190 (2d Cir. 2017).

retention practices related to penalties. However, the LB&I only partially agreed with the TIGTA's recommendation to study why Appeals was rejecting so many proposed penalties, noting that the LB&I and Appeals have essentially different missions and that many penalties will be removed in Appeals as a result of underlying issues.

Whatever its methodological flaws, the TIGTA penalties report and the LB&I's response indicate that key stakeholders in the IRS and Treasury believe penalties should be considered and asserted with greater regularity. Taxpayers should expect increased consideration and better documentation of accuracy-related penalties and will likely encounter fewer cases in which proposed penalties will be hamstrung by procedural deficiencies such as a failure to obtain § 6751(b)(1) approval. Together with the directive on transfer pricing penalties, this indicates that § 6662 penalties are no longer reserved for egregious cases but rather may and, presumably, will be more routinely applied when the § 6662 criteria for penalty application are satisfied.

2.8 Improving Documentation: LB&I FAQs

In April 2020, the LB&I released a set of six FAQs on transfer pricing documentation.[54] The FAQs highlight the message of the penalties directive—namely, that documentation will not suffice to defend against penalties unless it is adequate and reasonable—and note that one objective of that directive is to "incentivize taxpayers to improve the quality of their transfer pricing documentation."[55] The FAQs build on the directive by providing recommendations for transfer pricing documentation best practices.

The FAQs are instructive both with respect to transfer pricing documentation and with regard to the LB&I's risk-focused enforcement strategy. Importantly, the FAQs emphasize the important role that high-quality transfer pricing documentation may play in determining the course of an audit. Documentation may "help demonstrate low levels of compliance risk and in turn help support early deselection of the transfer pricing issue from further examination" and, for issues that are selected for audit, documentation may help the IRS to focus its inquiries so that "rather than an examination possibly taking years, issues might be raised and addressed within a much shorter time frame."[56] The focus on high-risk areas and avoiding inefficient audits is very much in keeping with the themes of risk sensitivity highlighted above.

In reading the FAQs, it is important to distinguish between recommended best practices that may help to avoid or facilitate an audit and the minimum requirements under the § 6662 regulations that must be met in order for penalties to be avoided. The FAQs provide some helpful reminders with respect to the latter such as that taxpayers applying unspecified TPMs to transactions for which specified methods exist must document why none of the specified methods was likely to provide a reliable measure of an arm's length result. The FAQs indicate that taxpayers frequently neglect this

54. Documentation FAQs.
55. *Id.* (introductory section).
56. *Id.*, FAQ 1.

requirement, rendering their documentation deficient under Treasury Regulation § 1.6662-6(d).

However, most of the recommendations in the FAQs relate to best practices that, while helpful, are not required in order to avoid the imposition of penalties. This is key because, while complying with these best practices will frequently be helpful in navigating potential IRS examinations, the cost of preparing robust documentation that goes beyond the requirements of the § 6662 regulations may not be justifiable in every case. Some of the FAQs' recommendations may be cost- and/or labor-intensive such as the suggestion that taxpayers document searches for methods that are rejected as well as for the method they ultimately select. While this may make sense in some cases, following this recommendation could easily cause the cost of preparing transfer pricing documentation to balloon.

Many taxpayers view transfer pricing documentation as a compliance exercise meant to avoid the imposition of penalties. While taxpayers should be cognizant of the significant additional benefits that documentation can provide, particularly in terms of audit defense, each taxpayer will need to weigh the cost of preparing documentation that goes beyond the minimum requirements against the anticipated benefits of doing so. For instance, robust documentation may make more sense for a transfer of valuable intangible property than it does for a routine, low-value service function.

3 CONCLUSION

Transfer pricing has had its share of high-profile cases in recent years, although this activity has largely been concentrated in a few areas. With the exception of the highly interesting APA issues involved in *Eaton*, recent major transfer pricing litigation has concentrated on cost sharing (*Altera*, *Amazon*,) and intellectual property licensing (*Eaton*, *Medtronic*, *Coca-Cola*). While *Altera* was focused more on abstract concepts of rulemaking and proper notice and comment, these cases are factual, for the most part highly, and involve significant dollar amounts. The recent taxpayer victories in *Amazon* and *Medtronic* (notwithstanding the Eighth Circuit setback) indicate that taxpayers continue to be more effective than the IRS in presenting transfer pricing analyses to the courts. At the same time, there are indications—such as the IRS-favorable dicta in *Amazon* and the *Medtronic* remand—that the strategic landscape may be shifting, and the IRS win in *Altera* may deflate taxpayers' appetite for future regulatory challenges. In this environment, taxpayers should watch with interest how the *Coca-Cola* and *Medtronic* matters develop.

These cases provide valuable insights, and the trends that they indicate are important. Yet, for many taxpayers, especially those without high dollar intellectual property issues, the procedural developments in how the IRS approaches transfer pricing cases may be more significant. There is much in these developments that are poised to ease the burden for taxpayers in the short term. Transfer pricing inquiries, in the absence of the mandatory IDR, are no longer a routine feature of all examinations for taxpayers with cross-border related party transactions. Exam and APA teams should launch fewer method selection challenges, and the exam should dedicate less time to issues that the APMA will be unlikely to prevail on in MAPs. Still, as discussed above, optimism must be tempered by an appreciation of the context of these developments both individually and as a whole.

The LB&I's new approach is grounded in principles of resource conservation and risk-tiering and represents a reshuffling rather than a retreat from transfer pricing controversy. Yet implementation issues may undermine the effectiveness of this approach. The penalties directive guides examiners to consider and assess penalties consistently and methodically, but the LB&I's historical practice has generally fallen short of that standard. Similarly, campaigns could be a targeted tool for addressing compliance in key areas, but their benefits are yet to truly materialize. It is too early to say whether the LB&I's reformulated approach will be effective, but it is clear that it has significant potential and should not be underestimated by taxpayers. If effectively implemented, this risk-based approach may substantially change the landscape for future transfer pricing litigation.

CHAPTER 4

Transfer Pricing Developments in Developing Countries and Emerging Economies

Emily Muyaa[*]

[*] The views expressed in this chapter are those of the author.

1 INTRODUCTION

Transfer pricing continues to be a key area of focus and scrutiny by most tax authorities globally and, therefore, calling for keen consideration by taxpayers. The recent years have witnessed some convergence in transfer pricing rules with most countries implementing rules that closely follow the guidance under the (Organisation for Economic Co-operation and Development) OECD Transfer Pricing Guidelines for Multinational Enterprises and Tax Administrations (OECD Guidelines) and the United Nations Practical Manual on Transfer Pricing for Developing Countries (the UN Manual).[1]

During 2019, various countries reviewed and revised their laws and systems in order to take into account the changes in other jurisdictions that would have a direct impact on multinational enterprises (MNEs) with operations in those countries. Notably, countries that were blacklisted by certain other countries and international organizations implemented changes to their laws and tax systems in order to introduce substance requirements and to enhance transparency through the introduction of documentation requirements, specifically country-by-country (CbC) reporting. Examples of jurisdictions that reacted to such blacklisting include the United Arab Emirates (UAE) and other jurisdictions in the Middle-East[2] and Seychelles in Africa.

In the same breath, the Inclusive Framework expanded to a current membership of 137[3] countries from all continents. Members of the Inclusive Framework are collaborating on the implementation of the OECD/G20 Base Erosion and Profit Shifting (BEPS) Project measures to tackle tax avoidance, improve the coherence of international tax rules, and ensure a more transparent tax environment. The members have committed to implementing certain minimum standards as contained in four actions as follows: (i) Action 5 dealing with harmful tax practices; (ii) Action 6 on preventing treaty abuse; (iii) Action 13, specifically the aspect on CbC reporting; and (iv) Action 14 on making dispute resolution more timely, effective, and efficient.

The implementation of the minimum standards is monitored through peer reviews that are undertaken on the various deliverables based on specified parameters.

1. The OECD Guidelines and the UN Manual were reviewed in 2017 in order to reflect the changes introduced pursuant to the G20/OECD Base Erosion and Profit Shifting (BEPS) Project. Both organizations continue to discuss transfer pricing issues and look for ways to improve the current guidance to reflect ongoing work, e.g., on financial transactions. For further discussion on the recent developments regarding the OECD, *see* Chapter 1 "Global Transfer Pricing Developments" in this book and, for the UN, *see* section 2 of this chapter.
2. Of the Gulf Cooperation Council members, only Oman was not included in the list published by the Dutch Government on December 28, 2018. The list set out certain jurisdictions considered by the Dutch Government as low-taxed and non-cooperative jurisdictions for purposes of certain anti-avoidance measures.
3. Updated list as of December 2019 by the OECD available at https://www.oecd.org/tax/beps/inclusive-framework-on-beps-composition.pdf, accessed January 17, 2020.

The review process is continuous, and the outcomes of each review (or stage of review) are published by the OECD on a regular basis.

Despite the continued focus on transfer pricing and the seemingly converging guidance, some issues abound for developing countries such as access to comparables data, capability for transfer pricing audits of complex cases and inadequate frameworks for the exchange of information.

This chapter begins by looking at the continuing work of the UN on transfer pricing and then gives a roundup of some developments across some developing countries by considering certain selected areas (such as documentation, dispute resolution, commodity transactions, simplification measures). The chapter then considers some of the challenges faced by countries in Africa in transfer pricing. The analysis of the challenges is done through an analysis of a recent case in Zambia that set out a number of pertinent issues relevant for most African or, even more broadly, developing countries.

2 UPDATE ON UN WORK ON TRANSFER PRICING

During 2019, the UN continued its work on the update of the UN Manual. The work on the update of the UN Manual has been largely driven by the need to bring the current UN Manual in line with the evolving international tax rules, especially following the ongoing developments and much needed guidance on various transfer pricing aspects. Changes to the UN Manual have also been instigated by feedback from developing countries on areas of practice that are of great relevance and that pose challenges on a day-to-day basis and thus requiring guidance. This is, for example, the case with the new guidance on centralized procurement activities.

Some of the key highlights of the UN's work on the update of the UN Manual are discussed briefly below. The update has been undertaken by the *Subcommittee on Article 9 (Associated Enterprises): Transfer Pricing* (TP Subcommittee), one of the subcommittees of the UN Committee of Experts on International Cooperation in Tax Matters (the UN Tax Committee). The various items of guidance are at various stages of preparation by the TP Subcommittee and/or approval by the UN Tax Committee or are pending tabling before that body.[4]

The UN Manual is intended to provide practical guidance and present such information in an easy to-use and -understand format.

2.1 New Chapter on Financial Transactions

The new chapter on financial transactions (will be Chapter B.8.) provides guidance on the transfer pricing issues of financial transactions and discusses the most critical

4. For the most recent published version of the drafts of the guidance presented to the UN Tax Committee during its 19th Session in October 2019, *see* the document E/C.18/2019/CRP.15 in, https://www.un.org/esa/ffd/wp-content/uploads/2019/09/19STM_CRP15_Transfer-Pricing.pdf, accessed January 15, 2020. Other items of guidance are still under discussion at the subcommittee level.

issues faced by developing countries. This can be seen from the choice of the types of transactions and instruments that are discussed.

The guidance discusses various aspects such as financing arrangements in multinational groups and notes that intra-group financial arrangements are important for taxpayers and tax administrations alike for various reasons including the following:[5]

- the significance (in terms of amounts involved and frequency) of these transactions for MNE groups;
- the fact that money is mobile and fungible, which makes it relatively simple for an MNE to shift debt to group companies and claim an interest deduction. This reduces taxable profits in the jurisdiction of the borrower and can, depending on the situation of the group lender, reduce the MNE Group's overall tax liability;
- the difficulty that tax administrations face in determining the true character and characteristics of certain financial instruments; and
- the concern that excessive interest deductions provide opportunity for tax base erosion.

Due to the above reasons, countries continue to devise rules to deal with the risks associated with financial arrangements. The scope of such rules varies.

Broadly speaking, the new guidance introduces the transfer pricing considerations for intra-group financial transactions by first describing commercial considerations relating to corporate financing decisions and then presenting some of the more common types of intra-group financial transactions as well as describing the operations of group financing departments/entities. The guidance briefly references corporate income tax approaches that address financing arrangements and then goes on to describe the application of the arm's length principle to financial transactions in general. As mentioned earlier, the guidance looks at some pertinent financial transactions that are considered to be of great relevance for developing countries, especially transactions involving intra-group loans and intra-group financial guarantees.[6]

The general guidance on the application of the arm's length principle covered in other parts of the UN Manual is emphasized throughout the guidance on financial transactions, notably the concept on accurate delineation of the transaction, and economically significant characteristics of financial transactions, which are also discussed more specifically in the context of the specific financial transactions covered in the guidance.

The guidance makes detailed consideration of the creditworthiness of associated enterprises, a pertinent issue when undertaking a transfer pricing analysis of financial

5. *See* paragraph B.9.1.4. of the document E/C.18/2019/CRP.15, available at https://www.un.org/esa/ffd/wp-content/uploads/2019/09/19STM_CRP15_Transfer-Pricing.pdf, accessed January 15, 2020.
6. *See* paragraph B.9.1.5. of the document E/C.18/2019/CRP.15, available at https://www.un.org/esa/ffd/wp-content/uploads/2019/09/19STM_CRP15_Transfer-Pricing.pdf, accessed January 15, 2020.

transactions, and considers the issue of risk embedded in financial instruments, also important when analyzing a financial transaction for transfer pricing.

With respect to the transfer pricing methods that are applicable to financial transactions, the guidance notes that the analysis and choice of method follow the guidance already provided in the UN Manual on transfer pricing methods.

The guidance gives a brief note on simplification measures and safe harbors for financial transactions. One notable aspect in this regard is the discussion on the analysis of the creditworthiness of the associated enterprises. In this regard, it is noted:

> Access to the credit rating of individual associated enterprises and the determination of the impact/effect of implicit support on intra-group financing transactions are not easily available and are based on judgements/determinations that are very hard to be verified by tax administrations. Therefore, another consideration for simplification could be to use the MNE Group credit rating as basis when reviewing the arm's length nature of the financial transaction between the respective associated enterprises, if taxpayers do not corroborate the credit rating used. This approach has the added benefits of providing certainty and reduction in administrative burden to both tax administrations and taxpayers ... . The same approach could be considered if taxpayers do not sufficiently corroborate the interest rate used on intra group loans (by prescribing a basis point margin on top of a base rate).[7]

The guidance continues the discussion by advising that the use of simplification measures and safe harbors should be carefully considered especially with regard to how the practice by countries interacts with the application of the arm's length principle.[8]

The guidance is complemented with a number of practical examples expounding on the different aspects set out thereunder.[9]

2.2 Revised Chapter B.2. on Comparability Analysis

The revision to Chapter B.2. not only updates the guidance in view of other revisions to other parts of the UN Manual and developments in the international arena but also brings into focus important aspects of the continued work and efforts of various international organizations to provide practical guidance on issues that are of relevance to developing countries.

Relevant to this chapter, the question on the search of comparables and lack of data has remained on the agenda of many developing countries. This issue poses serious challenges in the application of the arm's length principle and is a critical issue

---

7. *See* paragraph B.9.2.5.2. of the document E/C.18/2019/CRP.15, available at https://www.un.org/esa/ffd/wp-content/uploads/2019/09/19STM_CRP15_Transfer-Pricing.pdf, accessed January 15, 2020.
8. *See* paragraph B.9.2.5.3. of the document E/C.18/2019/CRP.15, available at https://www.un.org/esa/ffd/wp-content/uploads/2019/09/19STM_CRP15_Transfer-Pricing.pdf, accessed January 15, 2020.
9. The examples are still under discussion at the subcommittee level with the intention of presenting them to the UN Tax Committee for approval at its 20th Session. The main guidance (excluding the examples) was substantially approved at the Committee's 19th Session in October 2019.

in the sense that, even if other commonly mentioned problems (such as inadequate capacity) are solved, lack of data to properly undertake a benchmarking study could greatly hinder the sound application and operation of the arm's length standard.

In recent years, various international organizations[10] have combined their efforts in a bid to find solutions for issues identified by developing countries as relevant for them but which were not necessarily addressed by the BEPS Project (or at least not addressed sufficiently).

Relevant for the current discussion, the Platform for Collaboration on Tax has developed a toolkit[11] that sets out a number of strategies designed to address the issue of a lack of comparables data. The revised text of Chapter B.2. of the UN Manual provides stakeholders with an easy to read and understand guidance that covers selected guidance that is also available in the said toolkit.

2.3 Additional Guidance on Centralized Procurement Activities

The other pertinent work of the UN Subcommittee involves developing additional guidance especially regarding centralized procurement activities. This guidance, as noted earlier, was mainly driven by feedback received from a number of African countries.

Centralized procurement activities are said to cause challenges for countries due to the complex business models used by MNEs coupled with the issue of the lack of comparables data on which to properly base the transfer pricing study and price the transactions that are undertaken. The new guidance on centralized procurement activities is at an advanced level of discussion. Specifically, additional guidance is provided on how to analyze centralized procurement activities in an MNE Group, the factors that may affect compensation for those activities, and the transfer pricing methods that may be appropriate. The guidance is supplemented by various examples covering the issues set out in the guidance. Of key importance to note here is that reference is made to other parts of the UN Manual in which concepts of general application to transfer pricing are mentioned, notably, the concept of accurate delineation of the transaction.

The additional guidance will be included in the chapter on services of the UN Manual (Chapter B.4.) and was presented before the UN Tax Committee for the first time during its 19th Session in October 2019.[12]

One of the recent developments with respect to guidance on aspects related to procurement is seen in Nigeria's domestic provisions, emphasizing the importance of

10. Notably, the organizations under the umbrella of the Platform for Collaboration on Tax which comprises the International Monetary Fund (IMF), the Organisation for Economic Co-operation and Development (OECD), the United Nations (UN), and the World Bank Group (WBG).
11. *See* "A Toolkit for Addressing Difficulties in Accessing Comparable Data for Transfer Pricing Analyses", available at https://www.oecd.org/tax/toolkit-on-comparability-and-mineral-pricing.pdf, accessed January 15, 2020.
12. *See* Attachment E in the document E/C.18/2019/CRP.15, available at https://www.un.org/esa/ffd/wp-content/uploads/2019/09/19STM_CRP15_Transfer-Pricing.pdf, accessed January 15, 2020.

such transactions for developing countries. In 2018, Nigeria issued the Income Tax (Transfer Pricing) Regulations 2018 that replaced the 2012 Regulations with effect from March 12, 2018. Under the 2018 Regulations, it is stated:

> Where goods, assets, services or other supplies produced or traded by unrelated persons are procured by a connected person through another related person, the contemporaneous documentation to be maintained in respect of the transaction shall include documents (contracts, invoices, bills or similar documents) issued by the unrelated person from whom the items originated.[13]

This provision clarifies what has been a prevailing practice in Nigeria where the Federal Inland Revenue Service (Nigerian FIRS) requires information/documentation relating not just to the connected procuring entity but also the third party supplier. This practice, now supported by law, enabled the Nigerian FIRS to analyze the procurement value chain and satisfy itself that the functional and risk profile of the offshore intermediary company matches the compensation derived under a procurement arrangement.[14]

2.4 Other Developments Relevant for Transfer Pricing

Other UN work undertaken in 2019 (through the various subcommittees of the UN Tax Committee) that is relevant for transfer pricing include the following:

Revised texts on profit splits

The existing guidance contained in Chapter B.3.3. of the UN Manual on the transactional profit-split method is being revised in order to make it consistent with the work done in the context of the Inclusive Framework while providing examples that are more practical.[15]

Work on dispute resolution

The relevant subcommittee of the UN Tax Committee has been working on a comprehensive handbook on dispute avoidance and resolution at domestic and international levels.

13. Regulation 17(6) of the Income Tax (Transfer Pricing) Regulations 2018.
14. V. Adegite, Revised Transfer Pricing Regulations in Nigeria: Implications for Transfer Pricing Audit Process, 26 Intl. Transfer Pricing J. 4 (2019), Journal Articles & Papers IBFD, accessed January 17, 2020.
15. *See* Attachment C in the document E/C.18/2019/CRP.15, available at https://www.un.org/esa/ffd/wp-content/uploads/2019/09/19STM_CRP15_Transfer-Pricing.pdf, accessed January 15, 2020.

The continuing work focuses on proposals for mechanisms that can be used including, among other mechanisms, the mutual agreement procedure (MAP), arbitration in the context of the MAP, and other alternative dispute resolution mechanisms as well as looking at ways to make the MAP more effective.[16]

3 FOCUS ON SELECTED ISSUES

3.1 Documentation

This is one of the items that was widely picked up by most countries following the BEPS Project. The uptake reinforces, without a doubt, the role of documentation in transfer pricing. It is invariably the starting point when the taxpayer has to support its transfer pricing policy and also the starting point for the tax authority in its scrutiny of related party transactions.

Generally speaking, in 2019, most developments on transfer pricing documentation requirements for emerging economies were mainly to do with clarifications by tax authorities on the forms and formats of submission of documentation, etc. Most countries introduced enhanced documentation requirements in the period mainly between 2017 and 2018.

CbC reporting is one of the minimum standards under the Inclusive Framework. Implementation of transfer pricing documentation has, in the past three years, taken various forms including the following:

- basic form, i.e., setting out general information required for transfer pricing purposes (such as the requirements of the Zimbabwe transfer pricing regulations);
- requiring detailed information in the local file (implemented by countries such as Liberia);
- requiring three-tiered documentation comprising the master file, local file, and CbC report in line with BEPS Action 13 (as implemented by most developing countries globally—giving examples from each region—such as Malaysia, Mexico, Saudi Arabia, South Africa, etc.); and
- requiring only the CbC report (as is the case in Mauritius and UAE).

Also, during 2019, countries continued efforts to introduce transfer pricing regulations. Notable among these countries in Africa is Botswana. The transfer pricing regulations became effective on July 1, 2019. Prior to this period, Botswana only had a general anti-avoidance provision in its income tax law that allowed the tax authority to scrutinize the taxpayers' activities, including those related to transfer pricing. With the

16. For further details on the documents presented to the UN Tax Committee at its 19th Session, *see* document E/C.18/2019/CRP.18, available at https://www.un.org/esa/ffd/wp-content/uploads/2019/09/19STM_CRP18_new-chapters-5-and-6.pdf, accessed August 28, 2020.
See also document E/C.18/2019/CRP.17, available at https://www.un.org/esa/ffd/wp-content/uploads/2019/09/19STM_CRP17_domestic-dispute-resolution-mechanisms.pdf both links, accessed January 15, 2020.

introduction of specific transfer pricing regulations, better clarity and certainty have been accorded to taxpayers. The regulations are largely in line with the OECD Guidelines and *extend the application of the arm's length principle also to domestic transactions* but only in respect of international financial centers. The regulations provide documentation requirements consisting of a local file and a master file. The information required to be reflected in the local file follows that is required in the OECD Guidelines. The local file should be filed at the same time as the income tax return. Taxpayers are only required to file a master file if their transactions with related parties exceed BWP 5 million. Additionally, the master file is to be filed upon request by the tax authority, i.e., there is no statutory prescribed deadline for filing the master file. The regulations prescribe penalties for failure to submit the required documentation.[17]

On a more general note, the practice of extending transfer pricing rules to domestic transactions has gained prominence in the African continent in recent times. Some countries, such as Botswana, as noted in the paragraph above, and Kenya apply transfer pricing rules when one of the domestic-related parties is operating within a preferential regime. Other countries apply transfer pricing rules to domestic related party transactions without any differentiation. In the author's view, the practice such as that adopted by Botswana and Kenya is effective for curbing problems that arise with tax incentives such as tax holidays.[18] This is especially so as, in most cases, companies operating within preferential regimes are not often monitored for compliance with various (other) domestic legislation. Extending transfer pricing rules to these entities could help to ensure that, regardless of the fact that the companies are enjoying tax holidays, for example, the correct transactions are booked in the domestic entities' financial statements. Also, in the author's (theoretical) view, the strain on resources of applying transfer pricing rules to domestic transactions when there is no differentiating factor between the involved entities (e.g., no differentiation in the tax rate as in the case when (one of) the companies (is) are operating within a preferential regime) might not necessarily justify such practice. This might be a good area for future studies on tax policy decisions for transfer pricing purposes.

Zimbabwe issued the Income Tax (Transfer Pricing Documentation) Regulations 2019 (the Regulations) with Statutory Instrument 109 of 2019. The regulations require the submission of documentation containing specified information on related party transactions including the following key elements: an overview of the taxpayer's business operations; a description of the corporate organizational structure including group members; a description of the controlled transactions; insight into the selection of the transfer pricing method used; a comparability analysis; documents upon which the analysis relied; details of any advance pricing agreements (APAs); and any other information that may have a material impact on determining compliance by the taxpayer. The documentation should be submitted within seven days from notification/request by the tax authorities. The nature of the information required by

17. J. Amos, Botswana: Corporate Taxation section 7, Country Tax Guides IBFD, accessed January 17, 2020.
18. E. Muyaa, Chapter 2: Tax Holidays in Tax Incentives in the BEPS Era (M. Cotrut et al. eds., IBFD 2018), Books IBFD, accessed January 17, 2020.

Zimbabwe's legislation is largely the particulars that would be contained in a local file (based on the OECD Guidelines or the UN Manual). It is not surprising that Zimbabwe has not adopted the CbC reporting requirements. In considering implementation of BEPS recommendations, most countries, especially developing countries, have to consider what their priorities are in the general framework of revenue administration and collection. Furthermore, as Zimbabwe is not a member of the Inclusive Framework, there might not yet be a pressing need/commitment to implement CbC reporting requirements.

Other notable jurisdictions in Africa that have not yet implemented three-tiered documentation requirements (with specific emphasis on CbC reporting) include Ghana and Tanzania. These countries are also not members of the Inclusive Framework.

Although heightened documentation requirements (and other transfer pricing requirements) by governments has the potential of increasing the compliance burden for taxpayers in such jurisdictions, the requirements can also provide clarity and certainty for taxpayers and thereby enhance the ease of doing business. For this goal to be achieved, however, the requirements must be clearly set out, the cost and benefit both to the tax authority and the taxpayer must be balanced, and must necessarily be structured so as to achieve a purpose that is appreciable by all stakeholders.

One aspect that is to be considered is when a taxpayer is required to prepare and submit transfer pricing documentation. Should there be a materiality threshold in order to balance the cost and benefit dynamic, for example? When should the documentation be submitted to the tax authorities? The practice varies from country to country. Some countries only require submission of the documentation upon request (a majority of countries fall in this category, e.g., Zimbabwe as mentioned above). Some countries require submission of documentation upon the occurrence of a stated event (e.g., Morocco requires submission of documentation on the first day of a tax audit with further provisions on request after that date, as the case may require) or such other prescribed period.

In February 2019, Saudi Arabia released the final transfer pricing regulations and guidelines thereon. The regulations introduced a three-tiered approach to transfer pricing documentation in line with the recommendations of BEPS Action 13, i.e., a master file, local file, and CbC report. According to the regulations, transfer pricing documentation must be provided to the tax authorities upon request and within the period specified which shall not be less than thirty days from the date of such a request.

Saudi Arabia exempts small enterprises (defined as taxpayers whose value of the controlled transactions does not exceed SAR 6 million in a twelve-month period) and natural persons from the obligation to maintain the master file and local file. However, the tax authorities may nevertheless require such persons to maintain and submit such documentation in certain specified cases including when: (i) the controlled transactions are carried out with persons deemed to be residents or established in special economic zones in Saudi Arabia; (ii) controlled transactions are carried out with persons who are legally exempt or granted relief from tax and Zakat obligations; (iii) the tax authorities have reason to believe that any of the indicators of tax avoidance specified in the tax law exists; (iv) the taxpayer requests a corresponding adjustment;

or (v) the documentation is necessary for purposes of fulfilling the obligations of Saudi Arabia under an international agreement to which it is a party.[19]

The UAE introduced the requirements to file a CbC report through regulations issued in April 2019. It is important to note that the UAE does not have transfer pricing rules requiring application of the arm's length principle, understandably due to the fact that the country does not impose taxes on income. The need for CbC reporting is seen not only by the call for increased transparency and the attendant blacklisting by certain international bodies and jurisdictions but also by the fact of the UAE's membership in the Inclusive Framework and CbC reporting as one of the minimum standards that all members have committed to implement. The mode of implementation by the UAE is not much different from what most other countries have done in the recent past, i.e., prescribing thresholds largely along the OECD recommendations, etc. Additionally, the UAE's regulations prescribe penalties for failure to file CbC reports as a measure to enforce compliance with the transparency requirements.[20]

Morocco has introduced CbC reporting requirements through its Finance Law 2020. The threshold for filing a CbC report is a consolidated group turnover equal to or greater than MAD 8.125 billion. The CbC report must be filed with the tax authorities within twelve months following the end of the financial year using an electronically prescribed format.

Some countries continue to require taxpayers to file other specific documentation alongside their income tax returns (and in addition to the transfer pricing documentation). These specific returns/forms are intended to disclose specified information on related party transactions; for example, the method that is selected (including the profit level indicator where, e.g., the transactional net margin method is selected), the intensity of related party transactions, information on directors of the company, whether safe harbors prescribed by the domestic law have been used. Examples of countries that require such additional disclosure forms/returns in one way or another include Nigeria, Israel, Saudi Arabia, Uruguay, etc.

In Saudi Arabia, for example, all taxpayers, regardless of the value of the transactions involved, are required to electronically submit a disclosure form containing information on all controlled transactions along with their annual income tax return.[21] According to the transfer pricing regulations, the disclosure form must contain certain details, notably: information on related persons or parties to the controlled transaction; information on legal or beneficial owners of the taxpayer; total revenue, expenses and net profit/loss as reported in the annual income tax return for the reporting year; and mention of whether the taxpayer is required to maintain transfer pricing documentation as specified in the regulations. The disclosure form must be accompanied by an affidavit from a licensed chartered accountant certifying

19. A. Abdul Raheem, Transfer Pricing Regulations in Saudi Arabia, 26 Intl. Transfer Pricing J. 4 (2019), Journal Articles & Papers IBFD, accessed January 15, 2020, at p. 289.
20. For more details on the UAE regulations on CbC reporting, *see* B. Hassan, Transfer Pricing Documentation Requirements in the United Arab Emirates for Multinational Enterprises, 26 Intl. Transfer Pricing J. 6 (2019), Journal Articles & Papers IBFD, accessed January 15, 2020.
21. A. Abdul Raheem, Transfer Pricing Regulations in Saudi Arabia, 26 Intl. Transfer Pricing J. 4 (2019), Journal Articles & Papers IBFD, accessed January 15, 2020, at p. 289.

that the transfer pricing policy of an MNE group is consistently applied in relation to the taxpayer in Saudi Arabia. The disclosure form must be filed within 120 days from the end of the fiscal year. The language of the form must be the same as the language of the annual income tax return.

Most countries have implemented steep penalties for failure to provide transfer pricing documentation and/or for providing incomplete information. Although, in some exceptional cases, a country (e.g., Morocco) may not expressly state penalties for failure to provide documentation, by operation of other legal provisions, the taxpayer may lose the right to defend itself before various dispute resolution bodies should the taxpayer query the tax authority's findings.

The importance of transfer pricing documentation and the challenges faced by governments in implementing rules on such aspects is seen in the ongoing discussions by stakeholders. Some international organizations (under the umbrella of the Platform for Collaboration on Tax) have been on the forefront in developing handbooks and toolkits to assist jurisdictions with certain considerations when they are setting up their policies on various aspects of transfer pricing. For transfer pricing documentation, the toolkit developed by the Platform for Collaboration on Tax is a useful resource.[22]

On a more global level and according to the OECD, as of January 2020, over 2,400 exchange relationships have been activated in respect of CbC reporting. The first automatic exchange of CbC reports took place in June 2018. This was achieved under the framework of the CbC Multilateral Competent Authority Agreement, the EU Council Directive 2016/881/EU (between EU Member States) and through bilateral exchange agreements between the United States and various countries.[23] These numbers reflect a commitment by countries globally to enhance transparency in tax matters and specifically in respect of transfer pricing.

3.2 Dispute Resolution

Increased controversy in transfer pricing matters in recent years and the anticipation for heightened enforcement of the BEPS recommendations by many countries make the Action 14 measure on effective and efficient dispute resolution (especially through the MAP) ever so important. This is also one of the minimum standards under the Inclusive Framework, and peer reviews are ongoing and at various stages for most members of the Inclusive Framework.

During 2019, efforts continued in various fronts in respect of dispute resolution. Countries that are part of the Inclusive Framework have committed to the minimum

22. Practical toolkit to support the successful implementation by developing countries of effective transfer pricing documentation requirements (draft version) available at https://www.oecd.org/tax/beps/draft-toolkit-transfer-pricing-documentation-platform-for-collaboration-on-tax.pdf, accessed January 15, 2020.
23. *See* https://www.oecd.org/tax/beps/country-by-country-exchange-relationships.htm, accessed January 15, 2020. With respect to bilateral exchange agreements, for example, during 2019, India and the United States signed an agreement for the automatic exchange of CbC reports. This means that Indian constituent entities of U.S. parent entities no longer need to make a separate filing in India for the period after the agreement.

standard under Action 14. This measure has been majorly implemented through the Multilateral Convention to Implement Tax Treaty Related Measures to Prevent BEPS (commonly referred to as the MLI). Some countries have also amended their tax treaties (or entered into treaties reflecting the proposals) in order to reflect this commitment. For transfer pricing purposes, MAP is a welcome initiative, especially for African countries where there is still not much experience in this regard.

In terms of the practice on dispute resolution in the past year, during 2019, the Chinese authorities published a report setting out the statistics on APA to the period ending in 2018. According to the report, the MAP was also applied to cases under the APA mechanism.[24] In summary, the report indicated that APAs were used widely in related party buy-sell transactions, services, and for the transfer of the right to use or ownership of intangibles. It is notable that APAs have not been used for financing transactions.

Additionally, China's bilateral APAs were mainly with Asian countries (44), European countries (14), and North America (7). An interesting observation can be made with respect to China and dispute resolution. Despite the fact that China is a big investor into especially Africa (and has at least thirteen income tax treaties with various African countries), there is still no mechanism for certainty beforehand from a transfer pricing perspective. Perhaps Chinese investors obtain incentives in these regions in other forms (e.g., reduced withholding taxes, tax holidays, etc.) that balance the shortcoming of not having access to APAs. *See also* section 4.1 for further discussion on APAs and African countries.

Nigeria published its MAP guidelines in February 2019 through Information Circular No. 2019/01. The stated purpose of the guidelines is to provide guidance on obtaining assistance in order to resolve international tax disputes involving double taxation and inconsistencies in the interpretation or application of the provisions of a tax treaty between Nigeria and another contracting state. The guidelines also provide additional guidance on the application for corresponding adjustments pursuant to the article dealing with associated enterprises (Article 9 of the OECD/UN Model Conventions).

According to the guidelines,[25] the time limits for presenting a case to a MAP depend on the specific time stated in a particular treaty. When the time limit for presenting a case to invoke a MAP is not specified in the relevant tax treaty, the competent authorities of the contracting states will agree on the applicable time limit. Nonetheless, the case must be presented to the Nigerian competent authority within three years from the first notification of the action that results in taxation not in accordance with the provisions of the said tax treaty. The said time limits also apply to cases involving corresponding adjustment of tax or income resulting from a tax audit by the Nigerian FIRS.

Pursuant to paragraph 4.16 of the guidelines, the competent authority of Nigeria reserves the right to recommend to the other competent authority that a case under a

24. *See* PwC's release on, https://www.pwc.com/gx/en/tax/newsletters/pricing-knowledge-network/assets/pwc-tp-china-2018-apa-report.pdf, accessed January 15, 2020.
25. Paragraph 4.3. of the Nigeria MAP Guidelines 2019.

MAP be terminated for various reasons set out in the guidelines, including when the taxpayer has failed to provide all of the information necessary for the MAP and when the retrieval of documents necessary for the MAP is not possible due to lapse of time. This emphasizes the importance of documentation in transfer pricing and indeed for tax in general. The guidelines provide useful contacts for MAP purposes under paragraph 9.0 thereof.

3.3 Low Value-Added Services

This is one of the action points for which uptake has not been so high. For emerging economies, a notable jurisdiction that has implemented this recommendation is Israel. In a circular issued in 2018, low value-added services that meet the criteria set out in the circular are to be priced at a mark-up of 5% of total operating costs, including expenses that should be recorded according to Generally Accepted Accounting Principles (GAAP), such as stock options.[26] Although no benchmark analysis is required for these types of transactions, taxpayers are required to prepare transfer pricing documentation including an economic and FAR (functions, assets, and risks) analysis. If the taxpayer shows that the transactions meet the requirements set out in the circular, then no benchmarking analysis is required.

In Africa, so far, only Zambia has implemented a rule on low value-added services generally along the OECD recommendations on BEPS Action 10. Pursuant to an amendment to the transfer pricing regulations in 2018, an amount charged for low value-added services shall be considered arm's length if the following cumulative conditions are satisfied: (i) the amount is based on allocation to every person who receives a low value-added service of the group costs of providing such service; (ii) the allocation of such costs is based on an appropriate allocation method; (iii) the cost plus method is applied to the costs; and (iv) the mark-up on those costs is 5%.[27]

As mentioned above, this is one of the recommendations of the BEPS Project that was not taken on by most developing countries. This is not a shocking observation as the question surrounding services continues to draw great concerns for most governments. This is due to the fact that transactions involving services are, by their nature, very mobile and create great BEPS concerns for most countries. Such transactions also present a great burden on resources as these transactions are oftentimes selected for transfer pricing audits. Whereas the policy decisions of countries may vary and the priorities also vary in terms of implementation of the recommendations of the BEPS Project, most countries consider that payments for services are present risks that still require careful consideration before any "safe harbors" can be implemented. Some

26. Available at https://www.ey.com/gl/en/services/tax/international-tax/alert--israels-tax-authority-releases-circulars-on-transfer-pricing-methods-and-profitability-ranges-in-certain-local-transactions, accessed January 14, 2020.
27. Regulation 17(6) of the Income Tax (Transfer Pricing) (Amendment) Regulations 2018. For purposes of the Regulations, a "low value-added service" is defined in Regulation 2(a) as "a service that is not provided by any member of the group to unrelated customers, does not use or create intangible property, and does not involve the assumption, control or creation of significant risks."

countries consider that the burden is, in the short and medium term, offset by the fact that withholding taxes continue to be collected on such payments.

The trend might change in the coming years but, in the author's view, especially for Africa, it will take some time before legislative changes such as the ones implemented by Zambia take place. Also, based on reliable sources from the country, there have not been any practical implementations of the said provisions in Zambia as at the end of 2019.[28]

3.4 Rules Limiting the Deductibility of Interest and Other Expenses

Many jurisdictions continue to implement rules limiting the deductibility of various expenses notably interest and management expenses between related parties or, in unrelated party situations, when one of the parties is located in a "non-cooperative or low (or no) tax jurisdiction."

In this regard, OECD Action 4 is informative. In summary, the recommendations of Action 4 resulted in rules akin to earning stripping rules being implemented by various countries. Countries either introduced these rules for the first time while other countries amended existing rules in order to reflect the recommendations.

In Africa, for example, a number of countries substituted their thin capitalization rules with the earning stripping rules. Notable among countries that have taken this direction in the past three years include: Benin, Ivory Coast, and Uganda. Some countries, e.g., Senegal, have continued to supplement their existing rules, i.e., not replacing earlier rules; for example, interest deductibility is determined by, among other criteria, indicators based on the central bank rate, relationship with directors of the company (a transfer pricing rule).

In 2019, Uganda amended its rules limiting interest deductibility in order to remove financial institutions and insurance companies from the scope of application of the rules. According to the rule, which took effect on July 1, 2018, interest deduction in respect of all debts owed by a taxpayer who is a member of a group is capped at 30% of tax earnings before interest, tax, depreciation, and amortization (EBITDA) with excess interest allowed for carry-forward for up to three years.[29]

In June 2019, Malaysia issued rules (supplemented by guidelines issued in July 2019) limiting interest deductions on certain cross-border financial assistance. The limitation applies to cross-border financial assistance from associated parties as well as cross border financial assistance from third parties if such assistance is guaranteed by associated parties in or outside Malaysia. Interest deductions in any year of assessment is limited to 20% of tax-EBITDA (as defined) but will only apply if the interest expenditure incurred on such cross-border financial assistance exceeds a specified

28. In contrast, based on unofficial confirmations, some countries in Africa have expressed views that, in the event that they are not able to establish appropriate transfer pricing outcomes, e.g., in situations involving lack of comparables data, they may consider applying the OECD 5% mark-up to low-value added services.
29. R. Oscar, R. Kukundakwe & M. Makumbi, Uganda: Corporate Taxation Section 7, Country Tax Guides IBFD, accessed January 15, 2020.

threshold. Interest expenditures in excess of the threshold can be carried forward indefinitely provided that no substantial change in shareholding occurs. Individuals, licensed financial institutions, construction contractors, property developers, and certain other types of entities are exempted from the application of the rule.[30]

Peru's rule on the limitation on deductibility of interest expenses based on a fixed percentage rule (30% of EBITDA of the preceding year) will take effect from January 1, 2021. Under the rule, interest disallowed in a given fiscal year may be carried forward for a consecutive period of four years. At the moment, Peru applies a thin capitalization rule that limits the deductibility of interest subject to a debt to net equity ratio of 3:1. Effective January 1, 2019, the scope of the thin capitalization rule was expanded to also include interest paid to unrelated parties.[31]

Some countries have enacted provisions that limit deductibility of other expenses such as those relating to technical assistance rendered by non-resident companies to related companies established in those countries.

For example, in Algeria,[32] costs incurred by an Algerian company in respect of payments for services rendered by way of technical, financial, or accounting assistance by a company established abroad are deductible subject to the following limits: (i) 20% of the general expenses of the Algerian company or 5% of the turnover; and (ii) 7% of the turnover for engineering and consulting firms. This restriction does not apply to expenses relating to heavy installations in the context of an industrial activity, in particular plant assembly. Additionally, interest on loans borrowed by an Algerian company is deductible subject to the effective interest rates established by the Bank of Algeria. However, such interest is subject to two further conditions, i.e., the share capital of the borrower company has been fully paid and the sums placed at the disposal of the company do not exceed 50% of its share capital.

3.5 Commodity Transactions

Transfer pricing of commodity transactions has remained an issue of great debate for most countries. This was not left behind in the BEPS Project where this issue was discussed under Action 10. Subsequently, both the OECD and the UN updated their respective transfer pricing guidance to reflect the recommendations of the final report on that action point.

The period after the BEPS debate has seen countries either introduce rules on transfer pricing of commodity transactions or provide guidance or implement requirements aimed to ensure transparency in respect of such transactions. Brief examples are given below.

30. *See* EY Alert, available at https://www.ey.com/gl/en/services/tax/international-tax/alert--malaysia-releases-rules-and-guidelines-on-interest-expense-limitation, accessed January 17, 2020.
31. R.A. Villagra Cayamana, Peru: Corporate Taxation section 7, Country Tax Guides IBFD, accessed January 15, 2020.
32. R. Hamzaoui, Algeria: Corporate Taxation section 1, Country Tax Guides IBFD, accessed January 16, 2020.

In May 2019, the Inland Revenue Authority of Singapore published guidance (in the form of an e-tax guide) for commodity marketing and trading activities. The stated aim of the guidance is to analyze the economic value of taxpayers' commodity marketing and trading activities in Singapore and help taxpayers to comply with the arm's length principle and transfer pricing documentation requirement when such activities are carried out with related parties. The guidance emphasizes the pertinent concepts of accurate delineation of the transaction substance requirements (in calling for an analysis of the economic value of the transaction). The guidance also considers some of the models used for commodity transactions and indicates the methods that may be used by taxpayers for those transactions. It also sets out the documentation requirements for these transactions. The guidance is very practically supplemented by examples to illustrate the various concepts discussed. The specific focus on commodity transactions reinforces Singapore's position as a leading trading hub, and the guidance is welcomed in terms of providing clarity for taxpayers and tax authorities. It is also very good and informative guidance for countries that do not yet have elaborate guidance on commodity transactions.[33] Furthermore (from other developing countries' perspectives), it is important to consider how such rules might interact with the rules applied by typical commodity exporting countries in order to ensure compliance with the rules applicable to a given commodity transaction.

In 2019, developments in other emerging economies (especially those that already have advanced guidance regarding commodity transactions, such as Argentina) involved mainly provisions on compliance and providing further clarity on the applicability of rules relating to commodity transactions.

For example, in November 2019, Argentina gazetted a resolution[34] setting out the requisite documentation (*declaración jurada de venta al exterior*, DJVE) that exporters must file when exporting certain commodities. The resolution indicates that relevant information will be shared in real time with the federal tax authority. The measure aims to control exports carried out through foreign intermediaries that are subject to specific transfer pricing regulations in accordance with the amendments introduced by Law 27,430 to the Income Tax Law.[35]

Additionally, in 2019, Argentina also issued clarification that consideration of economic substance requirements when determining relatedness of parties for transfer pricing of commodities, i.e., justification for using the "sixth method" when a foreign intermediary is involved, is not unconstitutional and is founded on Argentina's Income Tax Law. This clarification was the basis of an opinion issued by the public prosecutor following a challenge by a taxpayer that the economic substance requirements were an artificial technicality that aimed to apply the "sixth method" to all transactions in which a foreign intermediary was involved. According to the taxpayer's argument, the corresponding statute, Law 25,784, explicitly covers intermediaries that lack the

33. Other countries that have implemented detailed rules on similar transactions in the past two years include Australia.
34. Resolution 128/2019 issued by the Ministry of Farming and Fisheries (*Ministerio de Agricultura, Ganaderia y Pesca*).
35. Argentina: Transfer pricing—control of commodities exports enhanced (November 25, 2019), News IBFD, accessed January 15, 2020.

necessary FAR in their jurisdiction of residence or whose main activity involves receiving passive income, reselling to related parties, or distributing the exports in Argentina. However, the corresponding statute does not specify that parties should be considered related based on economic substance criteria.[36]

4 SIMPLIFICATION MEASURES

Application of transfer pricing rules might present difficulties for countries for various reasons, e.g., the complexity of transactions involved, inadequate capability within the tax administration, lack or inadequate access to comparables data. Many countries continue to explore options to simplify the application of transfer pricing rules either by prescribing "safe harbors" or by allowing certainty, e.g., through APAs.

Developments in this regard are discussed briefly below.

4.1 Advance Pricing Agreements

Leaving aside Asian and Latin America countries, the issue of APAs continues to gain focus mainly from taxpayers in Africa. Whereas some countries in Africa have provisions in their tax laws allowing APAs between taxpayers and the tax authorities, there is no evidence that any APAs have been entered into in practice. Examples of countries in Africa that have provisions allowing APAs include: Nigeria, Tanzania, Malawi, Morocco, Ethiopia, etc. Kenya has proposed provisions on APAs in the Income Tax Bill 2018 that is pending deliberation in parliament.

However, and as mentioned earlier, the author is not aware of any APAs having been negotiated in any of the countries mentioned above. Whereas most governments appreciate that APAs could reduce the potential for controversy and admittedly also provide much needed reprieve for strained resources in the tax administration, what seems to be a common worry for not implementing APAs is the following:

- lack of capacity to undertake an analysis and subsequently negotiate properly with advanced tax administrations;
- lack of access to relevant information on which to subsequently test the viability of the APA, i.e., most tax authorities would like the comfort of being able to also check that the critical assumptions on which the APA was based are still viable. Does this perhaps suggest a lack of trust? Not necessarily. In the author's opinion, this is a valid expectation especially given the wide information asymmetry between taxpayers and tax authorities and the experience with respect to transfer pricing audits coupled with a rather dismal access to information exchange mechanisms.

APAs, if properly implemented and structured, can serve the purpose of providing much needed certainty in transfer pricing to both tax authorities and taxpayers.

36. R. Finley, Argentina: Transfer Pricing Rule Is Constitutional, Argentine Ministry Says (December 4, 2019), News Tax Analysts, accessed January 15, 2020.

However, the concerns raised above are also valid. Whereas these are not issues that can be quickly discussed theoretically, it is the author's opinion that, as tax authorities in Africa continue establishing themselves in terms of sophistication in undertaking complex transfer pricing audits, the worries surrounding APAs will diminish. There is also a no better way of knowing if APAs are good for a country without first having practical experience in them. In this regard, the author suggests for tax authorities and taxpayers in Africa to continue dialogue on APAs in a bid to build trust and, maybe then, a move toward more certainty and freeing up of tax authorities' resources to focus on increasing complex transfer pricing audits will be seen.

However, other developing countries, mainly in Asia and Latin America, continued their efforts in 2019 toward developing guidance on APAs. For example, in December 2019, Costa Rica took great efforts regarding APAs specifically by issuing a draft resolution for public comment. The resolution generally sets the scene for implementation of APAs. The draft resolution sets out the following: definition of an APA, procedure for requesting an APA; minimum content of the APA; minimum content to be included in the annual report that the taxpayer should file to the tax administration demonstrating that the APA conforms with its own transfer pricing policy; procedure for amending an APA and reasons for termination thereof, etc.[37]

See also the report on China's APA statistics discussed in section 3.2 in the context of dispute resolution.

4.2 Documentation

Another area where some countries continue to provide simplified requirements for taxpayers is regarding transfer pricing documentation.

Some countries only require transfer pricing documentation for certain taxpayers who meet a specified (materiality) threshold that could be based on, among other criteria, turnover, percentage of specified transactions to total turnover, etc. This is, for example, the case with the CbC report requirement for which countries generally only require the report if the consolidated group turnover exceeds a certain limit. This mode of application follows from the general recommendation on BEPS Action 13 by the OECD.

Some countries also apply thresholds in respect of requirements for the master file, local file, or other transfer pricing documentation. In 2019, examples of countries that implemented rules with thresholds in this regard include Saudi Arabia and UAE (*see* section 3.1).

The practice of requiring compliance with transfer pricing requirements generally or only in respect to certain aspects (in this instance, documentation) is commendable as it considerably relieves the compliance burden for taxpayers as well as enabling tax authorities to focus their resources only on cases that may present a material transfer pricing risk. For most emerging economies where transfer pricing audit resources

37. Costa Rica: Procedure and requirements to obtain APAs—discussion draft released (December 9, 2019), News IBFD, accessed January 15, 2020).

might be limited, in the author's view, such differentiation should be considered by governments, of course, subject to their policy decisions.

4.3 Deductibility of Certain Expenses

Countries continue to introduce rules limiting the deductibility of various expenses especially when the expenses are incurred between related parties and, in some cases, when the other party (although unrelated) is located in a low (or no) tax jurisdiction or non-cooperative jurisdiction (as defined in the particular country's legislation).

As an example, in 2018, Israel issued circulars prescribing the methods to be used for transfer pricing purposes but most notably prescribing profitability ranges for certain transactions. Profitability ranges were issued specifically with respect to low value-added services (*see* section 3.3), marketing services (a mark-up between 10% and 12% on total operating expenses, including expenses that should be recorded according to GAAP such as stock options) and distribution activities (an operating margin between 3% and 4% of total revenues generated in the relevant markets by the Israeli entity).[38]

A number of countries in Africa (mainly French-speaking West and Central African countries) have implemented rules limiting deductibility of various expenses, notably those involving provision of services.

Whereas rules limiting deductibility of certain expenses, e.g., interest and management expenses, can be viewed as simplification measures in the sense that they do away with the need to carry out a(n elaborate) transfer pricing analysis, their interaction with transfer pricing rules should necessarily be examined. Also, whereas certain rules (such as those limiting deductibility of interest following the recommendations in BEPS Action 4) are now widely accepted globally, this is not the case with respect to rules limiting deductibility of various other expenses, such as management expenses.

In the author's view, a careful analysis ought to be undertaken on how those rules align with the arm's length principle. This is in order to avoid situations of double taxation (when the corresponding jurisdiction applies rules founded on the arm's length principle) and also to avoid the risk of BEPS as a result of structures aimed at circumventing the said rules.

Examples of these rules, as seen in developments during 2019, are discussed in section 3.4.

38. Available at https://www.ey.com/gl/en/services/tax/international-tax/alert--israels-tax-authority-releases-circulars-on-transfer-pricing-methods-and-profitability-ranges-in-certain-local-transactions, accessed January 14, 2020.

5 SPECIAL FOCUS: BRAZIL AND INDIA

5.1 Introduction

For China, 2019 saw a focus on enforcement mechanisms for transfer pricing with no major reportable transfer pricing developments.

The key developments in 2019 with respect to Brazil and India are discussed below.

5.2 Brazil

During the past two years, the OECD has been working with Brazil in the planned accession of Brazil to the OECD. To do so, it is important that Brazil's transfer pricing system is closely approximated to the OECD transfer pricing rules, i.e., the arm's length standard. Without going into too much detail, the Brazilian transfer pricing system is predicated on (non-rebuttable) fixed margins. Broadly speaking, the system has the advantage of avoiding the common problems associated with the arm's length standard; administrability, access to data on comparables, certainty for the taxpayer, etc.[39] However, and as noted in the ongoing work between Brazil and the OECD, there are certain gaps in the Brazilian transfer pricing system that could result in double taxation and/or pose BEPS risk of loss of revenue.

In a joint statement issued by Brazil and the OECD (the Joint Statement), it is noted that the project involved an in-depth analysis of the Brazilian transfer pricing legal and administrative framework as well as its application. The work program was structured in three stages, namely:

- Stage 1: preliminary analysis of the legal and administrative framework of Brazil's transfer pricing rules.
- Stage 2: assessment of the strengths and weaknesses of Brazil's existing transfer pricing rules and administrative practices.
- Stage 3: options for alignment with the OECD transfer pricing standard.

The first step of the analysis (during Stage 2 of the work program) was the identification of the main areas in the Brazilian transfer pricing framework and the related rules and practices that constitute gaps and divergences from the OECD transfer pricing standard (gap analysis). The second step was to test the effectiveness of the existing rules and practices in view of the policy objectives of transfer pricing rules (assessment of effectiveness).[40]

The gap analysis identified thirty issues in the Brazilian transfer pricing system that, upon further assessment of effectiveness (based on policy objectives of transfer

39. For a detailed discussion on this, *see* L.E. Schoueri & R.A. (Jr.) Galendi, Challenges to Brazilian Transfer Pricing Rules upon Accession to the OECD, 26 Intl. Transfer Pricing J. 6 (2019), Journal Articles & Papers IBFD, accessed January 15, 2020.
40. Joint Statement p. 3.

pricing rules[41]), revealed that at least twenty-seven out of the thirty issues pose the risk of double taxation and, therefore, hinder trade and investment. Additionally, it was identified that a large number of the issues (twenty-three out of the thirty issues) pose the risk of loss of revenue especially due to the fact that the Brazilian transfer pricing rules do not provide for certain complex transactions (e.g., transactions involving the use or transfer of intangibles, intra-group service transactions, and transactions comprising business restructurings). The assessment also revealed other weaknesses in the system such as the fixed margin approach.

The Joint Statement further notes that, although the Brazilian transfer pricing system provides tax certainty from a domestic perspective, it fails to do so from an international perspective.[42] This is due to the fact that, on an international level, jurisdictions have generally agreed and apply the international best practice predicated on the OECD arm's length standard, which is not the case in Brazil.

Domestically, the Brazilian system is characterized by practicality, predictability, and tax certainty. These aspects result in ease of administration and tax certainty from a domestic perspective. The Joint Statement notes that certain features of the current system (such as the absence of the requirement for a comprehensive comparability (including functional and risk analysis) and the freedom of selection of the methodology for transfer pricing allows Brazil to overcome the problem of lack of access of data on comparables). However, from the assessment, it emerged that these perceptions of simplicity are relative and complexity does arise from other existing features, mainly the item-per-item approach, the strict standard of comparability, and documentation in certain situations. In some cases, the key features contributing to simplicity may undermine the primary objectives of transfer pricing rules, leading to potential double taxation and BEPS risks.[43]

Stage 3 of the report of the work program sets out the options for alignment of the Brazil transfer pricing system with the OECD standard. According to the Joint Statement: "Two options emerged that both aim to achieve full alignment based on the assumption that, otherwise, significant gaps would remain in the system, which would make it difficult for Brazil to both integrate global value chains and to accede to the OECD."[44]

According to the Joint Statement,[45] the first option would entail immediate alignment of Brazil's transfer pricing rules with the OECD Guidelines. The second option would aim to achieve the same result but through gradual implementation of changes to the Brazilian system in order to align it with the OECD standard. The second option also offers the opportunity to prioritize the different needs with respect to the tax

41. The Joint Statement (p. 3) notes that transfer pricing legislation has the primary dual objective of securing the appropriate tax base in each jurisdiction and avoiding double taxation (prevention of BEPS risks and prevention of double taxation) and other secondary objectives (ease of tax administration, ease of tax compliance, and tax certainty from a domestic and international perspective).
42. Only three out of the thirty identified issues give evidence of certainty from an international perspective.
43. Joint Statement p. 4.
44. Joint Statement p. 5.
45. *Ibid.*

structure, administrative aspects, expertise of the workforce, etc., as changes are progressively implemented. It is further noted as follows: "The options also consider how to maintain a number of elements of simplification, which provide ease of tax administration, ease of tax compliance and tax certainty (i.e. the fixed margins approach—for example, in the form of carefully tailored safe harbours or rebuttable presumptions)."[46]

The next step is a political one, i.e., for the parties to determine whether to align and how that should be done, and Brazil's specific implementation needs are important in charting a way forward. It will be interesting to see what the final outcome of this project will be, i.e., whether Brazil will align its transfer pricing rules with the OECD standard (and accede to the OECD). Considering that the request for accession was made by Brazil, it can be assumed that some form of alignment, possibly adopting the second option, will be undertaken in the near future. For MNEs operating in Brazil, this is a welcome development as alignment will result in more certainty from an international perspective (as noted in the Joint Statement) and an opportunity for Brazil to address issues that might, in the past, have hindered investment. Additionally, the findings of the project contained in the final report are also interesting for other countries especially those that employ safe harbors in the form of fixed margins (and that might not fully apply or consider the arm's length principle) to reassess their safe harbors to ensure that they align with international standards in order to address the risks identified in Brazil's case, i.e., double taxation and revenue loss.

5.3 India

Attribution of profits to permanent establishments

With respect to India, the most notable development in 2019 is the new guidance on attribution of profits to permanent establishments. Preliminarily, it is important to note that, like most (developing) countries, India does not endorse the OECD approach for attribution of profits to permanent establishments. Under the OECD Model (post-2010 Article 7 on taxation of business profits), profits are to be attributed to a permanent establishment of a non-resident in the source state based on a FAR approach. This approach varies from the position that applied prior to the revision (in 2010) of Article 7 of the OECD Model Convention that allowed taxation based on apportionment of profits using various factors.

For countries like India and other developing countries that are net capital importers and with a huge consumption capacity, apportionment of profits to a permanent establishment based on the FAR approach might not approximate the proper contribution that should be allocated to such countries. It is thought that computing the contribution that such a country should receive should be based on a

46. The full report on the findings of the project may be accessed on this link, available at http://www.oecd.org/tax/transfer-pricing/transfer-pricing-in-brazil-towards-convergence-with-the-oecd-standard.pdf, accessed January 17, 2020.

factor(s) that has a direct correlation with the situation of the market economy/country. This is the thinking behind so-called market jurisdictions and the call for a fair share of income to such countries.

Also, following the ongoing discussions and developments in the international arena on the taxation of large companies, the issue of nexus (i.e., not based merely on physical presence) has continued to gain focus. India has enacted rules on nexus that are not linked to physical presence, i.e., so-called "significant economic presence." These non-physical presence permanent establishments are also considered in India's guidance on attribution of profits to permanent establishments. The provision on "significant economic presence" was earlier proposed to be effective from the assessment year 2021-2022 but has now been deferred to 2022-2023.

India applies a fractional apportionment method provided for under Rule 10 of the Income Tax Rules and is also contained in the UN Model Tax Convention (Article 7(4) and OECD 7(4) pre-2010 Model) as well as some tax treaties in force for a number of countries. This method is different from the formulary apportionment method in the sense that the fractional apportionment method does not seek to consolidate the profits of the enterprise from different jurisdictions but rather only considers and seeks to apportion profits derived by the enterprise from India.

Broadly speaking, the guidance provides for the fractional apportionment of profits using a formula that gives weight to three key factors (looking at demand and supply), namely:

(1) sales;
(2) manpower (employees and wages); and
(3) assets.

For a "significant economic presence" permanent establishment, an additional factor is included, i.e., one based on users. Detailed rules apply to the determination of the attributable profits using the said factors.

Under India's domestic law, the above rule on fractional apportionment applies when the permanent establishment of the non-resident in India does not maintain separate books of account or financial statements or, in the tax authorities' opinion, when it is not possible to determine actual income from the books of account.

As discussions continue in the international arena on the rules to be applied to large MNE groups that undertake businesses not requiring physical presence, it will be interesting to see the developments from a transfer pricing angle especially when permanent establishments are involved. This is in consideration of the fact that most countries do not currently apply the authorized OECD approach for attribution of profits to permanent establishments, and many developing countries[47] continue to favor attribution based on apportionment of profits with foundations in domestic law and the UN Model Tax Convention.

47. Examples of countries in Africa with domestic rules on attribution of profits to permanent establishments based on apportionment include Ghana and Tanzania.

Secondary adjustments

Additionally, in September 2019, the Central Board of Direct Taxes issued a notification[48] amending the provisions on secondary adjustments for transfer pricing. Broadly speaking, India's secondary adjustments require taxpayers to repatriate cash equivalent to the primary adjustment made following a transfer pricing assessment. Failure to repatriate the cash within a prescribed time results in the excess amount arising from a primary adjustment being deemed to be an advance made by the taxpayer to the associated party. Accordingly, notional interest is charged on the outstanding amounts. The notification amended the secondary adjustment in order to provide clarity on when the cash should be repatriated in various instances (repatriation following conclusion of an APA, repatriation upon resolution of a transfer pricing case under MAP, determining the start date for the limitation period for the repatriation, and the applicable foreign currency exchange rate).

6 SPECIAL FOCUS: AFRICA

6.1 Introduction

More and more countries in Africa continue to implement domestic provisions requiring application of the arm's length standard to related party transactions and, in some cases, transactions involving non-cooperative jurisdictions and low (or no tax) jurisdictions.

However, these countries face challenges that might not be specific to only Africa but also to most other developing countries. The level of sophistication of transfer pricing rules and the practice varies from country to country with no specific notable trend. However, a general observation is that the practice of transfer pricing is far more developed in English-speaking African countries compared to their French- and Portuguese-speaking counterparts. For the author, this is not a very shocking observation as most capacity development efforts by most donors have focused and continue to focus on the English-speaking countries. Maybe this can be explained by language barriers (most donors and technical expertise are invariably drawn from countries where English is more widely used than French or Portuguese). However, it is important that the other two parts (French- and Portuguese-speaking countries) are also carried along and their capability developed. This will ensure more uniform and certainly informed applications of rules that impact cross-border transactions not just on a regional level but also on a global scale.

48. Available at https://tp.taxsutra.com/sites/tp.taxsutra.com/files/webform/%5BNotification.pdf, accessed March 12, 2020.

6.2 Some Notable Challenges

Even the most developed countries in Africa in terms of transfer pricing practice continue to face certain challenges that impact their revenue collection and, most importantly, might result in cases of double taxation for MNEs.

Constrained resources at the tax authorities cause enormous delays in transfer pricing audits. Some countries in Africa (such as Kenya) have considerably big teams dealing with transfer pricing (or international issues generally), but other countries depend on the transfer pricing auditors who deal with other (general) audit areas. This challenge coupled with limited capacity result in long protracted cases between tax authorities and taxpayers. This is in part also explained by the fact that the administrative (and judicial) bodies that deal with appeals also may not themselves have the capability of dealing with the complex issues raised by transfer pricing disputes. All of these issues continue to make doing business in these countries rather unfavorable and, therefore, affect trade and investment. It also results in loss of revenue and double taxation, i.e., it impacts all of the parties involved.

Access to information/data on comparables for a proper benchmarking study also poses considerable problems for Africa. This is due to the fact that it is not always possible to get internal (and also local) comparables which then means that the parties (tax authorities and taxpayers) have to resort to external (mainly foreign) comparables. The problem is further complicated by the fact that, in most cases, there are no local or even regional comparables. The use of foreign comparables raises concerns for most tax authorities and may not always be allowed. This leaves taxpayers in a dilemma as to how to support their transfer pricing policy. Even for countries where the use of foreign comparables is allowed, the difficulties with ascertaining the financial information of such comparables in order to determine if any comparability adjustments are required is an additional challenge for most tax authorities. Some countries tend to deal with this problem by allowing the use of interquartile ranges and adjusting the findings to the median in order to do away with the need for comparability adjustments.

Other special considerations on foreign comparables are discussed in the analysis of the *Nestlé Zambia* case (*see* section 6.3 below).

The problem of access to comparables data led the Platform for Collaboration on Tax to issue the toolkit on comparability aimed at providing guidance for stakeholders in situations involving lack of comparables.[49]

Academics and transfer pricing practitioners have not been left behind in trying to find a solution. The Transfer Pricing Economists for Development (TPED), a think tank on transfer pricing with a special focus on emerging economies, recently released their findings on research on the use of foreign comparables for a benchmarking study. The research by TPED aims to find a solution to what has been identified by most

49. *See* "A Toolkit for Addressing Difficulties in Accessing Comparable Data for Transfer Pricing Analyses", available at https://www.oecd.org/tax/toolkit-on-comparability-and-mineral-pricing.pdf, accessed January 15, 2020.

developing countries as a recurring problem hindering the proper application of the arm's length principle.[50]

6.3 Case Law Analysis: *Nestlé Zambia*

Nestlé Zambia was selected as it encompasses a number of issues that are of great relevance for most African countries ranging from selection of cases for a transfer pricing audit, the challenges faced in undertaking a proper benchmarking study, and generally accurate delineation of transactions.

On March 28, 2019, the Tax Appeals Tribunal of Zambia (the Tribunal) delivered its ruling in *Nestlé Zambia Trading Limited v. Zambia Revenue Authority* (Case No. 2018/TAT/03/DT).[51] Briefly, the appeal was triggered by the respondent's (hereinafter "ZRA") audit of the appellant (hereinafter "Nestlé Zambia" or the taxpayer) resulting in an upward adjustment of Nestlé Zambia's taxable profits for the years under review (2010-2014). The audit was triggered by Nestlé Zambia's loss-making position not just in respect of the years under review but going back to the years of its incorporation in Zambia.

As has been the trend in most jurisdictions, ZRA's attention was drawn to the numerous transactions between Nestlé Zambia and other related parties outside Zambia (mostly within Africa) involving commonly targeted transactions such as shared services, management fees, and royalties. The ZRA outlined three key points for its upward assessment of Nestlé Zambia, namely:

(1) that there were continuous negative operating margins for a period of more than five years;
(2) that there were continuous losses for a period of five years; and
(3) that the taxpayer had huge volumes of transactions with related parties.

The taxpayer did not agree with the assessment and appealed to the Tribunal for the assessment to be set aside based on six grounds, namely, that the ZRA:

(1) had failed to assess whether the taxpayer was compliant with the arm's length principle;
(2) erroneously assumed that the taxpayer could not operate at a loss for all of the years in question and failed to consider the reasons for the taxpayer's loss-making position;
(3) failed to objectively test the related party transactions and relied on excessive and unreasonable assumptions and estimates;

50. *See* the full publication available at https://tped.eu/proposed-framework-for-foreign-comparables-selection-and-adjustment, accessed January 16, 2020.
51. The information in this part is based on the Tribunal's decision and a summary of the decision available on the IBFD Tax Research Platform prepared by Sachin Sachdeva. The Tribunal's decision may be accessed via, available at https://tpcases.com/zambia-vs-nestle-trading-ltd-march-2019-tax-appeals-tribunal-case-no-2018-tat-03-dt/, accessed March 12, 2020.

(4) erroneously recharacterized the taxpayer as a limited risk distributor despite the fact that the taxpayer had provided evidence to the contrary;
(5) performed and used a benchmarking study that was comparable neither to the taxpayer's business conditions nor to the country's economic condition; and
(6) erroneously added back unrealized foreign exchange losses attributable to a loan that the taxpayer had not included in its financial statements and, therefore, were not deducted by the taxpayer.

The ZRA responded to the taxpayer's grounds of appeal with the following arguments chronologically:

(1) the pertinent related party transactions had been adequately tested. The ZRA specifically stated that the royalty payments made by the taxpayer to related parties (specifically Nestlé South Africa) contravened the arm's length principle;
(2) the taxpayer's loss-making position year-on-year was a result of the large amounts of payments to related parties, particularly with respect to royalties, management fees, and product costs;
(3) the adjustments were made pursuant to and in consonance with the relevant statutory provisions and, therefore, were not assumptions or estimates;
(4) the taxpayer was reclassified as a limited risk distributor due to various factors (based on analysis of its value chain and role played by its related parties) including the following:
   - the control and oversight of the taxpayer's operations was done by Nestlé Zimbabwe;
   - sourcing and invoicing of Nestlé products for the taxpayer were done through Nestlé Ghana;
   - inventory risk was shared with other Nestlé manufacturing companies;
   - the level of investment in the taxpayer was low;
   - there was only a lean staff complement in Zambia; and
   - customers managed their own logistical arrangements for picking up delivery of products from the taxpayer's warehouses;
(5) Nestlé's products were already known and available on the Zambian market long before the taxpayer was incorporated and, as such, the taxpayer was not developing the (Zambian) market; and
(6) the foreign exchange losses adjustment was a secondary adjustment performed to ensure proper allocation of profits as a result of the primary transfer pricing adjustment.

The issue that fell for determination by the Tribunal was whether the assessment by the ZRA was valid.

The Tribunal ruled in favor of the ZRA on ground (4) and in favor of the taxpayer on all other grounds.

The Tribunal dealt with grounds (1) and (3) jointly and observed that the ZRA acted erroneously when it aggregated the transactions as there was no close economic link between the transactions to justify the aggregation.

In considering ground (2), the Tribunal confined its position to the legislative provisions in place during the years under review and noted that adjustments could only be made if the loan was not employed for business purposes by the taxpayer. The adjustment made by the ZRA on the basis of the debt-equity ratio was found to have been erroneous.

The Tribunal ruled in favor of the ZRA on ground (4). Based on the testimonies from expert witnesses, the Tribunal concluded that a significant level of control was exercised by Nestlé Zimbabwe over the taxpayer with regard to the strategic directions of the taxpayer's business. In addition, the Tribunal held that the essential functions such as strategic management, sales and marketing support were provided by related parties. This observation further supported ZRA's argument about control over the taxpayer being exercised from outside Zambia. Further, the Tribunal concluded that, as Nestlé South Africa retained ownership, property in the products, and attendant risk in the know-how (as defined in the licensing agreement), the ultimate risk in marketing, distribution, storage and/or selling of the products lay with Nestlé South Africa and not with the taxpayer.

Regarding ground (5), the Tribunal found that the comparables used by the ZRA—representing businesses in Western Europe—was disproportionate and, as such, capable of producing an inaccurate transfer pricing adjustment. The Tribunal's finding on comparables is reproduced below:

> We do not find the use of businesses in Western Europe to benchmark the Appellant to have been proportionate as the situations of the Appellant and those of the businesses in Western Europe are, under the circumstances, incomparable and highly likely to materially affect the transfer price that was being enquired into during the transfer pricing audit conducted by the Respondent. Further, it is evident to us, that it would be very difficult to reasonably eliminate the potential huge differential arising from the transfer price adjustment. Therefore, it would not be possible to ensure that reasonably accurate adjustments can be made to eliminate the effect of any such differences.[52]

In its determination of ground (6), the Tribunal held that there was no legal basis to support the adjustment made by the ZRA, i.e., to add back the unrealized foreign exchange losses. The Tribunal noted that such adjustments can only be made in cases when the taxpayer has claimed a deduction in respect of the item in question, and there was nothing to show that the currency losses in question had been claimed by the taxpayer.

This case, the arguments of the parties, and the final decision set out some key points that are common in most transfer pricing cases in Africa as discussed below.

52. Paragraph 1 on page 30 of the decision.

Losses

It is not uncommon for a taxpayer to be selected for a transfer pricing assessment based on the fact that it has been in a loss-making position for a number of years, and the MNE group as a whole is profitable. For most developing countries, this continues to be a key risk assessment indicator. It is also not uncommon that a tax authority might consider perpetual loss making as a sign of profit shifting by the local entity to related parties especially those in favorable/lower tax jurisdictions.

It might well be that the local entity is genuinely making losses, and this could be due to various reasons, for example, that the entity is in its first years of operation (start-up) and, therefore, incurring huge expenses in, among other things, establishing its brand in the local market. This would especially be true if the group is not known in the jurisdiction of the local entity. In the current case, the ZRA specifically raised this point in their response to ground (5) of the taxpayer's appeal.

However, what happens if, after the audit, it is actually found that the losses were justified. So, for example, in this current case, would the ZRA have been in a more favorable position if they had, during the audit, advanced an additional ground to support their findings? What grounds would this have been? This necessarily leads us to the discussion of a point that is clearly stated in both the OECD Guidelines and UN Manual,[53] i.e., an analysis of the value generated by the loss-making local entity should be undertaken in a bid to find out if independent parties in similar circumstances would have expected that the local entity be remunerated for its function, if any, to the group. This would necessarily involve a clear analysis of the position of the local entity vis-à-vis the group of which it is a part. The question that would have been asked in the current case is: "What role did Nestlé Zambia play, what function did it perform for the group that made it comfortable to make losses since its inception?"

If the analysis revealed that indeed there was value in this arrangement, then it very well could be that the local entity should have been remunerated for providing a "service" to the group.

The concerns raised by loss-making companies are, arguably, what has caused some countries to introduce provisions to ensure that a certain amount of tax is collected regardless of the taxpayer's profitability. In Tanzania, for example, an alternative minimum tax was introduced by the Finance Act 2012 and is payable by entities which have been in a loss position for the current year and the three preceding years. From 2018, the alternative minimum tax applies at the rate of 0.5% of gross revenues.[54]

Searching for comparables

In the current case, the ZRA relied on comparables from Western Europe. First, it is notable that the ZRA did not consider the taxpayer's study but went straight ahead to preparing their own separate benchmarking study. As noted in the ruling, the margins

53. Paragraphs 1.129-1.131 of the OECD Guidelines and B.2.4.5. of the UN Manual.
54. Section 4(2)(a) read together with paragraph 3(3) of the First Schedule to the Income Tax Act 2004, as amended.

that the ZRA came up with were lower than those that the taxpayer's own study had come up with. However, the taxpayer still refuted the ZRA's approach stating that the use of comparables from Western Europe was disproportionate because, among other reasons, the economic circumstances were not comparable.

The approach by the ZRA was lenient when compared with most other tax authorities in the region. Based on the author's experience working with African Governments, it is highly unlikely to get internal comparables in most cases. Additionally, there are no local or regional comparables available for a benchmarking study. In such cases, therefore, the tax authorities turn to foreign comparables. As the use of foreign comparables raises the question of subjectivity given the differences in the geographical market, risk, etc., most countries tend to look for comparables from countries/regions that they consider to be closely comparable to Africa. The practice of such countries is to select/allow the use of foreign comparables from, for instance, Asia or Eastern Europe (not Western Europe as was used by the ZRA). This choice of the region then allows some comfort in that not many (or none at all) comparability adjustments might be required. Some countries couple this practice with the use of interquartile ranges and, in some instances, using the median.

The ZRA's approach in this instance resulted in lower margins (not a surprise given the fairly stable market conditions and country risk profiles of Western European countries) which would definitely have disadvantaged the ZRA's adjustment. However, this was not accepted by the taxpayer, a position that was supported by the Tribunal.

It will be interesting to see how the practice will evolve in the region after the findings of the Tribunal in this case. The toolkit on comparability is a welcome resource for tax authorities and taxpayers alike (*see also* section 2.2 of this chapter).

Recharacterization of entities/transactions

The ZRA recharacterized the taxpayer as a limited risk distributor. A proper FAR analysis invariably allows for a determination of what an entity is, i.e., in this case, whether a fully-fledged or limited risk distributor. The starting point is, of course, the contracts and only when the contractual terms and the conduct of the parties are not aligned should a discussion on recharacterization be considered.

However, and also as noted by other commentators,[55] in similar audits in the region, it is normally a limited risk distributor model that would risk getting challenged by tax authorities. This is due to the fact that, in most instances, it might be viewed that the limited risk distributor (as characterized in the contractual agreements) is undertaking more (value) functions, assuming higher risks, and utilizing more assets than is stated in the contracts, i.e., the conduct of the parties would suggest that the limited risk distributor is not what the contract indicates. This would come with an upward adjustment of profits to reflect the additional FAR of the local entity.

55. *See*, for example, KPMG's commentary available at https://assets.kpmg/content/dam/kpmg/xx/pdf/2019/04/tnf-zambia-apr26-2019.pdf, accessed January 17, 2020.

This item, along with the one on "searching for comparables" above reveal practice by the ZRA that is not common in most other countries in the region.

Interaction of transfer pricing with other rules

In this instance, the issue on thin capitalization of the taxpayer was raised. The ZRA argued that the taxpayer would not, if it were an independent party in similar circumstances, i.e., being highly thinly capitalized, have been paying out such huge expenses. It is to be noted that, during the period covered by the assessment, Zambia's thin capitalization rules based on the debt to equity ratio applied only in respect of mining companies. In all other instances, transfer pricing rules were applied, i.e., the determination was whether the transactions were in accordance with the arm's length principle.

In the current case, the ZRA applied the debt to equity ratio (reserved only for mining companies) in its argument for making the adjustment. Due to the fact that this approach was not supported by law, the Tribunal allowed the taxpayer's argument. Would the outcome have been different if the ZRA had undertaken a proper transfer pricing analysis of the various transactions, including the one on financing, i.e., not aggregating them and not resorting to the debt to equity ratio argument? In the author's view, the outcome would definitely have been different.

Probably, going forward, the ZRA's position might change. Effective January 1, 2019, Zambia applied a rule to limit the deductibility of interest expense that follows closely the OECD recommendation under Action 4 of the BEPS Project. According to that rule,[56] interest deduction is limited to 30% of EBITDA. The interest deduction limitation applies to all companies except companies under the insurance, banking, and financial services industries.

7 CONCLUSIONS

The initiative under the Inclusive Framework is a welcome one. Developing countries (or, more generally, non-OECD member countries) have the opportunity to contribute to the ongoing debate on matters that are shaping the international tax landscape. However, the structure of the initiative is not without fault, notably, that developing countries only joined the debate when most of the rules had already been devised by the OECD. As such, it is debatable whether such earlier rules sufficiently considered the needs of developing countries especially in terms of the priorities for these countries. Additionally, the ongoing debate takes on extra resources and might strain the already wanting resource levels.[57]

As noted by the International Monetary Fund (IMF), the Inclusive Framework embodies effective features in operating through soft law standards that are supported by mechanisms to ensure effective global implementation and that the Inclusive

56. Section 29 of the Income Tax Act, Chapter 323 of the Laws of Zambia.
57. *See also* IMF Policy Paper: Corporate Taxation in the Global Economy available at http://www.imf.org/external/pp/ppindex.aspx, accessed January 14, 2020) at p. 44 for further insights.

Framework holds the potential of enhanced cooperation beyond the implementation of BEPS for which it was created. However, the IMF also notes that realizing the full potential of the Inclusive Framework would require taking on issues not covered by BEPS but of particular interest to developing countries. Such issues include those on service fees that remain of great relevance to developing countries.[58]

Priorities of countries also vary, and certain issues that most developing countries considered relevant were either not covered in the BEPS Project or were not sufficiently covered. However, there have also been increased efforts by the Platform for Collaboration on Tax to revisit some of the areas identified by developing countries as being of importance and that should be prioritized. In this respect, some notable work includes that on offshore indirect transfers. This is an area that has seen countries especially in Africa amend their domestic rules in order to include anti-avoidance measures on indirect transfers of shares.

As noted in section 6 of this chapter, there are still special challenges facing developing countries. Capacity and access to comparables data for transfer pricing remain high on the list of pressing issues. There have also been considerable efforts in the recent past to develop capability and toolkits on comparability. The efforts of all stakeholders involved in these processes are highly commendable, and it is hoped that the efforts will continue in order to reach countries that are still in dire need of assistance for tax matters.

As efforts continue globally for transparency, one of the greatest challenges, for Africa especially, is the framework for enabling exchange of information (including CbC reports) for transfer pricing purposes. Countries in Africa continue to sign multilateral agreements allowing exchange of information and are entering into bilateral arrangements for exchange of information and CbC reports. The efforts of the African Tax Administration Forum in this regard is notable in terms of providing guidance on various tax issues and encouraging African countries to implement a framework for mutual administrative assistance.

The issues raised throughout this chapter interrogate crucial issues for consideration by developing countries, issues which necessarily go back to the basics: the relevant/pressing priorities for these countries. This also extends to the discussions regarding the tax challenges of the digitalization of the economy.

Transfer pricing practice and laws are expected to continue toward convergence. However, efforts to obtain certainty for all the stakeholders who are involved are paramount. This can be achieved by ensuring that laws are structured clearly, the enforcement bodies are clearly set out, and that tax matters between various local government institutions are aligned so that the applicable position is clear for tax authorities and taxpayers alike. This is especially important as more and more alignment and cooperation continues to be seen between various government ministries in ensuring transfer pricing compliance is achieved.

58. *Ibid.*

CHAPTER 5

Recent Developments on the Tax Challenges Arising from the Digitalization of the Economy: New Nexus Rules

Isabel Verlinden & Stefaan De Baets

1 INTRODUCTION

Languages change over time and can be understood though through tough thorough thought ... at least that is what one sees when googling "funny language quotes." Although meant to target the English language, it seems to work even better when addressing the Organisation for Economic Co-operation and Development (OECD) language that is used in reports and papers addressing the digitalization of the economy. In 2015, what was still called "the tax challenges of the *digital economy*" was labeled "tax challenges of *digitalization*" in 2018. In 2019, barely one year later, it became the "tax challenges of the *digitalisation of the economy*." There is, however, one constant element in the language change, and it is one of the most fearful things for consultants to face: scope creep. Indeed, with every change, the scope is becoming wider and wider. The economy as a whole focuses on the development of customer relationships, the improvement of their experiences, the collection and analysis of customer data, the maintenance of physical infrastructure to that end, etc. (Communication) technology and digital means are everywhere; the digital economy—informally often referred to as being dominated by the GAFAs (Google, Amazon, Facebook, Apple) or FANGs (Facebook, Amazon, Netflix, Google)—could not and should not be ring-fenced.

It is, therefore, not really a wonder that the concept of nexus is creeping wider and wider as well. It was (and still is) very much connected to a brick and mortar situation (permanency and fixed place). This fixedness may not (fully) capture the digitalization issue as the deployment of remote economic activity is at the heart of numerous business models in that area. Nexus rules may hence need to be revisited; the digital economy has become the economy in itself and does not need a fixed and permanent place to be present in a given market. Hence there was a shift in language from a narrow to a broad concept—digital economy to digitalization of the economy—including enlarging the scope of nexus rules.

In this contribution, the authors discuss the issues related to creating new nexus rules in connection with the OECD/G20 work on tax challenges arising from the digitalization of the economy. Profit allocation rules related to it are discussed elsewhere in this publication. Needless to say, the reader should keep in mind that nexus rules and profit allocation are closely linked.

In the following sections, the authors give an overview of the work done on the creation of the new nexus rules at the OECD, EU, and national levels. They then address the vision of scholars and practitioners on the matter. Finally, they develop some personal thoughts before concluding on the topic while acknowledging that things are still very much in a flux.

The nexus approach discussed in this contribution differs from the wording around nexus under Base Erosion and Profit Shifting (BEPS) Action 5[1] which requires that preferential tax regimes provide benefits only where the taxpayer undertakes substantial activities. For example, tax benefits arising from intellectual property regimes can only be granted to the extent that underlying research and development expenditure activities are undertaken primarily by the taxpayer itself or in the tax jurisdiction granting the tax benefits. This "nexus" approach is clearly linked to a fixed presence. The new nexus approach that is being developed is destined to allocate taxing rights in cases where no fixed presence whatsoever is available in the source state.

2 NEW NEXUS PRESENTED IN THE OECD DOCUMENTS

2.1 Action Plan on BEPS

Let us take a time machine and return to the past when the BEPS reports still had to be written. The OECD was granted the G20 mandate to design new international standards to ensure the coherence of corporate income taxation at the international level[2] and penciled its plan of action through fifteen different actions supported by three pillars: coherence (Actions 2-6), substance (Actions 7-10) and transparency (Actions 11-14). Two actions remained in the analysis phase: Action 1 on Addressing the Tax Challenges of the Digital Economy and Action 14 on Developing a Multilateral Instrument to Modify Bilateral Tax Treaties.[3] In the presentation of the different tracks under the BEPS Action Plan, the description of the relevant work to be undertaken already mentioned reviewing the nexus rules:

> Issues to be examined include, but are not limited to, the ability of a company to have a significant digital presence in the economy of another country without being liable to taxation due to the lack of nexus under current international rules, the attribution of value created from the generation of marketable location-relevant data through the use of digital products and services, [...].[4]

For this work, a dedicated group called the Task Force on the Digital Economy (TFDE)[5] was created. It produced the BEPS Action 1: 2015 Final Report on Addressing

1. OECD (2015), Countering Harmful Tax Practices More Effectively, Taking into Account Transparency and Substance, Action 5, 2015 Final Report.
2. OECD (2013), Action Plan on Base Erosion and Profit Shifting, p. 13.
3. This contribution will focus only on BEPS Action 1 and the tax challenges of the digital economy or—as the project was later renamed—on the tax challenges arising from the digitalization of the economy.
4. *See supra* n 2, pp. 14 and 29.
5. The Task Force on the Digital Economy (TFDE) was initially a subsidiary body of the Committee on Fiscal Affairs (CFA) in which non-OECD G20 countries participate as associates on an equal footing with OECD countries. It was established in September 2013 to develop a report identifying issues raised by the digital economy and detailed options to address them by September 2014. *See* https://oecdgroups.oecd.org/Bodies/ShowBodyView.aspx?BodyID = 7608&BodyPID = 11936&Lang = en&Book = True for the composition and mandate of the TFDE, accessed January 14, 2020. In 2016, the TFDE became a subsidiary body of the Inclusive Framework.

the Tax Challenges of the Digital Economy (2015 Report). The 2015 Report[6] recognizes that the digital economy enabled access to markets with less physical presence (absence of the "brick and mortar" element), allowed collection of analysis of data at an unprecedented scale, and has increased customer and user participation impact as well as the degree of network effects. Rather surprisingly, the section on nexus in the 2015 Report starts with recognizing that the "[a]dvances in digital technology have not changed the fundamental nature of the core activities that business carry out as part of a business model to generate profits." This confirms, in fact, earlier findings published in an OECD publication on e-commerce.[7]

2.2 E-Commerce: Transfer Pricing and Business Profits Taxation (2005)

Based on a review of a subgroup of the Comité on Fiscal Affairs and a Technical Advisory Group (TAG) on the challenges that are posed on the tax systems by Internet electronic commerce, this chapter discusses how governments need to focus on addressing them in a spirit of collective cooperation. Already in 2005, the message was that the allocation of taxing rights should be based on mutually agreed principles and a common understanding of their application. The report also warns that such consensus may affect countries' abilities to enforce taxation but, without it, the internet and other new communication technologies may pose a serious challenge to governments in maintaining their revenue bases.

2.2.1 Transfer Pricing

The subgroup examined how the OECD Transfer Pricing Guidelines (OECD TPG) would apply to different electronic business models and concluded that the existing guidance[8] (at that time) "is capable of dealing with the issues raised by electronic commerce." The main conclusion was that the communications revolution did not present fundamentally new or categorically different transfer pricing issues although it could make the more difficult problems more common. The OECD publication on e-commerce does recognize some of the problems for which the OECD TPG may be inadequate:

- Functional analysis to assess comparability: it can be difficult to know who is doing what and where; transactions become more complex, and functional analysis becomes more difficult to implement.
- Transactional approach: the mobility of functions adds to the difficulty of attaching particular transactions to a particular jurisdiction.

6. OECD (2015), Addressing the Tax Challenges of the Digital Economy, Action 1, 2015 Final Report, paragraphs 253-261. This publication does not reflect a consensus view.
7. OECD (2005), Tax Policy Studies E-Commerce: Transfer Pricing and Business Profits Taxation.
8. At the time of the OECD publication on e-commerce (2005), the 1995 version of the OECD transfer pricing guidance was applied.

- Comparability analysis: it becomes more difficult to determine what the transaction actually is and even more difficult to find out enough about a potential comparable third-party transaction; can the comparability standard still be met?
- Differing tax treatment for permanent establishments (PE) and subsidiaries:[9] a possible approach might be for the multinational enterprise (MNE) group income and expenses to be allocated among the various parts of the group regardless of the composition of the group (PE, subsidiary, or a combination) but distinguishable from a global formulary apportionment method.
- The effect and importance of intangibles as the economy becomes knowledge-based.
- Mutual Agreement Procedure (MAP) and granting corresponding relief may become more difficult.
- Small businesses may enter into international trade more easily (with, as a consequence, more audits, disputes, and MAP cases).
- Increasing use of tax havens: increase of anti-avoidance rules as a support measure but profit allocation in accordance with the arm's length principle (ALP) is still required to determine the distribution of primary taxing rights.

2.2.2 Nexus Issues and Profit Allocation

The treaty issues in the OECD publication on e-commerce were discussed in a TAG that consisted of OECD Member States, non-OECD economies, and business representatives. It reiterates the common conditions of nexus and PE as we know them till today for treaty purposes: the definition of a PE contains both a geographical element and a temporal element. With regard to the geographical element, the reference to "fixed place of business" means a fixed physical location; the temporal element means that the presence of the enterprise through the fixed physical location must be more than temporary in relation to the business that is conducted.

For that matter, a website in itself does not constitute a PE.[10] Web hosting services provided by an internet service provider (ISP) do not constitute a PE for the enterprise for which the website is run through the servers of the ISP.[11] Also, the activities performed through a potential PE should not be of an auxiliary or preparatory nature.

The OECD e-commerce publication mentions that there are exceptions to the PE nexus (e.g., the dependent agent PE) and some categories of profits may even be taxed in the absence of a PE.

---

9. The OECD report on e-commerce was published before the 2008 and 2010 Reports on the Allocation of Profits to Permanent Establishments although discussions on this issue were ongoing at that time.
10. OECD, Model Tax Convention on Income and on Capital, paragraph 123. Not all countries share the view expressed in the OECD Commentary and claim that a website may constitute a significant economic presence.
11. *Ibid.*, paragraph 124.

2.3 The 2015 OECD BEPS Report Addressing the Tax Challenges of the Digital Economy

On October 5, 2015, together with the other BEPS Reports, the OECD released the Final Report Addressing the Tax Challenges of the Digital Economy (2015 Report).[12] One of the policy challenges identified with regard to direct taxation originating in the "digital economy" is whether the existing nexus rules (condition of fixedness and permanency) are appropriate for tax purposes[13]—scale without mass. As can be read in the 2015 Report: "the digital economy has, however, enabled access to markets with less reliance on physical presence than in the past."[14] The 2015 Report does not want to overstate or understate the issue of nexus—recognizing that a large quantity of sales can be made without physical presence—and raises the question of whether, indeed, the current nexus rules are still fit for purpose. The 2015 Report mentions the enhanced collection and processing of customer and user data/data, in general, user and customer participation, and network effects. Another issue raised concerns about the gathering of data and whether a nexus should be created in the jurisdiction of where the data is gathered, in particular in light of the growing role of data (and the potential value or value-added thereof).

What is also questioned is whether activities that were almost automatically being considered of an auxiliary or preparatory nature are still rightfully benefitting from that status as some of those activities (e.g., local warehousing) may become part of the core business of the MNE in times when supply chains are shortened, and phones and spreadsheets are replaced by algorithms.[15]

However, the issue of nexus is not limited to tax treaties; domestic law may also not recognize a nexus absent the features of fixedness and permanency. The authors refer to the discussion on digital services taxes (DSTs) in the relevant section of this contribution.

The 2015 Report also recognizes that new business models may give rise to nexus issues and cites cloud computing services (infrastructure-as-a-service, software-as-a-service, and platform-as-a-service transactions) as an example.[16]

Three possible approaches are presented in the 2015 Report, but no recommendations were withheld at that stage. The approaches[17] are the introduction of:

(1) new nexus rules based on the concept of a significant economic presence (SEP);
(2) a withholding tax on certain digital transactions; and
(3) an equalization levy.

---

12. OECD (2015), Addressing the Tax Challenges of the Digital Economy, Action 1, 2015 Final Reports, 2015.
13. *Ibid.*, paragraphs 253-261.
14. *Ibid.*, paragraph 259.
15. The World is not flat: Special Report: Global Supply Chains, The Economist, July 13, 2019, 12 pp.
16. *Ibid.*, paragraph 272.
17. *Ibid.*, paragraphs 277 and following. A discussion on withholding taxes and equalization levy falls outside the scope of this contribution.

The SEP starts from a purposeful and sustained interaction with the source jurisdiction through technological or automated tools. Several elements need to be considered to determine whether an SEP—and hence a new nexus—exists. These elements are based on revenue and on (number of) users.

The principle behind a revenue-based approach is that revenue is linked to a (strong) user base or network, and the data retrieved from that base or network enhances the services rendered in the jurisdiction. Revenue will be a basic factor but not the only factor and must be combined with other elements such as the transactions covered (broad or narrow scope), level of the threshold (level of gross revenues from transactions with users in the jurisdiction), and administrative issues with regard to the threshold (identification, registration, compliance, etc.).

Digital factors could also be used to establish whether an SEP exists. Such factors could, e.g., consist of domain names, digital platforms, or payment possibilities in the jurisdiction concerned.

Finally, user (or consumer) based factors could be employed based on active users,[18] online contract conclusions (analogous to a dependent agent), and data that is collected. It would seem, however, that the collection of the relevant information of these factors may cause administrative difficulties as the enterprise is not situated in the jurisdiction concerned.

None of the other options analyzed by the TFDE, namely: (i) a new nexus in the form of an SEP, (ii) a withholding tax on certain types of digital transactions, and (iii) an equalization levy were recommended at this stage. It is expected that the measures developed in the BEPS Project will have a substantial impact on BEPS issues previously identified in the digital economy, that certain BEPS measures will mitigate some aspects of the broader tax challenges, and that consumption taxes will be levied effectively in the market country.

2.4 The 2018 OECD Interim Report on Tax Challenges Arising from Digitalization

The 2018 OECD interim report on tax challenges arising from digitalization[19] (2018 Interim Report) does not contain a separate discussion of the nexus issue. Nevertheless, because the new nexus rules and new allocation of profit rules are intrinsically linked, the 2018 Interim Report can do nothing else than refer to the nexus issue and related challenges.

The 2018 Interim Report recognizes the broad acknowledgment of the continuing evolution of digital technologies as well as the need for further consideration and monitoring of how these changes are impacting value creation across the economy. It also mentions, at that time, the lack of agreement among countries over the tax implications of scale without mass and greater reliance on intangibles. Additionally,

18. The 2015 Report, however, indicates that detailed metrics are needed to identify an active user.
19. OECD (2018), Inclusive Framework on BEPS, Tax Challenges Arising from Digitalisation: Interim Report.

there was no agreement on whether data and user participation should be considered as contributing to value creation.

The lack of consensus can be demonstrated through the positions presented by three groups of countries:[20]

> Position (1): There is no big issue. Any challenge is characteristic for certain business models and could be solved through a well-targeted change of the existing tax rules including a re-consideration of the rules relating to profit allocation and nexus. Most of the countries in this group rejected the idea that, in the market country, a sufficient link is established to create a tax nexus through user participation, and profit allocation should continue to be aligned with value creation.
>
> Position (2): There is a big issue, and it is not limited to highly digitalized business models. It raises both a nexus and a profit allocation issue. Data and user participation, however, should be treated in the same way as other business inputs sourced from an independent third party in the business' supply chain.
>
> Position (3): What's the fuss? BEPS has largely addressed the concerns of double non-taxation although it is still too early to fully assess the impact of all of the BEPS measures. There is currently no need for any significant reform of the international tax rules although there is room for further analysis.

Based on these three diverging positions, the Inclusive Framework (IF) agreed to review the profit allocation and nexus rules.

The 2018 Interim Report indicates[21] that certain countries are of the opinion that a physical presence is no longer needed for the "service PE" as defined in Article 5(3)(b) of the United Nations Model Tax Convention (UN MTC). Some countries have reasoned that services "used" or "consumed" in the source jurisdiction can include services performed from a remote location when, for example, the permanency criterion is met. In other words, compared to the "mainstream" PE, the geographical requirement is not met, but the temporal element is satisfied.

It is needless to say that the nexus issues will have an impact on the PE definition which, in turn, will have an impact on the allocation of profit. An open question is whether the nexus issues will also influence the authorized OECD approach.

2.5 The Policy Note

On January 29, 2019, the OECD released a two and a half page policy note[22] on options to further work on addressing the tax challenges of the digitalization of the economy. The webcast,[23] held on the same day, on the policy note explicitly indicated that the

20. *Ibid.*, pp. 171-172.
21. *Ibid.*, pp. 138-139.
22. OECD (2019), Addressing the Tax Challenges of the Digitalisation of the Economy, Policy Note.
23. OECD Tax Talks # 11, available at http://www.oecd.org/tax/oecd-tax-talks-january-2019.htm, accessed January 20, 2020.

proposals may go beyond the ALP and consider new types of nexus irrespective of a physical presence. The policy paper—and webcast—explicate the proposals under two pillars:

(1) Pillar 1 on nexus and profit allocation, destined to allocate more taxing rights to market or user jurisdictions, contains three proposals:
   (a) User Participation Approach: Revising the rules on nexus and profit allocation based on "active user participation"; to be applied to highly digitalized businesses. The profit allocation would be based on a residual profit split methodology with formulaic features.
   (b) Marketing Intangibles Approach: Revising the allocation rules based on market-related intangibles without requiring a physical nexus or presence in the market jurisdiction; to be applied to a wider scope of companies than highly digitalized businesses. The profit allocation would be based on a residual profit split methodology with formulaic features.
   (c) SEP Approach: revising the nexus and allocation rules on the basis of the existence of an important economic relationship with a market country. The profit allocation would be based on a formulaic approach.
(2) Pillar 2[24] on addressing the continued risk of profit shifting to no or low taxation jurisdictions through the following rules:
   (a) Income inclusion rule.
   (b) Denial of base eroding payments at source.
   (c) Coordination rules to avoid double taxation.

The policy note already stresses that taxation under the new rules should be linked to economic profit while, at the same time, double taxation should be avoided through effective dispute prevention and resolution mechanisms.

The policy note ended with the message that a solution must be delivered in 2020.

2.6 Public Consultation Document on the Digitalization of the Economy

On February 13, 2019, as announced in the policy note, the OECD released its Public Consultation Document on the tax challenges of the digitalization of the economy.[25] It allows for only a seventeen-day window for interested parties to submit their comments and observations.

The document describes in more detail the different proposals on Pillar 1 and Pillar 2 announced in the policy note. The Public Consultation Document confirms that the three proposals under Pillar 1 (the User Participation Approach, the Marketing Intangibles Approach, and the SEP Approach) require changes to the current nexus rules based on geographic and temporal features.

24. Pillar 2 falls outside the scope of this contribution.
25. OECD (2019), Addressing the Tax Challenges of the Digitalisation of the Economy, Public Consultation Document.

All in all, despite the importance of addressing new nexus rules, the discussion thereon is relatively short and comprises only one paragraph:

> 82. New nexus requirements would be required to implement the profit allocation proposals. The essential task would be to provide user or market jurisdictions with the right to tax the additional income, even if the entity earning that income would have no taxable presence under existing treaty principles. This could conceivably be achieved by amending or supplementing the Article 5 definition of "permanent establishment," allied with changes to the distributive rules in Articles 7 and 9. However, those existing provisions look at transactions between enterprises or parts of an enterprise, whereas the new proposals look at the combined profit of multiple entities within an MNE group. Therefore, an alternative approach might be to introduce the new nexus through a new standalone rule allocating taxing rights over the additional income. In all cases, the proposals recognise the need for a new nexus which would be based on an alternative threshold. There are similarities between this and nexus rules based on a concept of significant economic presence [...] which should be further explored. Of course countries may also need to amend their domestic laws, such that any new article can become operational and there may be benefits in coordinating the development of any such domestic rules.

This paragraph draws attention to the fact that not only treaty changes are needed, but changes to domestic legislation may also be needed in order to apply the new nexus rules under construction.

A public consultation was held on March 12 and 13, 2019. The OECD received 211 contributions following its call for comments on the Public Consultation Document.[26]

Strangely enough, although new nexus rules are considered as an important feature in establishing rules in addressing the tax challenges of the digitalization of the economy, the agenda of the public consultation left no room for a separate discussion on how the new nexus rules should be designed. Instead, they were covered in general under the three proposals under Pillar 1: the User Participation Approach, the Marketing Intangibles Approach, and the SEP Approach. The few interventions on nexus during the public consultation stressed the potential friction of the new rules with the existing ones and the likely difficulties and complexities to be encountered when designing new rules.

In its submission to the public consultation, PwC stressed that it would be more efficient to first determine a principled framework against which income could be allocated to a country and only then set a nexus threshold that is consistent with those principles and at a level that relieves the administrative burden on taxpayers and tax administrations from merely incidental activity.[27]

---

26. The agenda of the public consultation, the contributions received, and the slides presented during the public consultation held on March 13 and 14, 2019 are available at https://www.oecd.org/tax/beps/public-consultation-tax-challenges-of-digitalisation-13-14-march-2019.htm, accessed January 21, 2019.
27. PwC submission to the Public Consultation Document on Addressing the Tax Challenges of the Digitalisation of the Economy, p. 23, available at https://www.pwc.com/gx/en/tax/tax-policy-administration/beps/assets/response-to-oecd-consultation.pdf, accessed January 21, 2019.

2.7 The Programme of Work

The story continues. On May 31, 2019, the OECD released the Programme of Work[28] seeking a political agreement on a Unified Approach by the end of 2019.[29] The next step would be the implementation of a political agreement by the end of 2020.

In line with the policy note, the Programme of Work describes three major work streams, one of which is work on new nexus rules. The other two work streams are profit determination and allocation as well as implementation and administration.[30]

The work stream on the new nexus is intended to develop a taxable (hence the link with allocation rules) non-physical presence in market jurisdictions including:

(1) Revision of the PE definition (Article 5 OECD Model Tax Convention) and allocation rules (Article 7 OECD Model Tax Convention).
(2) Development of a stand-alone rule establishing the new and separate nexus through either a taxable non-physical presence or a source concept. This would require:
   (a) defining a taxable non-physical presence separate from a PE;
   (b) defining a new concept of income taxable in the source country;
   (c) identifying interactions between the taxable non-physical presence and income taxable in the source country with the existing rules.
(3) Development of indicators demonstrating a remote but sustained and significant involvement in the market country's economy through:
   (a) temporal and monetary thresholds; together with
   (b) additional indicators evidencing the involvement in the economy of the source country and going beyond the revenue generated through the mere selling activity.
(4) Influence on other articles of the OECD Model Tax Convention, for example, Article 9 on Associated Enterprises (Transfer Pricing).
(5) Measures to ensure tax certainty, administrability, and effective dispute prevention and resolution.

2.8 The "Unified Approach"

Anxious to expedite the process toward a consensus position, the OECD Secretariat prepared a consultation document containing a high level *Secretariat Proposal* for a "Unified Approach" under Pillar 1 (Unified Approach).[31] The Unified Approach was published on October 9, 2019. It combines the three proposals under the Programme of Work (User Participation Approach, Marketing Intangibles Approach, and SEP) and

28. OECD (2019), Programme of Work to Develop a Consensus Solution to the Tax Challenges Arising from the Digitalisation of the Economy—OECD/G20 Inclusive Framework on BEPS.
29. The G20 approved the Programme of Work on June 9, 2019.
30. As mentioned before, although these two work streams are intrinsically linked to the new nexus, a discussion thereof falls outside the scope of this contribution.
31. OECD (2019), Public Consultation Document—Secretariat Proposal for a "Unified Approach" under Pillar One.

recommends a departure from the ALP and the Separate Entity Approach under certain circumstances and advocates the use of formulaic or "simplified" approaches.[32]

The scope of the Unified Approach is wider than highly digital business models and is broadly focused on "large consumer-facing businesses." As the term "large consumer facing businesses" is only broadly defined as, for example, businesses that generate revenue from supplying consumer products or providing digital services that have a consumer facing element in the document, it indicates that further work needs to be carried out on scope and carve-outs (e.g., extractive industries, commodities, and possibly financial services). With regard to the size criteria, reference is made to the EUR 750 million threshold used for country-by-country reporting (CbCR).[33] For businesses within the scope of the Unified Approach, it would create new nexus rules that are independent of physical presence but largely based on sales and possibly including country-specific sales thresholds adjusted in such a way that smaller economies may also benefit. The new nexus rule would be designed as a stand-alone provision on top of the existing PE definition.[34]

Continuing the tenure of the previous reports, the Unified Approach is a reminder that no traditional physical presence in the market is needed to interact with users and customers and to create value. The new nexus rules would be applied when there is a sustained and significant involvement in the economy of the market state irrespective of its physical presence in that market state. That involvement could be demonstrated through a revenue threshold but also considering certain activities (e.g., online advertising directed at non-paying users in another country). The new nexus rules would also be applicable to businesses with sales in a country through related or unrelated distributors. The Unified Approach justifies this for achieving neutrality between different business models and capturing all remote involvement in a market country.

2.9 The Public Consultation

Following the request for comments from stakeholders, the OECD Secretariat received 304 contributions from business, academia, civil society, and consultants.[35] The opinions expressed in the written contributions vary from a (very) low nexus threshold and adapting the threshold to the market in question to a (very) high nexus threshold with increased complexity should the threshold differ per country concerned. Additionally, the issue of discrimination was touched upon. Several contributions mentioned that, when sales through unrelated parties create a taxable nexus, this approach will make the nexus approach very complicated. The business of the unrelated distributor is not under the control of the MNE, and information may be hard—if not

32. A discussion of the (formulaic) approaches, referred to as Amount A, Amount B, and Amount C, falls outside the scope of this contribution.
33. OECD (2019), Public Consultation Document—Secretariat Proposal for a "Unified Approach" under Pillar One, p. 7.
34. *Ibid.*, pp. 5 and 8.
35. For an overview of the contributions, *see* Barry Larkin, OECD Buried under Avalanche of Pillar 1 Tax Reform Comments—Tax Notes International, January 13, 2020, pp. 153-170.

impossible—to retrieve. One suggestion is to "stop the nexus" at the first third-party distributor.

The public consultation related to Pillar 1 was held on November 21 and 22, 2019. On the issue of scope and nexus, most commentators indicated that the concept of large consumer facing businesses should be clarified. A good illustration of the difficulties that businesses might face was presented by the LafargeHolcim Group, a company probably safe to be called operating a bricks and mortar business. No one can unambiguously tell whether cement should be labeled a commodity. They have different business lines some of which may be out of scope, some may be in or out, and others (client facing) might be in.[36] Although the nexus question was formally put on the table—and certainly can be construed as one of the most important issues to be solved—it received relatively little attention during the public consultation.

The PwC contribution[37] raised several issues with regard to nexus. As a preliminary remark on the nexus issues, the contribution clarifies that whatever nexus standard is agreed upon, it should be linked to the expected allocation of profits (e.g., profits allocated to the location of customers would lead to an incoherent approach if the threshold is based on the number of users). Introducing local (country-specific) revenue thresholds independent of a global threshold will increase the administrative and compliance burden.

In order to create a sustained threshold to answer to the requirement of a significant and sustained involvement in the market country, PwC suggested taking into account:

(1) the preceding taxable year, or
(2) the average ratio for the preceding three taxable years (allowing mitigating the impact of cyclical changes or losses in one or more years).

Companies may operate several activities or business lines some of which may be in scope and others out of scope. If the approach would not allow for segmentation, profit unrelated to the consumer facing activity can be brought into the approach. Segmentation seems to be a mandatory feature of Amount A[38] leading to a fair allocation of profit generated from customer-oriented activities.

36. The presentation of LafargeHolcim Group at the public consultation can be found on, https://www.dropbox.com/s/sysgbgqdo3q23xk/presentations-oecd-public-consultation-pillar-one-november-2019.zip?dl=0&file_subpath=%2FDay+1%2FItem+3+Karine+Uzan+Mercie+-+LarfargeHolcim+Group.pdf, accessed January 22, 2018.

37. Available at https://www.pwc.com/us/en/tax-services/publications/insights/assets/Oecd-pillar-1-paper-pwc-response-final.pdf, accessed January 22, 2020.

38. The new rules would introduce an approach based on Amount A—linked with the new nexus—and Amounts B and C—linked with a nexus based on physical presence:

> Amount A can be described as a part of "deemed residual profit" to be allocated to market states under the new nexus rules based on a formulaic approach. It would start with defining profits that come in scope of the new nexus approach determined as a proportion of revenues to profits (a). As a second step, a fixed deemed share of profit representing a remuneration for "routine returns" would be eliminated (b). What is left after the second step ((a)-(b)) will be labeled "non routine returns" and will partly be used for further allocation among the market

MNEs that already have a physical presence in a certain market country (subsidiary or PE) should not be in scope of Amount A; the market country is already capable of sharing in the exploitation of the marketplace in the country.

With regard to ensuring that smaller economies can also benefit from the new approach, a measure based on country-specific factors, for example, gross domestic product (GDP), could be used. The following criteria could be also used:

(1) the number of consumers (e.g., a business with less than X consumers in the local jurisdiction should be out of scope); and
(2) the number of transactions (e.g., a business that concludes fewer than X business transactions with persons resident in the local jurisdiction should be out of scope).

3 STATEMENT BY THE OECD/G20 INCLUSIVE FRAMEWORK ON BEPS ON THE TWO-PILLAR APPROACH TO ADDRESS THE TAX CHALLENGES ARISING FROM THE DIGITALIZATION OF THE ECONOMY

On January 31, 2020, the OECD released the Statement by the OECD/G20 Inclusive Framework (IF) on BEPS on the Two-Pillar Approach to Address the Tax Challenges Arising from the Digitalisation of the Economy (the Statement).[39] It confirms the IF (only the main issues with regard to Pillar 1 are mentioned here):

(1) endorses the Unified Approach as the basis for the negotiations of a consensus-based solution to be agreed in 2020 but also notes the requirement of improved tax certainty including effective and binding dispute prevention and resolution mechanisms and minimizing complexity;
(2) expresses concerns about a potential safe harbor approach as suggested in the letter of December 3, 2019 of U.S. State Secretary Mnuchin;
(3) recognizes that difficult issues still need to be resolved, including:
   - the binding nature of dispute prevention and resolution mechanisms (and their scope);
   - possible weighting of the quantum of Amount A to account for different degrees of digitalization between in scope business activities; and

states (c). The deemed "non routine returns" will be split on the basis of a fixed ratio (determined at an international level with possible differences for different industries or business lines) in a portion to serve as a deemed remuneration to market countries under the new taxing right (c1) and in a portion to remunerate other elements such as intangibles, capital, and risk (c2).
Amount B is a fixed (formulaic) remuneration for "baseline marketing and distribution activities" (not defined) in the market country.
Amount C includes remuneration in excess of Amount B.

39. Available at http://www.oecd.org/tax/beps/statement-by-the-oecd-g20-inclusive-framework-on-beps-january-2020.pdf, accessed January 31, 2020.

- regional factors in computing and allocating Amount A (through regional segmentation).

The chapter gives some (non-exhaustive) examples of what it considers to be in scope under Amount A activities, namely, the automated digital services and consumer facing businesses. It uses the EUR 750 million threshold as an example but delinks it from the CbCR concept. A further carve-out will be considered when the total aggregated in-scope revenue is less than a certain threshold. Further, a *de minimis* amount on the total profit from the in-scope activities could be determined. The computation of Amount A and application of the new nexus rule will involve additional thresholds.

Table 5.1 Scope of the Unified Approach

Automated Digital Services	*Consumer Facing Businesses*
- online search engines; - social media platforms; - online intermediation platforms, including the operation of online marketplaces, irrespective of whether used by businesses or consumers; - digital content streaming; - online gaming; - cloud computing services; and - online advertising services.	- personal computing products (e.g., software, home appliances, mobile phones); - clothes, toiletries, cosmetics, luxury goods; - branded foods and refreshments; - franchise models, such as licensing arrangements involving the restaurant and hotel sector; and - automobiles.
Further work is required on the definitional issues.	

The Statement confirms that extractive industry and commodity products as well as financial services are not in scope (due to protective regulations and great deal of financial transactions are realized between commercial actors).

The new nexus will be drafted as a stand alone rule to spillover effects on other existing tax or non-tax rules. It will be based on indicators of a significant and sustained engagement with market jurisdictions. In order to limit the administrative burden, the IF will examine simplified reporting and registration-based mechanisms (e.g., as a one-stop-shop) and exclusive filing in the ultimate parent jurisdiction.

The revenue threshold shall be in line with the size of the market with a *de minimis* amount and will be the only threshold for automated digital services. With regard to the consumer facing businesses, no new nexus will be created if the MNE is merely selling consumer goods in a market jurisdiction without a sustained interaction with the market; sales in itself will not generate a significant and sustained engagement.

Further work is needed on possible additional factors, in particular the existence of a physical presence of the MNE in or marketing directed at the market country.

4 EUROPEAN UNION

On March 21, 2018, say straight after the publication of the OECD BEPS Interim Report on the tax challenges arising from the digitalization of the economy, the European Commission (EC) published its digital package containing two proposals for directives and one recommendation:

(1) Proposal for a Council Directive laying down rules relating to the corporate taxation of a significant digital presence.[40]
(2) Proposal for a Council Directive on the common system of a DST on revenues resulting from the provision of certain digital services.[41]
(3) Commission Recommendation relating to the corporate taxation of a significant digital presence.[42]

The draft directive on the corporate taxation of a significant digital presence represents a long-term, comprehensive solution within Member States' corporate tax systems. It provides rules for establishing a taxable nexus for a non-physical commercial presence of a digital business ("a significant digital presence"). More specifically, a digital platform would constitute a significant digital presence (or nexus) if it meets one or more of the following criteria:

(a) the proportion of total revenues during the tax period and the amount resulting from the supply of the digital services to users located in that Member State during that tax period exceeds EUR 7 million;
(b) the number of users of one or more of those digital services who are located in that Member State during the tax period exceeds 100,000;
(c) the number of business contracts for the supply of any such digital services that are concluded during the tax period by users located in that Member State exceeds 3,000.

Furthermore, the proposed directive sets out the principles for attributing profits to that significant digital presence on the basis of a functional analysis for profit attribution based on a profit split method as a default mechanism (activities include the collection, storage, processing, analysis, deployment, and sale of user level data; the collection, storage, processing, and display of user-generated content; the sale of online advertising space; making third-party created content available in a digital marketplace; and the supply of any digital service not listed in those activities). The proposed directive will apply to all taxpayers who are subject to corporate tax in one or more

40. Available at https://ec.europa.eu/taxation_customs/sites/taxation/files/proposal_significant_digital_presence_21032018_en.pdf, accessed January 22, 2020.
41. Available at https://ec.europa.eu/taxation_customs/sites/taxation/files/proposal_common_system_digital_services_tax_21032018_en.pdf, accessed January 22, 2020.
42. Available at https://ec.europa.eu/taxation_customs/sites/taxation/files/commission_recommendation_taxation_significant_digital_presence_21032018_en.pdf, accessed January 22, 2020.

Member States and to entities resident for tax purposes in a non-EU jurisdiction with respect to their significant digital presence in a Member State. It will not apply if an entity is tax resident in a non-EU jurisdiction that has a double tax convention (DTC) in force with the Member State in which there is a significant digital presence unless that DTC includes similar provisions in force on a significant digital presence and the attribution of profits to those of the draft Directive. Through the recommendation, the EC invites EU Member States to amend their DTCs with non-EU jurisdictions to reflect a significant digital presence and profit attribution per the directive.

The second proposed directive represents a targeted, short-term solution and introduces, at the EU level, a DST at a rate of 3 % on gross revenue (net of value-added tax (VAT) and other similar taxes) derived in the EU from certain activities (placing advertising on a digital interface targeted at users of that interface; making available to users a multi-sided digital interface that allows users to find and interact with other users and which may also facilitate the provision of goods or services directly between users; and transmitting data collected about users and generated from users' activities on digital interfaces).

Only entities with both total annual worldwide (i.e., not only within the EU) revenue above EUR 750 million and total annual taxable digital revenues in the EU above EUR 50 million would be subject to the DST regardless of whether they are established in a Member State or in a non-EU jurisdiction. Furthermore, the proposed directive sets out rules on the DST's place of taxation that is based on the location of the taxable service's users. It also proposes a simplification mechanism in the form of a one-stop-shop for taxable persons with DST liability in one or more Member States. The DST becomes due on the next working day after the end of the tax period. Although this proposal is presented as a temporary measure, it may well become permanent. For example, if a non-EU enterprise meets the thresholds, but the relevant double tax treaty has not been changed in the way the EU wants it to change, the temporary measure will still be applicable. It takes two to tango. If the treaty partner does not agree to change the treaty, then the treaty does not change. It would seem anything but plausible, just as an example, that the U.S. would agree to change the treaty in that sense.

The EC indicates it recognizes the need for a new tax framework that is not only up-to-date with digital business models but also provides an international solution to the challenges of taxing the digital economy. The EC also states that it is working closely with the OECD to support the international solution development.

Those proposals have been resting for quite some time, leaving the possibility to come to a solution at the global level. Additional recent communication, with the new EC in place, featuring Ms. Ursula von der Leyen as President of the European Commission, Executive Vice-President Ms. Margrete Vestagher (Coordinating the Commission's work to achieve fair digital taxation), and Commissioner Mr. Paolo Gentolini as Commissioner for Economy, the issue of taxing the digital economy in the EU is "back from the trenches." They seem to feel that it resonates well in a political discourse around "fairness" and definitely in times of crisis in political legitimacy. For example, the mission statements of Commissioners Gentolini and Vestagher refer, in general, to fair taxation and indicate:

(1) Commissioner Vestagher[43] must *coordinate the work on digital taxation to find a consensus at the international level by the end of 2020 or propose a fair European tax.*
(2) Commissioner Gentolini[44] must
  (a) Make sure that tax policies are *fair, fit for the digital economy, and make it easier for businesses* and people to work across borders.
  (b) [...]
  (c) Lead international efforts to find an agreed approach on digital taxation working with the OECD and the G20. *If no consensus emerges by the end of 2020, you should lead on the proposal for a fair European digital tax.*
  (d) Focus on making our tax systems simpler, clearer, and easier to use. As part of this, lead efforts on making a *common consolidated corporate tax base* a reality.

[...]

The EU Commission is also being chased on the "digitized economy" by the European Parliament (EP). For example, just before Christmas 2019, the EP accepted a resolution[45] and published a press release entitled "Parliament keeps up pressure to tax digital economy more fairly."[46] The press release indicates that:

> [I]n the resolution, MEPs express their concern that there is no common approach at EU level on the ongoing international negotiations and call on the Commission and Member states to agree on a joint and ambitious EU position, while making their own positions publicly known. The Parliament supports Commission President Ursula von der Leyen's commitment to propose an EU solution, should an international deal not be reached by the end of 2020. MEPs say that at international level, the EU's position should aim to ensure that the Single Market functions smoothly, notably by safeguarding a level playing field for all types of firms. They demand that firms pay a fair share of tax where the actual economic activity and value creation take place and that the income from taxes is fairly distributed across all the member states.

Two major elements can be retained. The first one is that, if there is no international (IF) solution by the end of 2020, the EU will go its own way. The second one is that the EU solution should not be limited to digital businesses (hence the confusion on the title of the press release). The EP further confirms its ongoing support for the C(C)CTB. Just to remind, in matters of direct taxation, the EU Member States still have full sovereignty.

43. Mission letter to Margrethe Vestager—Executive Vice-President for a Europe fit for the Digital Age, December 1, 2019, available at https://ec.europa.eu/commission/commissioners/sites/comm-cwt2019/files/commissioner_mission_letters/mission-letter-margrethe-vestager_2019_en.pdf, accessed January 22, 2020.
44. Mission Letter of Ursula Von der Leyen to Paolo Gentolini—Commissioner Designate for Economy, December 1, 2019, available at https://ec.europa.eu/commission/commissioners/sites/comm-cwt2019/files/commissioner_mission_letters/mission-letter-paolo-gentiloni_en.pdf, accessed January 22, 2020.
45. Resolution available at https://www.europarl.europa.eu/doceo/document/TA-9-2019-0102_EN.html, accessed January 29, 2020.
46. Press release available at https://www.europarl.europa.eu/news/en/press-room/20191212IPR68924/parliament-keeps-up-pressure-to-tax-digital-economy-more-fairly, accessed January 29, 2020.

The EP has also asked the EU Member States to speak at the OECD with one voice. This may prove to be not so easy, however.[47]

5 ON THE UNILATERAL FRONT: DST AKA TAXES WITH CASCADING EFFECT

Several jurisdictions have prepared or are in the process of preparing DSTs on all kinds of digital services including advertising services; sale of any audio, visual or digital content in digital media; and services provided in digital media for listening, watching, playing, or recording or using them in digital media; provision and operation of digital environments where users can interact with each other; or mediation services provided in the digital environment for the above-mentioned services. The nexus rules in these DSTs may vary (widely) leading to uncertainty and complexity; in other words: chaos. The more cynically enhanced may observe similarities with the viral spread of low emission zones throughout the EU. While the intention may be noble and have a convincing rationale, the execution shows an inherent lack of consideration for consistency and coherence. These would be the necessary building blocks for a sustainable robust solution that can be explained to and lived-up by all with fewer torturous explanations and at a lesser cost.

A description of all DSTs and the different nexus rules may lead us too far. Table 5.2 contains a (non-exhaustive) summary of DST legislation drafted, suggested, or imposed in different jurisdictions as known per January 31, 2020.

The list contains a comparison of the DST rates, thresholds to be considered for becoming a taxpayer under the DST, and taxable base calculations in these jurisdictions (if available).

Table 5.2 Digital Service Tax in Different Jurisdictions (Non-exhaustive List)

Country	*DST Rate*	*Note*	*Thresholds and Nexus*	*Taxable Base*
Austria	5%	–	It will be applied to any company with a revenue of EUR 750 million (USD 826 million) worldwide and EUR 25 million in digital advertising revenue in Austria.	–

47. Elodie Lamer, EU to Discuss Digital Taxation on Regular Basis—Tax Notes Today International, January 21, 2020—and EU to Give Scattered Response to Digital Tax—Tax Notes Today International, January 22, 2020.

Country	*DST Rate*	*Note*	*Thresholds and Nexus*	*Taxable Base*
Chile	10%		Digital services provided by persons or entities domiciled or resident abroad to Chilean natural persons. Digital services include digital intermediate between providers and users of services that may be concluded by electronic means; paid entertainment services for digital content, including images, movies, series, videos, music, games, and other digital entertainment provided through download, streaming, or other technology; certain advertising and promotional services and the use and subscription of internet platform services; and data storage services, including cloud services.	

Country	*DST Rate*	*Note*	*Thresholds and Nexus*	*Taxable Base*
Czech Republic	7%	–	Total consolidated revenues of more than EUR 750 million of the group (or a stand-alone organization) of which the provider is a member. Total revenues of the group from which the provider is a member (or a stand-alone entity that is not a member of a group) from the taxable digital services from the Czech Republic of more than CZK 50 million (approximately EUR 2 million).	The tax base will be determined according to the ratio of revenues obtained in the Czech Republic to total revenues.
France	3%	The rate is the same as in the draft EU Directive.	It has been said that the enterprise can be taxpayer only if two thresholds are met together at the individual level or consolidated group level in relation to the previous year: - Revenue for taxable services provided worldwide is higher than EUR 750 million. - If the revenue for taxable services localized in France is higher than EUR 25 million.	Taxable income should originate in France. It will be found pro-rata using the amount paid by users.

Country	*DST Rate*	*Note*	*Thresholds and Nexus*	*Taxable Base*
Hungary	7.5%		Tax on advertising services available over the internet, television, radio, billboards, newspapers, vehicles, and others. Trading revenue of more than HUF 100 million.	
Italy	3%	The rate is the same as in the draft EU Directive.	A taxpayer is one of the taxable persons either at the group level or at an individual level and is a business enterprise that meets both of the following conditions for one year (one calendar year): (i) The total reported worldwide income for the relevant taxable year exceeds EUR 750 million; (ii) The total taxable income in the Italian territory in the relevant fiscal year exceeds EUR 5,500,000. Activities covered: online advertising, intermediation platforms, and sale of data.	Italian taxable income includes total gross income.
Malaysia	6%	–	–	–

Country	*DST Rate*	*Note*	*Thresholds and Nexus*	*Taxable Base*
India (equalization levy)	6%		Threshold INR 100,000 (EUR 1,200) Activities covered: online advertisement, any provision for digital advertising space or any other facility or service for the purpose of online advertisement and includes any other service as may be notified by the central government.	
Poland	3%	The rate is the same as in the draft EU Directive.	–	–
Romania	3%	The rate is the same as in the draft EU Directive.	–	–
Spain	3%	The rate is the same as in the draft EU Directive.	It will be applied to companies with annual revenues of at least EUR 750 million worldwide and more than EUR 3 million in Spain. Activities covered: online advertising, intermediation platforms, and sale of data	–

Country	*DST Rate*	*Note*	*Thresholds and Nexus*	*Taxable Base*
Turkey	7.5%	-	The taxpayers will be subject to DST on their digital services revenues if: - the revenue obtained for those services in Turkey exceeds TRY 20 million and - worldwide revenues of more than EUR 750 million. Activities covered: online advertising, intermediation platforms, and sale of data.	Digital services that are provided in Turkey.
U.K.	2%	-	- The total global revenue generated by the group is greater than GBP 500 million; and - U.K. income is higher than GBP 25 million. Activities covered: social media platforms, online marketplaces, and internet search engines	Total income in the U.K. (GBP 25 million will be subtracted from revenues).

What seems to be lacking in several of these unilateral initiatives is an unambiguous commitment that the DST application will be abandoned once the OECD finds a multilateral solution for taxing the digital economy if the "Unified Approach" published under Pillar 1 by the OECD Secretariat is adopted. The abandonment of the DST, however, is one of the main criteria to make the Unified Approach a success on a global scale.

Further, the Canadian and Israeli Governments are considering to introduce a DST similar to the French model. The Treasury Secretary of Kenia stated that the digitalization of Kenya's economy gives rise to base erosion and decreased tax revenue and announced a draft of tax measures providing a platform for taxation of income generated from the digital economy.[48]

Some countries intend to introduce or have introduced domestic or treaty provisions on digital or online presence. For example, Israel[49] introduced measures that, in the absence of a double tax treaty, online services provided by a non-resident enterprise from a remote location (absent physical activities in Israel) to in-country customers may constitute an SEP. Such an SEP or "digital presence" includes but is not limited to significant online contract conclusions; significant use of digital products and services; localized websites (e.g., in Hebrew, local discounts and marketing, local currency and payment options); and multi-sided business models (the company generates significant revenue that is closely related to the volume of online activities performed by users located in Israel). There is no threshold requirement for local sales.

The Slovak Republic[50] introduced an SEP based on specific activities carried out by online platforms, intermediation services for transportation, and accommodation.

The SEP in India[51] expands the domestic definition of a nexus through the introduction of an alternative threshold that permits taxation of the profits of a non-resident enterprise on a source basis irrespective of the level of physical presence of that enterprise in the taxing jurisdiction. The SEP can be based on local revenue or on the number of local users.

6 SOME VIEWS OF SCHOLARS AND PRACTITIONERS

6.1 Nexus in General

A qualifying connection—or nexus—must exist between the country claiming the taxation right and the taxable facts. It is necessary that the condition of nexus or genuine link is fulfilled to allow a country to exercise its taxation and tax collecting powers. Otherwise, those powers could be considered unlawful from the perspective of

48. PwC, No slowdown in unilateral tax measures targeting digital activities in 2020, p. 3, available at https://www.pwc.com/us/en/tax-services/publications/insights/assets/pwc-no-slowdown-in-tax-measures-targeting-digital-activities-in-2020.pdf, accessed February 5, 2020.
49. Lee A Sheppard, Digital Permanent Establishment and Digital Equalization Taxes—Navigating the Tax Challenges of the Digital Economy—Special Reports—Tax Notes International, April 1, 2018, p. 15.
50. *Ibid.*, p. 16.
51. Public consultation on the proposal for amendment of rules for profit attribution to permanent establishments, available at https://www.indianembassyusa.gov.in/pdf/taxcorner/Public_consultation_apr18.pdf, accessed February 5, 2020 and Reuven S. Avi-Yonah & Ajitesh Kir, India's New Profit Attribution Proposal and the Arm's-Length Standard, Tax Notes International, June 17, 2019, p. 1183.

public international law.[52,53] As Mines indicated in The Encyclopedia of Taxation and Tax Policy: "Nexus describes whether a taxpayer, property, or activity has sufficient connection with a state to be subject to that state's jurisdiction."[54] A legitimate tax claim ought to be based on the relationship to a person (personal attachment) or on the relationship to a territory (territorial attachment).[55] Policy makers reached the conclusion that mere physical presence over a specific period is enough to warrant a jurisdiction's right to tax. International tax law allows income of non-residents to be taxed in the source state provided there is a clear connection between the income and the source state.[56] If there is no physical presence, the connection is not strong enough to warrant a taxable presence (leading to the absence of source income over which a jurisdiction may exercise its taxing rights).[57]

However, it could be argued whether the taxation and tax collection rights are indeed limited. Already in 1986, Arnold mentioned that government's taxation powers are limited only by other governments' countervailing interests as well as practical enforcement and collection difficulties. He stated that international law does not put any limitations on a country's individual taxation powers and, in most countries, no constitutional limitations exist.[58] Hence, questions that arise are whether countries can establish their own nexus rules or whether the nexus and ensuing taxation rights are limited by international (tax) law.

When the nexus principle is limited by international tax law, countries have to respect those limitations (e.g., in double tax treaties) in taxing powers in the absence of a nexus.[59] In that case, it is obvious that the creation of new nexus rules permitting the taxation of the digitalization of the economy would necessitate changes to the existing treaties as well as domestic legislation allowing for taxation on the basis of the new nexus. "Taxation is preserved by a tax treaty with reference to certain largely physical notions of presence; absent these, it is an international free-for-all".[60] If not, then it would apparently suffice that countries introduce domestic rules generating a nexus (e.g., through a DST or SEP) but would, at the same time, lead to a chaotic situation; different rules would apply for every country. Gadžo (2018) also concludes that countries can lawfully impose income tax on manifold bases. "The decision on

52. Stjepan Gadžo, The Principle of "Nexus" or "Genuine Link" as a Keystone of International Income Tax Law: A Reappraisal, Intertax, Volume 46, Issue 3, p. 195 (2018 Kluwer Law International BV).
53. Wolfgang Schön, One Answer to Why and How to Tax the Digitalized Economy, p. 9 Max Planck Institute for Tax Law and Public Finance, Working Paper 201, June 10, 2019.
54. *Supra* n 52, p. 195 and Paul Mines, *The Encyclopedia of Taxation and Tax Policy*, p. 269 (Joseph J. Cordes, Robert D. Ebel & Jane Gravelle eds., The Urban Institute, 2005).
55. Wolfgan Schön, Persons and Territories: On International Allocation of Taxing Rights, British Tax Review, pp. 554-562.
56. Jeroen Lammers, OECD Unified Approach Leaves Market Jurisdictions Out in the Cold, Tax Notes International, January 13, 2020, p. 173.
57. *Ibid.*, p. 174.
58. *Supra* n 52, p. 195 and Brian J. Arnold, The Taxation of Controlled Foreign Corporation; An International Comparison 1, Canadian Tax Foundation, 1986.
59. *Supra* n 52, p. 208.
60. J. Scott Wilkie, The Way We Were? The Way We Must Be? The "Arm's Length Principle" Sees Itself (for What It Is) in the "Digital" Mirror, Intertax, Volume 47, Issue 12, pp. 1089-2019 (Kluwer Law International BV).

which among these bases will actually be relied upon is largely a matter of tax policy".[61]

According to Schön, extending the taxing rights of market countries is only a matter of international tax policy and not a constraint under international law.

There is not even a necessity to distinguish between digital and non-digital sales and services delivered in a cross-border situation as the mere existence of customers and users would generate that link. International law does not require a threshold based on "significant economic presence," "user participation" or "marketing intangibles." The simple fact that profits are derived from the sale of goods or services to a customer country would be sufficient to fulfill this broadly understood requirement of international law.[62]

For example, this is demonstrated in VAT/GST.

6.2 Approaches for the New Nexus

Turning back now to the Unified Approach and the attempt of developing new nexus rules, in short, the approach seems to want the best of both worlds. On the one hand, it seems to largely maintain the current taxing rights based on the existing nexus and profit allocation rules[63] (applicable to the supply side). On the other hand, new nexus rules—largely based on sales—would create a market state nexus assorted with remedies (Amount A, Amount B, and Amount C) to avoid spillover effects or to remedy double taxation.[64]

As indicated in the OECD BEPS Action 1 Report on the Digital Economy, the digital economy should not be ring-fenced, in particular as the whole economy is digitalizing. Yet, it would seem that the new nexus rules under the Unified Approach lead to a different kind of ring-fencing. "By referring to *highly digitalized business and consumer-facing business*, the new nexus in the Unified Approach does not cover all types of business, therefore, it ring-fences the objective (the tax subject) and subjective scope (the taxpayers)." This would also be true if no reference is made to digital models, but it introduces thresholds as an indicator of a genuine connection with a country while, at the same time, the new rules devise exclusions from its scope. Introducing thresholds and exclusions allows for the possibility to bring future digital business models in scope of the approach when an approach based on identifying specific digital models needs to change the provisions of the treaties.[65] *The corporate income tax should reflect economic reality and not what jurisdictions want that reality to be.*[66]

61. *Supra* n 52, p. 209.
62. *Supra* n 53, p. 9.
63. Under profit allocation rules, both transfer pricing and allocation of profits to PEs are understood.
64. Ana Paula Dourado, The OECD *Unified Approach* and the New International Tax System: A Half-Way Solution, Editorial, Intertax, Volume 48, Issue 1, p. 3 (2020 Kluwer Law International BV).
65. *Ibid.*, p. 5.
66. *Supra* n 56, p. 179.

Not only should the international approaches on nexus under Pillar 1 be amended. Countries may need to take additional domestic measures under the new nexus rules in order to be able to exercise the taxing rights that shall be allocated to them under the revised nexus rules. As treaties do not introduce new taxing rights as such, they need to *translate the new guidance into national law. In order to allow such a new system to work, it has to be introduced simultaneously in a significant number of countries. Hence, the new taxing right has to meet the basic legal requirements of all of the countries that are involved.* However, that is yet not all. In order to complicate things a bit more, EU Member States must also comply with the fundamental freedoms. Another issue that pops up is non-discrimination. The new nexus rules apply to consumer facing businesses, broadly defined, with some carve-outs. The approach is also limited to MNEs of a certain size (revenue of EUR 750 million) and a (varying per country) local sales threshold. Do these thresholds pass the non-discrimination test? Moreover, will it pass the (illegal) state aid test in the EU? It does not come as a surprise that commentators are critically stating that the concept of "consumer facing" is vague, not transparent and complex.[67]

As indicated above, the main criterion seems to be revenue thresholds, but it is not entirely clear—to put things mildly—which types of revenues are meant. As the new nexus would not only rely on physical presence but would also include a virtual element based on sales in a market, reliance on significant people functions and the traditional functional analysis is not an option.[68]

Some commentators are of the opinion that the new nexus rules should not contain thresholds but be based on sales in a given jurisdiction instead. However, a *de minimis* rule could be introduced to carve out enterprises with minor business profits in a certain country. This would be simple and proportionate.[69]

With regard to potential carve-outs, commodities, extractive industries, and possibly financial services are given as examples, but a crystal-clear technical foundation of why these industries (or why only these industries) are left out is unfortunately missing. It is maybe too early to determine what carve-outs or exclusions should be envisaged, and it might be better to wait until the Unified Approach as a whole is clarified. In its submission on the Unified Approach, PwC notes that:

> It appears [that] the focus of Pillar 1 is highly digitalised business models and transactions where the ALP is not delivering the outcomes that countries consider appropriate in some cases. However, without further clarity about where the ALP

67. Hartmut Förster, Stefan Greil and Arnim Hilse, Taxing the Digital Economy—The OECD Secretariat's New Transfer Pricing A-B-C and Alternative Courses of Action, International Transfer Pricing Journal, Volume 27, Issue 1, (2020 IBFD), pp. 3-18 at p. 5 and Leopoldo Parada, The Unified Approach Under Pillar 1: An Early Analysis, Tax Notes International, December 16, 2019, pp. 984–985.
68. Stefan Greil, Raphael Müller and Marcel Olbert, Transfer Pricing for Digital Business Models: Early Evidence of Challenges and Options for Reform, World Tax Journal, Volume 11, Issue 4 (2019) Published online November 11, 2019, accessed January 28, 2020.
69. Pasquale Pistone, João Félix Pinto Nogueira, Betty Andrade and Alessandro Turina, The OECD Public Consultation Document "Secretariat Proposal for a 'Unified Approach' under Pillar One": An Assessment, Bulletin for International Taxation, Volume 74, Issue 1 (2020) Published online November 15, 2019, accessed January 28, 2019.

is considered not to be delivering the desired outcomes (i.e. is it related to generation of high profit margins, or is it related to the deemed value of the market?), there is a less principled basis for establishing carve outs.[70]

6.3 Setting the Cat among the Pigeons

Could Pillar 1 be a safe harbor? At least that is what U.S. State Secretary Mnuchin proposed in his letter of December 3, 2019. This letter was immediately followed by a diplomatic rebuttal by OECD Secretary-General Angel Gurria. It is meanwhile called the "Mnuchin letter" in common parlance and has definitely ruffled some feathers, and it is still not off the table. One issue is that taxpayers would have the option to use or not use a safe harbor. With regard to a nexus, the question that arises is whether taxpayers can choose to have a taxable nexus in a country. Most countries will likely struggle with that option, not in the least as it would be hard to design a legislative framework to accommodate that.

7 SOME THOUGHTS

The digital progress has made it possible for MNEs to remotely deploy substantial economic activity and hence build up a strong footprint in the economy of a country in this way without a physical presence. It can easily be understood why the current international tax system is no longer fit for its purpose, and a tailoring to the imperatives of today's economy is needed. The revision of the international tax system touches upon the nexus rules—or, said otherwise, the right to tax a subject—and the allocation of profit rules. Both the nexus and allocation of profits are closely linked.

The proposed revision of the nexus rules will lead to the coexistence of two approaches:

(1) the physical nexus—to be applied on Amount B and Amount C—based upon a fixed presence; and
(2) the virtual nexus—to be applied on Amount A—based upon a (virtual) presence deploying a downstream activity affecting a jurisdiction.

The physical nexus is the system as we have known it until today. The virtual (or digital) nexus is unprecedented.

The coexistence of physical and virtual nexuses may trigger several issues, however. First of all, if there is a physical nexus or presence in a country, the question is whether that would automatically lead to the coexistence of a virtual presence as well. That would mean that a country could claim two taxing rights over the same subject. This would call for clear dividing rules on which nexus has priority over the other. The easiest way should be to determine that, when a physical nexus is present

70. Nana Ama Sarfo, Pillar 1 Carveout Chaos, Tax Notes Today International, January 13, 2020 and *Supra* n 36, p. 8.

in a country and is remunerated at arm's length, no virtual presence should be deemed to exist.

A crucial area for debate will be whether "consumer facing" creates a sufficient nexus or genuine link to generate taxing and tax collection rights. From the discussion in the previous sections, it becomes clear that it is not sufficient that the virtual nexus finds its place in the international tax arena without being made available and applicable under domestic tax law. Although, from a policy and political perspective and given the sovereignty of countries, the introduction of a virtual nexus should not pose insurmountable problems, it is the likely differences in domestic law and the amalgam of interpretations of international rules by countries that would be anything but desirable. When looking at the myriad of nexus rules defined in the unilateral DSTs, it can only be hoped that country delegates in IF discussions can come to an agreement and define what is meant under the new nexus at the international level. However, as the current mediatized debate shows, tax politics may hamper the development of sound tax policies.

The virtual nexus would be "largely based on sales" if the OECD Secretariat's Unified Approach is followed. Although from a layman's perspective the use of sales to determine the virtual nexus may look plausible, it may be equally worrisome. It may sound like a simple question, though what is actually meant by "sales" and how it is to be determined is less trivial.

For cases when an MNE sells directly (this includes sales through related distributors) into a certain market state without having a physical presence there, the use of "sales" could serve as an approach to allocate a nexus to the market state (if other conditions such as local thresholds are met, of course).

The situation can be less straightforward, though. Assume an MNE is using independent franchisees in a given market without having a physical presence in that market. Would that automatically mean that the MNE has a virtual nexus in the market state? Would that not mean that the market state is venturing to assume the right to tax both the independent franchisee (on physical nexus) and the MNE, the latter based on a virtual nexus? If so, these would be two bites of the apple.

In this relationship, the MNE may still be able to keep track of the sales to the franchisee and from the franchisee to the customer. The appropriateness of taxing the MNE in this case could be argued based on a virtual nexus which would also mean two bites of the apple. Further, the tax paid in the market country must be compensated in the residence state of the MNE to avoid double taxation.

The situation can be even more complicated. Assume an MNE (situated in country X) sells consumer-oriented widgets to an unrelated distributor in country Y. The unrelated distributor on-sells the widgets to consumers in country Y but also to country Z where the distributor nor the MNE has a presence. Who comes in scope of the nexus rules largely based on sales in country Z? Is it the distributor—who is able to keep track of the sales of the widgets in countries Y and Z? Is it the MNE—who is unable to keep track of the sales of the widgets in countries Y and Z? Or both?

In any way, the MNE may be faced with taxation in countries where it is not even aware that it was virtually present. The Unified Approach claims that the new nexus rules would also be applicable to businesses with sales in a country through related or unrelated distributors to achieve neutrality. It is important to keep in mind here that two different business models are in place (related distribution versus unrelated distribution). It could be wondered, therefore, whether the neutrality is rather distorted and not enhanced. Stopping at the first third party intervening in the transaction might be a reasonable approach. The January 31 OECD Statement acknowledges that this deserves further attention.[71]

These oversimplified examples illustrate the complexities that may arise when the new nexus rules would be purely sales based without having regard to the business model or structure.

The OECD indicated in the recent past that the digital economy could not be ring-fenced. It is hard to disagree with that. Parts of the economy should not be ring-fenced; the principles of fair, proportionate, and sustainable taxation should be applicable to all businesses. Having said that, the path chosen to develop measures that ring-fence the consumer facing industry may not be free from criticism.

At regular intervals, reference is made to the threshold of EUR 750 million revenue that is used for CbCR purposes to indicate whether an MNE should fall into the scope of the new rules. Although there are certainly arguments in favor of using the same threshold (clarity, transparency, simplicity), care should nevertheless be taken that there are no unwanted spillover effects when the thresholds for CbCR and the Unified Approach are linked. For example, assume that, after the revision of the CbCR, the IF would decide to lower the threshold. That would mean that the threshold for the Unified Approach would also be lowered. Therefore, both thresholds could be set at EUR 750 million revenue but should be unrelated to each other. The Statement of January 31, 2020 seems to go in that direction.[72]

The discussion, including the one on the nexus, seems to be morphing from a discussion on the tax challenges of the digital economy into one on developing increased taxing rights over consumer facing industries. The new nexus rules should respect the non-discrimination approach. The Unified Approach risks driving a wedge between consumer facing and non-consumer facing businesses, between supply side and demand side, between an approach based on value creation and a sales-based approach. The nexus issue may also influence the business model that enterprises may apply. The nexus rules—and the Unified Approach more in general—may distort the way business is doing its ... business, leading to uncertainty and controversy and hence contributing to the very tax "chaos" that the project is intended to avoid. This is rather strange as the mandate of the Committee of Fiscal Affairs (valid until July 31, 2020) indicates[73] encouraging the elimination of tax measures that distort international trade and investment. Introducing them would be a very undesirable result.

71. *Supra* n 39, p. 13, paragraph 41.
72. *Supra* n 39, p. 12, paragraph 35.
73. Mandate of the CFA, available at https://oecdgroups.oecd.org/Bodies/ShowBodyView.aspx?BodyID=963&BodyPID=12053&Lang=en&Book=True, accessed January 29, 2020.

8 CONCLUSION

What is currently available in the Unified Approach with regard to the new nexus rules, not based on physical presence but largely based on sales, is prone to clarification. It is not clear what is precisely meant with large "consumer facing" businesses. At least for certain groups, it is not clear whether it is consumer facing as they market the same product to a very diverse customer base.

What precise thresholds will be used to determine the nexus—and how they will be used—is not yet being discussed. The use of country-specific thresholds seems to be defendable to allow smaller economies to have their share of the cake but is likely to give rise to more complexity. Perhaps it would be useful to develop an adjustment mechanism based on, for example, GDP, rather than each country defining its own base. There should be no link between CbCR and nexus, although both global thresholds could be, e.g., set at EUR 750 million independently. Finally, the new nexus should only apply where an MNE has substantial market presence in a sustained manner over a number of years.

The system should remain neutral and be simple and should respect the principle of proportionality. The introduction of the new rules may influence the way business is handling its transactions. Taxation should seek to be neutral and equitable between different forms of business activities.[74] By trying to resolve the issue of a large economic footprint in a country without physical presence may trigger distortion in other areas.

74. *Supra* n 12, p. 20.

CHAPTER 6

Recent Developments on the Tax Challenges Arising from the Digitalization of the Economy: New Profit Allocation Rules

Giammarco Cottani

Translation is that which transforms everything so that nothing changes

Gunter Grass

1 INTRODUCTION: BACKGROUND

For almost a hundred years, the international allocation of taxing rights applicable to multinational enterprises (MNEs) has relied on two fundamental pillars: (i) the permanent establishment (PE) concept[1] and the arm's length principle (ALP[2]). By December 2020,[3] the centrality of those concepts to the international tax system is likely to change. Such target date was set by the Organisation for Economic Co-operation and Development (OECD) Inclusive Framework (IF[4]) in order to come up with a full reshaping of the consensus-based regime underlying fair and efficient international tax systems and to overcome some of the shortcomings of the first phase of the base erosion and profit shifting (BEPS) Project as highlighted by the Final Report on Action 1 in addressing the tax challenges of the digitalization of the economy[5] (Action 1). In particular, at the center of the debate is whether international income tax rules, developed in a "brick-and-mortar" economic environment more than a century ago, remain fit for purpose in the modern global economy.

The fundamental elements of the global tax system that determined where taxes should be paid (namely, "nexus" rules based on physical presence) and what portion of profits should be taxed (namely, "profit allocation" rules based on the ALP) have served their purpose well in that they have enshrined tax certainty and helped to eliminate double taxation thereby stimulating global trade.

According to the OECD, though, three important phenomena facilitated by digitalization—(i) scale without mass, (ii) reliance on intangible assets, and (iii) the centrality of data—posed serious challenges to elements of the foundations of the global tax system. Arguably, the outcome of Action 1 left many countries, particularly those not possessing a significant skillset at their disposal at the level of tax administrations, with an underlying discontent in not being capable of capturing "a significant

1. The PE concept may be found in Article 5 of the OECD and UN Model Tax Convention. The notion was already subjected to a significant revamp when, in 2015, the OECD published the Final Report on Action 7 of the BEPS Project, *Preventing the Artificial Avoidance of Permanent Establishment Status*, available at https://www.oecd.org/tax/beps/beps-actions/action7/, accessed August 28, 2020.
2. The ALP has been subjected to further sophistication with the release of Final Report on Actions 8-9-10 of the BEPS Project, Aligning Transfer Pricing Outcomes with Value Creation, available at https://www.oecd.org/tax/beps/aligning-transfer-pricing-outcomes-with-value-creation-actions-8-10-2015-final-reports-9789264241244-en.htm, accessed August 28, 2020. It shall be noted that both actions never questioned the legitimacy of either the PE notion or the effectiveness of the ALP, although acknowledging the shortcomings, in terms of lack of physical presence, triggered by the advent of new, highly digitalized business models.
3. *See* the ambitious deadline as outlined by the OECD Statement released on January 30, regarding the Two-Pillar approach to address the tax challenges arising from the digitalization of the economy, available at https://www.oecd.org/tax/beps/statement-by-the-oecd-g20-inclusive-framework-on-beps-january-2020.pdf, accessed August 28, 2020, whereby it is stated, in paragraph 1 [...] "Members of the Inclusive Framework affirm their commitment to reach an a agreement on a consensus-based solution by the end of 2020."
4. For a full list of the Member Countries, available at https://www.oecd.org/tax/beps/inclusive-framework-on-beps-composition.pdf, accessed August 28, 2020. As it is already known, with the introduction of the standard of exchange of information and the BEPS Project, the OECD, with the political support of the G20, has gained a predominant role in international law making. In order to address the concerns of legitimacy of the OECD and the G20 vis-à-vis developing countries, the OECD introduced the BEPS Inclusive Framework in which non-OECD, non-G20 countries participate on an equal footing in the implementation of these initiatives.
5. *See* the BEPS Final Report on Action 1, available at https://www.oecd.org/tax/beps/beps-actions/action1/, accessed August 28, 2020.

piece" of the cake (*rectius*, the taxable income) generated by interacting with customers in local jurisdictions. Stated otherwise, simply outlining policy options was no longer enough.

The above explains why, in March 2017, this timeline was accelerated at the initiative of the G20 Finance Ministers who asked the OECD/G20 IF, working through its Task Force on the Digital Economy (TFDE), for an Interim Report, which was delivered in March 2018 (the Interim Report). It contained an in-depth analysis of new and changing business models and possible implications for the international tax system (in particular nexus and profit allocation rules). The Interim Report also repeated the conclusion from the Action 1 report that it would be difficult, if not impossible, to ring-fence the digital economy from the rest of the economy. While members of the IF did not agree on the conclusions to be drawn from this analysis, they committed to continue working together on the development of a consensus-based long-term solution by 2020 with an update in 2019.

To progress toward a consensus-based solution, IF members made a number of proposals, some of which focused on the allocation of taxing rights through modifications to the rules on nexus and profit allocation and others on unresolved BEPS issues. The IF agreed on a Policy Note in January 2019 that grouped the proposals into two pillars—(i) one of nexus and profit allocation and (ii) another on ensuring a minimum level of taxation (the Global Anti-Base Erosion (GloBE) proposal[6])—and contained an agreement to examine them as a possible basis for consensus.

On Pillar 1, which is the subject of this contribution, the Policy Note recognized that the allocation of taxing rights between jurisdictions is at stake.

Following the January 2019 Policy Note, the IF continued working on the proposals on a without prejudice basis, considering how the gaps between the different positions of jurisdictions could be bridged and, in March 2019, sought inputs from external stakeholders through a public consultation process.

Based on those inputs, the IF delivered a detailed Program of Work (the May PoW) in May 2019. This was endorsed by the G20 Finance Ministers and Leaders in June 2019.

For Pillar 1, the May PoW identified and allocated work to explore the different proposals articulated by members of the IF. It acknowledged the commonalities between the proposals. However, it noted that available options would need to be reduced and some gaps bridged in order to deliver a consensus-based solution on Pillar 1. It further emphasized the need for an agreement on the outlines of the architecture of a Unified Approach by January 2020 in order to arrive at a consensus-based solution by the end of 2020.

Mindful of this goal, the Secretariat developed an approach to facilitate progress toward consensus on Pillar 1 (the so-called Unified Approach) that built on the commonalities identified in the PoW, taking account of the views expressed during the

6. For further details on the mechanics of the GloBE proposal, *see* J. Englisch, J. Becker, *International Effective Minimum Taxation: The GLOBE Proposal International Effective Minimum Taxation*, available at https://papers.ssrn.com/sol3/papers.cfm?abstract_id = 3370532, accessed August 28, 2020.

March public consultation and the need to deliver a solution that is acceptable to all members of the IF.

After discussions in the Steering Group of the IF, the proposal was discussed by the TFDE and further in the IF meetings in September and October 2019 and subsequently released to the public for comments on October 9, 2019.

Eventually, on January 31, 2020, the 137 countries comprising the IF released a statement (the January Statement) expressing strong support for reaching a multilateral agreement with respect to Pillar 1 and Pillar 2, reaffirming their commitment to reach a consensus-based solution by the end of 2020.

2 PILLAR 1 PROPOSAL: PROFIT ALLOCATION RULES

With specific reference to the Pillar 1 proposal, the OECD original proposal in the PoW focused on highly digitized businesses and explored three separate proposals based on "user participation," marketing intangibles', and "significant economic presence."

However, after the November 2019 public consultation organized by the OECD Secretariat,[7] it was apparent that a consensus on any of the three proposals was unlikely to be reached, particularly since they appeared to disproportionately impact U.S.-based MNEs operating highly digitized businesses.

In October 2019, the OECD Secretariat released a proposal for a "Unified Approach" under Pillar 1. The Unified Approach introduced a revised profit allocation rule applicable to all MNEs that are "in scope" with potential carve-outs for certain industries. For taxpayers in scope with a sufficient nexus to particular jurisdiction(s) (based on revenue or other thresholds), an appropriate return for routine activities will be excluded from the overall profit. The remainder will be deemed to be non-routine profits, a portion of which will be allocated among different eligible market jurisdictions based on variables such as sales.

More particularly, under the Unified Approach, a market jurisdiction may be entitled to tax the following three types of amounts:

(1) *Amount A*: The portion of deemed residual profit (i.e., a group's overall profit less a return for routine activities) that is allocated to a market jurisdiction.
(2) *Amount B*: A fixed return (which may vary by industry or region) for certain routine marketing and distribution activities taking place in a market jurisdiction.

7. The November 2019 OECD Public Consultation drew significant attention from both business, academia, and Non-governmental Organisations. Most notably, the Secretariat received 304 submissions exceeding 3,000 pages covering both technical and policy aspects of the proposal. Pending such process, respondents raised concerns on certain technical aspects of the proposed approach, including its complexity. Addressing these concerns and working on issues such as tax certainty, simplified compliance, dispute prevention and resolution, and elimination of double taxation is essential, and this note identifies different work streams to achieve this. Nevertheless, many were supportive of its objectives and guiding principles provided it would effectively prevent the proliferation of unilateral measures, avoid double.

(3) *Amount C*: Any profit attributable to activities in a market jurisdiction that go beyond routine marketing and distribution activities, to be calculated based on the ALP, which should not duplicate Amount A above.

Arguably and from a general standpoint, the new OECD proposal seems to trigger a seismic shift moving away from the ALP. In particular, it seems that the IF infers that further change in the transfer pricing system is necessary. Indeed, following the 2015 BEPS reports, the international tax framework has a transfer pricing system that has been improved in a number of respects, yet is one that contains some important gaps and potentially serious shortcomings. Two main issues indeed emerged after the final reports on BEPS in 2015 were delivered: those of (i) complexity and (ii) potential vulnerability to avoidance.

Regarding complexity, certain tensions exist between the wholly separate and independent assumptions made by the ALP and the integrated group-wide approach typically taken for managing the business dealings of MNEs. In particular, post-BEPS complexity levels in terms of (overly) compliance requirements became rather significant, including coping with the numerous functional analyses and detailed documentation requirements mushrooming around the world. With respect to vulnerability to the avoidance of the ALP, that seems to be "the issue" for the following reasons. Countries perceive that MNEs are at relative ease in entering into contrived tax planning arrangements involving (i) the creation of low-taxed group entities and (ii) the transfer to such entities from within the MNE group of significant amounts of value (in terms of capital or asset contributions).

The envisaged Unified Approach should put a stop to this alleged BEPS behavior. Against this background, is it really needed, or, stated otherwise, does the current framework of profit allocation rules not provide for the answers sought by the international (political foremost) community? Some critical issues should be discussed that may put into question whether the IF's new standard of allocation of taxing rights is fit for its purpose. For the sake of clarity, the current contribution will not address issues associated with the recognition of the new taxing right, Amount A, but the profit allocation issues associated with it.

3 AMOUNT A AND ITS INTERPLAY WITH THE NOTION OF VALUE CREATION

It seems that the way for the introduction of Amount A, and the related arguments warranting for the recognition of taxing rights in favor of market countries, was paved by the concept, endorsed since the inception of the 2013 BEPS Action Plan, of "value creation." More in detail, since the inception of the BEPS Project, the traditional "benefit principle" that is at the heart of corporate tax systems has been refined by the latter notion.

According to this new principle, the allocation of taxing rights between countries should be based on the level of value created by the local business units of a multinational firm on the territories of their respective jurisdictions. The theory behind this concept of value creation appears to be that the generation of "value" somehow reflects not only the contributions of the taxpayer's business units to the overall profit of the firm but also the amount of benefits received from the local government in that process.

As a result, it seems that at both the OECD and the European Union level, there appears to be agreement that the idea of "value creation" shall be the "northern star" guiding a new balance of international taxing rights. It is apparent that "value creation" has been a useful political device under the BEPS Action Plan regarding the exclusion of tax havens from claiming jurisdiction over a firm's profits.

Indeed, shell companies simply do not perform any substantial economic activity. However, it is very ambiguous how to divide the "taxable income cake" under the "value creation" paradigm when several jurisdictions compete with each other, can each fairly show that the taxpayer exercises actual economic functions in their territory, and that the taxpayer benefits from public goods provided by local government. This seems to be a pretty strong assumption by the OECD which infers that such concept, once endorsed at the political/IF level, can then allow for the allocation of a "quantum" of taxing rights under Amount A. Arguably, that seems to be the very first quasi-departure from the ALP as the reliance of users/subscribers/consumers in a market jurisdiction warrant an allocation of taxing rights.

However, what the OECD takes for granted, instead, are voices of strong disagreement within the tax community. For instance, certain advocacy groups have heavily criticized excessive reliance on the role of users in the value chain[8] and, indeed, they may have a point as, otherwise, the side effect of such an approach would be negative, reverse "ring-fencing," generating detrimental opportunities for planning.

From the author's standpoint, though, it would be preferable that the definition of scope of enterprises subject to Amount A be sector neutral. This would be accomplished by ensuring that the levels of deemed routine return and the deemed non-routine return to be allocated under Amount A are the same for all sectors. In this respect, for example, the author believes that there should not be a different percentage allocation of profits under Amount A for highly digitalized businesses compared to any other enterprise that also falls within the scope definition and generates the same non-routine returns through the use of non-trade intangibles.

Arguably, the goal of the Unified Approach is to combine elements of three distinct theories of taxation beyond the traditional nexus rules and the ALP and that the "user engagement" proposal was one of those three theories. From a profit allocation standpoint, however, it is the author's convincement that the Unified Approach should rest principally on actual financial results achieved by larger enterprises utilizing non-trade intangible property (IP) to achieve non-routine returns. A tax system should rest its critical definitions on actual economic activity and actual profits and not on some hypotheticals that need to be assessed against economic evidence.

8. *See* Digital Economy Group written submission at the OECD October 2019 Discussion Draft on the Unified Approach on Pillar I.

3.1 The Mechanics of Profit Allocation under the Unified Approach Proposal: An Overlap of Two Antithetic Worlds

As mentioned, under the Unified Approach, a market jurisdiction's share of an MNE's taxable income will comprise up to three elements. A jurisdiction can claim the first (Amount A) if the MNE meets the threshold for the new non-physical concept of nexus in that jurisdiction. Assuming that the elements for the existence of Amount A (i.e., the new taxing right) are met, the determination of Amount A is based on a formulaic application of the concepts of the residual profit split method familiar to transfer pricing practitioners (although, given its formulaic design, it is similar to the transfer pricing method in name only).

It starts with the MNE group's overall global profit as reported in the group's consolidated financial statements. Next, from that global group profit, the amount deemed to constitute residual profit is identified. This step will be based on a predetermined rate or percentage that will serve as the cutoff for routine profits, and the amount of global profit over that cutoff will be the group's deemed residual profit.

Once that amount of the group's residual profit is determined, a share—again, based on a prespecified fixed percentage that could vary by industry—will be deemed allocable in total to the market jurisdictions possessing the new taxing right.

Finally, the total residual profit as determined under the preceding steps will be allocated among the relevant market jurisdictions via a formula based on the sales in each jurisdiction (and possibly other factors that serve as indicia of consumer or user involvement with the relevant MNE).

Both the October 2019 consultation document and the January 2020 statement by the IF leaves open the possibility that the calculation of Amount A may be performed at the level of a given business line for an MNE rather than for the MNE as a whole. That is to prevent distortions when the MNE has multiple (and disparate) business lines that differ in terms of profitability and markets served. Similarly, the documents also mention the possibility of performing the calculation on a regional basis (relying on regional segmentation of financial statement data).

Importantly, both documents describe the residual income captured by Amount A as coming out of the tax base of jurisdictions that, under existing income allocation rules (the ALP), claim non-routine profits—e.g., as owners of IP. Amount B would apply to a market jurisdiction only when an MNE has a PE in that jurisdiction as a result of some combination of sales, marketing, and distribution operations. For Amount B, the Unified Approach stipulates a fixed baseline return (e.g., as a fixed percentage of sales) for routine market-facing activities. The OECD documents do not specify how that baseline would be determined or how the return should be determined and whether that fixed remuneration should vary by industry or region.

Finally, and unlike Amounts A and B, Amount C will be determined under the application of the ALP. It allows taxpayers and (more likely) tax authorities to allocate income to a market jurisdiction above the baseline return for routine sales and distribution types of activities. That is intended to reflect facts and circumstances when the scope of an MNE's functions and activities in a jurisdiction are viewed to exceed the routine level covered by the baseline return under Amount B. Given its reliance on the

ALP, Amount C also applies only to countries that meet the current rules based on physical presence via a PE.

At first glance, the new rules to allocate an MNE's taxable income to market jurisdictions under each constituent element of the Unified Approach depart quite significantly (at least with respect to Amount A and Amount B) from the ALP.

Amount A is indeed determined under a formulaic method that unambiguously falls outside the ALP while Amount B is determined in a manner that can be reconciled as a simplified and safe-harbor-like application of the ALP (one that takes discretion and flexibility away from taxpayers).

Both the need for Amount C under a given set of facts and the determination of the amount respect the ALP. Thus, even in determining the income allocation for market jurisdictions, the Unified Approach does not abandon the ALP entirely in a politically savvy compromise which should try, at least in part, to save the status quo of the current international framework. Whether this will also come at the expense of simplifying the implementation of international tax rules remains to be seen.

Further, and outside the scope of the Unified Approach, the income allocation to and among source jurisdictions—or those where an MNE locates manufacturing operations, research, and development facilities, personnel who perform and deliver specific types of services (internally or externally), and IP—will continue to be governed by the ALP (at least to some extent). The continued scope and relevance of the principle—that is, the extent to which it will govern income allocation to (and among) source jurisdictions (as well as among market jurisdictions via Amount C)—will be constrained by the formulaic rules of the Unified Approach.

The principle's remaining scope will be determined by the extent to which the formulaic measures under the Unified Approach act as binding constraints on the income allocation that would have otherwise resulted from an unencumbered application of the ALP. The portion of an MNE's global pre-tax profit that will be allocated under the formulaic rules of Amounts A and B is what the Unified Approach scope income amount is intended to measure.

The reallocated income is intended to measure a related but different effect of the OECD's proposed rules.

The question about the effective administrability of the new system is due to the fact that the Unified Approach will add a separate income allocation standard (based on a formulaic approach) that will operate *in conjunction with* the ALP (and constrained in the manner described above). As a result, the overlap of two apparently odd systems will generate an income allocation outcome different from the status quo (or any future outcome generated by an unconstrained application of the ALP).

3.2 Amount A Computation: Some Critical Considerations

3.2.1 Financial Segmentation

The starting point of the Secretariat's proposal for determining Amount A is the identification of the MNE group's profits (full consolidated or segmented information) from financial statements. Financial statement information represents a formal and independently verified set of data that businesses and markets use for a variety of purposes unrelated to tax. This information is generally available and uses reliable financial figures, including profits.

It makes sense to rely on the use of segmented financial information only to the extent that the segmented information is required or otherwise disclosed in publicly issued financial statements. Any segregation not subjected to the rigor of a financial audit would be burdensome and susceptible to disputes. Such position stems from the fact that any use of segmented financial information should be solely at the option of taxpayers because using this information to compute one or more of the amounts under the proposal would necessarily result in additional administrative burden for taxpayers.

The relevant accounting principles should only be those that the enterprise uses in its audited statements. Any measurement standard that allows multiple jurisdictions the discretion to determine consolidated or segmented profits through methods other than by reference to published financial statements will result in significant controversies between Member States and between Member States and taxpayers. The author sees no merit to the idea that a separate set of accounting standards could be developed for the sole purpose of complying with the proposed Unified Approach.

More importantly, the design features of Amount A should be selected in light of the intent of its proponents that Amount A represents only a modest portion of the MNE's non-routine returns. Features of any formula to calculate Amount A should reflect the intent that, as a matter of economics, the portion of Amount A to be allocated should not include any return to trade intangibles, capital, or risk.

As the IF has repeatedly stated that there is no expectation that the Pillar Project should be approached on a "without prejudice basis," it seems an upward climb pushing the computation toward global formulary apportionment or destination-based taxation not least because the agreement among 137 countries may seem difficult to achieve.

In all cases for which an Amount A will be allocated to a market state, the functions, assets, and risks actually giving rise to the non-routine return will continue to exist and operate in the surrender state (or states). Even though Amount A will be determined beyond the ALP, any such amount must properly acknowledge the functions, assets, and risks performed in the surrender states and elsewhere outside the market jurisdictions.

The focus on consumer-facing businesses reflects the fact that an underlying policy principle of the Unified Approach is to address non-routine returns arising from the development and exploitation of marketing intangibles. If there were to be any differential allocation by sector, the allocation should be reduced for those enterprises with high research and development expenses. Enterprises with high research and development expenses will have greater returns to trade intangibles which, in principle, would reduce the portion of non-routine return that is potentially allocable to a market state. Enterprises that provide digital services generally make heavy R&D and infrastructure investments and undergo heavy investment cycles before a product can be brought to market. Any new taxation scheme must preserve an appropriate return to the innovation exercised and risk capital deployed for the state that supported those investments.

The author, therefore, supports the Secretariat's observation that one of the most important objectives in the implementation of the Unified Approach would be to keep the compliance and administrative burdens as low as possible while properly taxing profits where they are due. This is an especially important consideration in the design and implementation of Amount A since this is an entirely new concept that will cause some disruption for both tax administrations and taxpayers alike.

However, it is also worth noting that, notwithstanding the fact that one of the Secretariat proposal's main aims is "simplicity, stabilisation of the tax system, and increased tax certainty in implementation,"[9] any serious deviation from consolidated international tax principles (related to both nexus and income allocation as well as adoption of international accounting rules that are truly applicable on a global basis) warrants careful consideration of all possible drawbacks involved in its concrete implementation before proceeding.

Indeed, the introduction of new international standards (completely unrelated to the PE concept or to the ALP) will inevitably increase complexity not only in the transitory period but also as follows: (i) MNEs will need to have the relevant time to be placed in the position to review the transfer pricing policy that has already been amended to reflect the BEPS Action 1 recommendations, and (ii) MNEs will be required to bear extra compliance burdens due to the implementation of the Unified Approach. For instance, the application of the three-tiered approach by the UA will require necessary coordination (*rectius*, grandfathering) with the existing advance pricing agreements (APAs) and/or mutual agreement procedures (MAPs) concluded by taxpayers and tax administrations.

Furthermore, the introduction of a holistic and simplified approach should, in any case, take into consideration the ever-greater complexity of business models. Indeed, businesses are increasingly operating under matrix organizational structures in which the geographical and product scope are intertwined, and the global functions of the headquarters perform relevant activities (and thus bear the related costs). It is, therefore, recommended that regional and geographic differences are factored into the developments of the new system (although such considerations are more relevant for Amounts B and C rather than Amount A).

Lastly, a key operational aspect of Amount A is related to the ways that the consolidated profit generated by the MNE group is allocated. For the determination of Amount A, it is essential to arrive at a common definition of the MNE group being subject to the determination of the consolidated profit.

For determining the basis of profit allocation, there are potentially four separate avenues, i.e., determining a common tax base, following an international standard, following the residence state's standard, or determining the profit in each state separately. However, relying on a foreign state's accounting system would raise a number of legal issues related to their recognition while determining the basis for profit

9. *See* Secretariat Proposal, at paragraph 10.

allocation in all states on a stand-alone basis would result in a tremendous administrative burden for MNEs.

Therefore, alternatives should be considered but not new solutions. For instance, one option may be represented by the residence states' consolidated accounts with a possibility to adjust these accounts if considered appropriate by the host state. Another possibility would be to take international accounting standards as the reference for all states which they could then translate into their national accounting systems, if considered necessary. These occasions may be rather rare as many differences between international accounting standards and local accounting standards are balanced over time rather than being permanent (except goodwill or provisions for pensions).

Another important technical aspect related to Amount A is the possible need for segmentation of its accounts. In fact, according to the January 30, 2020 Statement by the IF's Project of Work,[10] the scope of application of the first tier of rules for profit allocation would be limited to (i) automated digital services and (ii) consumer-facing businesses while all other activities would fall out of scope of Amount A. Segmentation would allow excluding profits from out-of-scope activities when an MNE group performs both in- and out-of-scope activities.

From the Amount A standpoint, MNE groups may perform both in- and out-of-scope activities and hence generate in- and out-of-scope revenue. In order to ensure that the agreed scope of Amount A applies as intended, it would be necessary to segment the revenue of those MNE groups.

Two immediate considerations shall be flagged. It seems clear that significant underlying political considerations have erased one of the major outcomes of the Action 1 Final Report on BEPS and, namely, that "it is impossible to ring-fence the digital economy."[11] First, limiting the application of Amount A to categories that may be (especially consumer-facing businesses) loosely defined triggers the effect of negatively ring-fencing the application of the rules aimed at reshuffling the international tax order. Second, the author wonders what is the rationale of referring to the Unified Approach as a solution for "addressing the tax challenges of digitalization" as there is the reallocation of taxing rights between residence and source state at stake with a clear bias in favor of the latter in advancing a new system akin to destination-based taxation.

3.2.2 *Amounts B and C: Critical Considerations*

Assuming Amount B is a fixed baseline return, it could be calculated either as a percentage of operating margin in the local jurisdiction or as a function of costs. A cost-based approach may better reflect activities performed in a jurisdiction.

10. *See* paragraphs 22 and 29.
11. *See* press-release on Final Report on Action 1 BEPS [...] "As the digital economy is increasingly becoming the economy itself, it would not be feasible to ring-fence the digital economy from the rest of the economy for tax purposes," available at https://www.oecd.org/publications/addressing-the-tax-challenges-of-the-digital-economy-action-1-2015-final-report-9789264241046-en.htm, accessed August 28, 2020.

For example, MNE car manufacturers may sell cars in local jurisdictions through their own dealerships or through franchise arrangements with third-party dealerships. Using a cost basis for the Amount B return would produce a larger Amount B for the local affiliate of a manufacturer that sells at the retail level (e.g., through wholly owned storefronts) compared to a local affiliate operating under a franchise or wholesale business model that would earn comparatively less because it has lower costs. However, using a cost approach would create additional burdens on MNEs and tax authorities for ensuring that costs are reflected accurately, including additional record-keeping and reporting requirements.

A more straightforward approach to calculate a baseline return under Amount B would be to establish a return based on the operating profit margin. This approach, however, would less accurately reflect differences in local activities and cost structures related to the MNE business models mentioned above, particularly if returns were based on local gross margins. Using a net margin approach may result in a slightly better reflection of activities performed in the local jurisdiction by incorporating certain costs but would still not be an accurate proxy for such activities. Therefore, in order to balance ease of administration with approximating activities performed in the local market, the author recommends a cost-based approach with a safe harbor for the net margin approach.

Additionally, the author believes Amount C should be considered to represent the arm's length return above Amount B and would be determined according to existing transfer pricing rules. In order to maintain consistency with Amounts B and A, Amount C should then be adjusted to reflect other returns earned by the relevant entity that are unrelated to sales in its jurisdiction and thus should not affect its market allocation.

From a more economic standpoint, a helpful reference in delineating the notion of "functionality" (and, to a larger degree, to that of value creation) is the economic indicator of showing a positive correlation between SGA/Sales[12] intensity and return on sales (ROS) results for independent distributors. Theoretically, it corresponds to the concept of value creation through additional activities and risk bearing.

Lastly, with respect to both Amounts B and C, each of these amounts should be determined based on local book reporting. For Amount C, this would be consistent with current transfer pricing practices and, for both Amounts B and C, using book reporting would maintain consistency with the Amount A base, resulting in less risk of overlap between each of the amounts.

3.3 What If Amount B Becomes the Center of the New World

Arguably, it seems that, although politically the way has been paved for having a new taxing right, Amount A, departing from the ALP, raises doubts whether its implementing viability still persists.

In particular, it seems to the author that, when analyzing Amount A in further detail, it is not readily apparent from the January 2020 document how the routine

12. SG&A refer to supervisory, general, and administrative expenses.

group profit margin relates to deemed routine returns in each market jurisdiction (Amount B). As a general matter, this author believes that routine group profit margin should represent a sufficiently high percentage of operating profits so that it exceeds Amount B; this will minimize double taxation or double counting risk.

In view of the above principle, the actual calculation of the routine group profit margin will be a very important component of the Pillar 1 approach and should result in a profit proportion large enough to encapsulate Amount B while involving easy-to-administer calculations. One option is to base the calculation of a return on costs—e.g., operating expenses and internal costs of the MNE. Other approaches may include a fixed percentage of sales, a percentage of operating margin (determined by an agreed-upon percentage based on industry or business line), or the lesser of a cost-based return and the percentage of sales/operating margin. Using the percentage of sales or operating margin metric would be easier to administer, but a "lesser of the two" approach could more accurately approximate routine returns.

From a practical standpoint, keeping in mind the ultimate goal of simplicity and ease of administrability of the system, the solution would also consider a return to "origin" in that profit allocation should not necessarily be grounded on a potentially subjective application of formulaic percentages but rather on a more refined application of the ALP. There are indeed conceptual merits in believing that an important feature to achieve consensus on the Unified Approach is to retain at least part of the framework created by the final reports on BEPS Actions 1, 8, 9, and 10.

Reference is made in particular to the application of a modified profit split method that relies on the identification of the key drivers of the value chain of each MNE to determine the attribution of taxing rights over an actual residual profit computation. In this respect, the author suggests streamlining the envisaged mechanism of profit computation by moving from a three-tier to a two-tier formula, excluding Amount C from the computation. The latter tier may be factored in the determination of Amount A provided it is grounded on the application of the ALP, therefore, avoiding the risk of double counting of profits.

This would require making Amount B the cornerstone of the new system (extending its application to both baseline marketing activities and low-value-adding manufacturing functions) together with a refined application of the profits computation under Amount A. The author would advocate not pursuing the attribution of residual profits by means of a formulaic methodology as it is believed that the ALP (when accompanied by a detailed value chain analysis) is better served to guarantee an allocation of (residual) profits, which would be perceived as equitable and fair by both developed and developing countries, including market countries. It is helpful to emphasize the importance of reconsidering whether Amount A would always apply in all of those instances in which an MNE group already has a taxable presence in a market country. This is because the author perceives that there is a potential risk for double taxation as the new nexus rule of Amount A would apply on top of the taxing rights over baseline marketing functions already acknowledged with Amount B. The latter tier should, in this author's view, apply irrespective of whether an MNE has a physical presence in a market country.

The overarching objective of the Pillar 1 is to maintain a level playing field between countries by ensuring the international tax framework guarantees fairness and avoids double taxation. For this reason, it does not make much sense to advocate either (i) a carve-out applicable to certain industries or (ii) a carve-out applicable to transactions focusing only on business-to-consumers as both the October 2019 and January 2020 documents seem to infer.

As to new profit allocation rules, the author suggests then to start from Amount B as the centerpiece of the new international tax framework for the remuneration of baseline marketing activities. The computation of Amount B may be implemented by leveraging the important work carried out by the OECD in 2013 on the use of bilateral and multilateral safe harbors. In particular, the author suggests using the following profit level indicators (PLIs) with industry-based fixed margins: (i) ROS of 1%-3% for low-value-adding distribution activities and (ii) return on total costs (RoTC) of 5%-8% for low-value-adding manufacturing and market support activities.

The new mechanism must contemplate that the burden of proof for Amount B shifts to the tax administration in the event they want to adopt a different/greater percentage than the safe harbor. The author believes that such a solution would also allow factoring the quantum of profits associated with manufacturing activities in the allocation of taxing rights. In this regard, the author respectfully suggests taking the latter functions into account as the consultation document seems to be too unbalanced in focusing on distribution activities in market countries.

It will be important to also include, for a proper delineation of the connection between Amount A and Amount B, what is deemed to be the reference to "baseline marketing and distribution activities." If that is the case, this will also require an important coordination exercise with the current transfer pricing framework of Chapter I of the TPG. Therefore, section D2 (paragraphs 1.60 onwards) elaborated on the notion of "accurate delineation of the transaction" to move away from transfer pricing labels which, instead, will become the core once again of the new system of Amount B.

The actual (and not deemed) residual profit to be excluded from the computation of Amount A shall be determined by resorting to a residual profit split methodology. As anticipated above, the latter shall be anchored to the ALP as the only accurate way to reflect the impact of intangibles and capital in the value-creation process of every MNE. The author believes the current reference by the consultation document to formulaic percentages would increase the risk of arbitrary attribution of profits with an increased risk of controversies by countries that would become even more difficult to manage if compared with the current state of play with respect to MAPs. Lastly, the new taxing right, while sticking at least in part to the ALP, would require moving away from the identification of the "significant people functions" as, nowadays, many digitized businesses do not need individuals in a market country to carry out distribution activities. As a result, the author instead suggests focusing on the identification of "significant functions" performed at the group MNE level irrespective of the locations of the individuals who carry them out.

More in detail on Amount B, a compromise alternative to the above approach could be computing the latter amount in a formulaic manner while maintaining a strong correlation to the ALP.

It is a challenging task to select a formulaic approach for Amount B as business economics vary widely by industry, geography, and product lines. Moreover, the types of activities considered to be "routine marketing and distribution" may have slight variations by industry, business, or region. For instance, a single distributor net income target expressed as a percentage of sales for all taxpayers is problematic due to this variability.

Rather than a fixed starting point expressed as income as a percentage of sales, an alternative better approach may be to derive the Amount B income allocation as a function of earnings before tax that is calculated using an allocation and segmentation approach consistent with Amount A. This alternative approach may more appropriately address how to calculate a distributor return for a variety of business models in a formulaic way. As a simple explanation, low profitability businesses (5% or below) cannot afford, long term, to pay their distributors much above 1% of sales (e.g., automotive dealers), but most distributors may not be able to stay in business for multiple years with compensation much below 1% of sales. Conversely, very high margin businesses may well incent their distributors well above 3% of sales commission to pursue incremental highly profitable sales (e.g., pharmaceutical, technology firms, and others).

The author acknowledges that a formulaic approach may not accurately describe all industry and taxpayer circumstances but could be refined to describe perhaps 80%-90% of all outcomes. This is the inherent trade-off in the adoption of a simplified formulaic method.

There a couple of last considerations. In the author's view, the Unified Approach to calculating Amount A remains too complex to explain to the public. As it may be inferred from the above, the author believes that there is an arbitrary distinction being drawn between market intangibles and trade intangibles. If Amount A is instead thought of in terms of a *market access fee* it may be simpler to use a fixed percentage of the group operating profit or loss by industry sector, i.e., there would be no need to separately calculate routine returns, returns to capital, risk or intangibles. This does not remove the complexity of the reallocation between countries but at least the basis for the taxable income is transparent and simple.

Overall, equating Amount A to the new nexus and other countries where tax returns are already filed may have the effect of displacing withholding tax credits for the country that has a correspondingly reduced taxable income, and this will result in double taxation. The author, therefore, recommends that, jointly with a move toward an international tax system that includes more scope for the reallocation of income, the role and function of withholding taxes should be critically reviewed. Ultimately, there is no policy justification for withholding taxes (that act as source-based taxation rights) if taxing rights are going to be rebalanced to source countries.

The current 2020 January document entails that Amount B is relevant only when there is a limited risk distributor (LRD) operating model. This has to be read in conjunction with a Pillar 2 minimum tax rate which, once set at an effective level, would remove the tax arbitrage incentive from using a LRD model, albeit sound commercial reasons may sit behind the choice of the operating model. Pillar 2 in combination with Amount A for LRD models may have the most practical impact in reducing the number of tax disputes insofar as the mechanics of the three tiers of profit allocation are well coordinated with each other.

Lastly, on Amount B, if regional or industry classifications would be introduced, it would be helpful if the final guidance could be very clear on the ordering of screening criteria. In particular, it should be clarified whether it is necessary to elevate geographic screening or use narrow industry classification codes since the results from a broadened approach will look very different from some current expectations of typical benchmarking. For example, instead of wholesalers of after-market car parts being used as apparent comparables for national marketing subsidiaries of global car manufacturers, a set of comparables that include marketing activities involving mobile telecommunications products or kitchen appliances that show relevance to the economics of the delineated functions, assets, and risks may be proposed more reliably under a broadened approach. Instead of computer assemblers being used as apparent comparables for chip manufacturers, one may propose more reliably under a broadened approach a set of comparables that include food manufacturing and which demonstrate similar key financial ratios. Instead of comparables from the same country or region, one may propose more reliably relevant comparable from other countries, as at times for certain industries, geographic differences are immaterial.

4 CONCLUSIONS

From a general standpoint, the "Unified Approach" is the first step of a process that may lead to a gradual fading out, or at least reconsideration, of a number of longstanding international tax concepts, such as the PE notion as a single international nexus for taxing business profits. In particular, the OECD project seems to suggest introducing a new self-standing clause creating a new nexus for highly digitalized consumer-facing business as well as for automated digital services, capturing the active participation of such business to the economic life of a country. From an international tax standpoint, such a future clause would prevail as *lex specialis* over the existing provisions on business income as endorsed by Article 7 of the OECD (and UN) Model Tax Conventions.

Against the background mentioned above, though, some words of caution are needed. For the time being, the project is envisaging December 2020 to achieve a political consensus at the G20 level as embedded in a final report.[13] This entails that, before the new international tax architecture will see the light with domestic implementation at the country level, at least two to three years at best will be required (as

13. *See* the Communique of G20 Finance Ministers Meeting held in Saudi Arabia on February 21-22, available at https://g20.org/en/g20/Documents/Communique%CC%81%20Final%2022-23%20February%202020.pdf, accessed August 28, 2020, whereby it is stated that [...] "We encourage further progress on both Pillars to overcome remaining differences and reaffirm our commitment to reach a consensus-based solution with a final report to be delivered by the end of 2020. We stress the importance of the G20/OECD Inclusive Framework on BEPS agreeing on the key policy features of a global and consensus-based solution by July 2020, which would form the basis of a political agreement. We reiterate the importance of international cooperation to complete this work and ensure tax certainty."

such changes will require changes to both the model tax convention as well as constitutional amendments). Moreover, the political momentum underlying the project seems, by pushing to find a solution by "all means," to overlook the need for simplicity required by tax administrations (particularly those representing developing or transitioning economies) in managing the overall system.

Although, initially, the Unified Approach seemed to be contemplating a simplification of the system[14] by almost making sure that a departure from the ALP would have occurred. However the current ongoing discussions seem to point at a solution where, on the one hand, the ordinary transfer pricing regime would remain in place (with the application of Amounts B and C), whereas the new taxing right (i.e., Amount A) would respond to the new logic of a formulaic approach. The author doubts that such a new system, although understandable from a tax policy standpoint, would result in simplicity of administration for both taxpayers and tax administrations.

The effectiveness of any (domestic or international) tax policy analysis lies in its (relative, when talking about taxes) ease of administrability and capability of being successfully implemented. To this end, having systems that are at odds with each other (namely, a formulaic approach for Amount A and the conventional application of the ALP on the others) require a new linking point in order to be effective; such a new link may be represented by a reconsideration of the notion of "value creation" that became so central since the outset of the BEPS Project in 2013.

In particular, the author believes that, to capture the impact of digitalization, rethinking value creation would be necessary. In particular, the understanding of the term "functionality" would need to be modified, i.e., not limit it to people's functions. Rather, the understanding of functionality should be extended to automated processes as well as to the provision of data. Therefore, value, value creation, and the model that encapsulates these concepts irrespective of where functions are physically located (at least for Amount A purposes) must be understood.

Therefore, the demand side is included in the contribution analysis for a reason: it allows (more) profit allocation to market and source countries as all value is created jointly. User participations in the various users' jurisdictions (without any physical presence) are likely to enhance the value of intangibles especially in the case of platform business models, therefore, subconsciously contributing to the value-creation process.

When it comes to the introduction of the new taxing right (Amount A), assuming there is to be a new nexus rule, the author generally supports the notion that it should be a stand-alone rule that is separate from PE standards. That being said, care should be taken to ensure that market jurisdictions do not discriminate against taxpayers subject to the new nexus rule relative to residents carrying on similar activities (i.e., market jurisdictions should be subject to a nondiscrimination obligation comparable to

14. *See* paragraph 17 of the OECD Secretariat Proposal for a Unified Approach published for public consultation in October 2019 where it was clearly stated that "Moreover, there seems to be agreement that the arm's length principle is becoming an increasing source of complexity and that simplification would be desirable to contain the increasing administration and compliance costs of trying to apply it."

that found in Article 24(3) of the OECD Model Tax Convention with respect to the taxation of profits allocable to those jurisdictions under the new rules).

Similarly, countries should agree that the application of the new nexus rule will not create commercial registration or value-added tax obligations that would otherwise not apply nor have any other legal effects beyond those necessary for the taxation of Amount A.

The international convention would need to be rethought in order to assume that users are value co-creators and to reflect back to the original idea of taxing profits in the country where resources are located and directed. The cornerstone for rethinking has been laid due to the OECD's value creation concept. The suggestion here would be, rather than turning the new model upside down, improve the international tax system with tools that are already existing (*see* the OECD sample memoranda of understanding on bilateral safe harbors[15]) which may turn out to be pretty helpful when it comes to the application of Amount B, for instance.

Transfer pricing safe harbors can, in principle, reduce the reliance on benchmarking studies and can be designed to align with a country's fiscal policy objectives and sources of economic activity. However, eligibility criteria can be difficult to determine, and tax administrations may tend to design narrow entry definitions that can reduce their effectiveness. As an aside, descriptive eligibility criteria can be difficult to draft and interpret; instead, just like the use of economically significant financial ratios in the context of screening for comparability, financial ratios could also be used to determine eligibility appropriately and clearly (e.g., marketing spend above a certain ratio to total costs would lead to non-eligibility). Nevertheless, improvements to eligibility criteria may not improve the effectiveness of the safe harbor as much as a safe harbor that is more universal in design but with specific exemptions. Such an approach, for example, as outlined below may be feasible.

It is noticeable that the examples of transactions for which safe harbors may be appropriate all have the absence of significant risk in common. In turn, the absence of significant risk means that the expected profitability across a wide range of activities is likely to be predictable and stable within a narrow range and may be less affected by any market differences between countries, leading to greater prospects of the adoption of common approaches across countries.

It may be worthwhile to consider harnessing this common feature to provide guidance on designing an effective safe harbor that covers all intra-group activities when control of economically significant risks is not exercised in the country. An exception would be certain specified sectors that may be important for the country's economy or present other policy concerns or risk factors. Such a safe harbor would likely require the taxpayer to provide supporting material which could include contract terms and a risk statement modeled on the principles of Chapter I of the OECD

15. *See* OECD Transfer Pricing Guidelines, 2017 Annex I to Chapter IV. Sample Memoranda of Understanding for Competent Authorities to Establish Bilateral Safe Harbours, available at https://www.oecd-ilibrary.org/taxation/oecd-transfer-pricing-guidelines-for-multinational-enterprises-and-tax-administrations-2017/annex-i-to-chapter-iv-sample-memoranda-of-understanding-for-competent-authorities-to-establish-bilateral-safe-harbours_tpg-2017-19-en, accessed August 28, 2020.

guidelines. Resources could be spent for defining appropriate PLIs and various profit levels, but such an approach brings complexity.

If one of the key reasons for turning to safe harbors is to avoid the difficult task of finding reliable comparables, or indeed any comparables, it may be sensible to adopt a one-size-fits-all solution: that is, one PLI (the author suggests mark-up on total costs) and a fixed mark-up rate.

The author also advocates for the possibility of using Amount B as the means to standardize remuneration on the low-value-adding distribution of activities (of goods AND services) and significantly reduce controversy around the notion of "LRDs." In this respect, despite the OECD guidance on business restructurings introduced in 2010 and refined in 2017 and the work mentioned above for expanding the use safe harbors for low-risk distribution activities, tax administrations continue to scrutinize LRD. From a tax administration perspective, some MNE groups tend to rely on LRD models to trigger a reduction in taxable amounts for countries where the surrendering entity is located (i.e., stable but low returns).

Although there is no anecdotal evidence confirming the number of audits and MAP disputes focused on LRDs as opposed to other distribution models, baseline distribution activities would also include distribution arrangements with routine levels of functionality, no ownership of intangibles, and no or limited risks.

From a taxpayer's perspective, the ultimate goal is to have a system in place that will avoid double taxation and guarantee certainty. In this respect, the dynamics surrounding the application of Amount C will play a major role. Undoubtedly, the new system of international allocation of taxing rights will require the set-up of an advance dispute prevention process that is modeled as a voluntary process akin to a multilateral APA with specific timelines and an obligation for competent authorities to come to an agreement.

Thus, a taxpayer has a choice to opt into or stay outside the process. This may also be a necessary feature for some countries so that the taxpayer is always free to pursue domestic remedies (even if that means ending up with double tax). The process could be included in a new multilateral convention (and/or in coordinated domestic law). While multilateral APAs and the MAP are already a solution on the basis of existing treaties, certain representative features of the new process and the obligation to agree are not. In conclusion, the author believes there should be effective mechanisms to ensure the elimination of both economic and juridical double taxation with respect to Amount A.

In this respect, a new provision will be needed for eliminating juridical double taxation with respect to Amount A. For example, if Amount A is taxed by a market jurisdiction directly to a non-resident entity within the group that lacks a physical presence in the market jurisdiction, that entity should be entitled to double tax relief in its country of residence. The tax benefit that should be available in the residence country may take the form of an exemption, deduction, or foreign tax credit.

Guaranteeing that this double tax relief is available will require a very clear set of rules on which jurisdictions are considered "surrender" jurisdictions and how their double tax relief obligations will be calculated. One approach to identifying the entities to be taxed on Amount A by the market jurisdictions could be to identify members of the group that have profit margins above the Amount A "deemed routine" profit margin level as determined by entity level profit and loss statements prepared in accordance with the group parent company International Financial reporting Standards or local Generally Accepted Accounting Principles.

Each market jurisdiction could then tax its share of Amount A to those entities in proportion to their profit amounts above the deemed routine level. Those entities' residence countries should then be obligated to give those entities double tax relief for an amount equal to the aggregate Amount A taxed to those entities by market jurisdictions. This may require changes to source and/or characterization rules that are applicable in the residence jurisdictions. Amount A profits allocated to the market jurisdiction may not be viewed as being properly sourced there under traditional sourcing rules in the residence jurisdictions and, therefore, may not otherwise be eligible for double tax relief. Similarly, if Amount A profits are considered to be distributed out of entities that have been taxed directly on them by market jurisdictions to other members of the group and potentially subjected to tax in the latter members' residence countries (e.g., as dividends or CFC or Pillar 1 inclusions), those other members of the group should be entitled to double tax relief in their residence countries.

Rules may also be needed to take into account the taxes that the market jurisdiction may have imposed on outgoing payments (e.g., if a subsidiary in the market jurisdiction paid royalties on intangibles and if the group's profits from those intangibles were effectively taken into account in calculating Amount A reallocated to the market jurisdiction, any withholding taxes imposed on the royalties should be refunded by the market jurisdiction). If those withholding taxes were imposed on a group payee that is the entity on which the market jurisdiction will be imposing the Amount A tax, the market jurisdiction could instead credit the withholding tax against that Amount A tax liability and refund any excess.

It seems that the technical issues to be addressed are multiple while the time is scarce: it is hoped that the OECD Secretariat will be successful in building consensus with 137 countries and getting through a process of which the failure would not result in a plan "B" but in Plan "C," which would stand for Chaos.

CHAPTER 7

Recent Developments on Transfer Pricing and Intra-Group Financing

*Amanda Pletz & Diana Kabir**

* The chapter expresses the views of the authors and not the views of NERA. The authors also thank Emmanuel Llinares, Gary Lambert, and Georg Dettmann for their contributions.

Intercompany financing transactions have been a much-discussed topic in recent years. Due to the wide range of complexities surrounding the pricing of financing transactions, it has become apparent that the general transfer pricing guidelines that are available cannot be applied as a simple broad stroke to these intricate arrangements. Consequently, organizations such as the Organisation for Economic Co-operation and Development (OECD) and the United Nations (UN) have begun focusing more on the issue of financial intercompany transactions.

In February 2020, the OECD released the final "Transfer Pricing Guidance on Financial Transactions" that was a response to additional mandated work as part of the Base Erosion and Profit Shifting (BEPS) Actions 8-10. The document is intended to be an addition to the OECD Transfer Pricing Guidelines and includes guidance for transfer pricing issues on treasury activities including loans, cash pooling, guarantees, and captive insurance companies.

Similarly, in April 2019, the Committee of Experts on International Cooperation in Tax Matters released a new draft chapter on financing transactions for the UN *Practical Manual on Transfer Pricing for Developing Countries*.

These developments have created pause for thought as the recent OECD and UN thinking and relevant case law are considered, and the authors provide an analytical framework on how to effectively deal with some complexities stemming from financing in a transfer pricing context.

1 KEY CONSIDERATIONS: OECD GUIDANCE AND THE UN TRANSFER PRICING MANUAL

The OECD released its guidance on financial transactions to cover transfer pricing issues on financial transactions as a follow-up to its previous work on the BEPS Action Plan, focusing on the alignment of transfer pricing outcomes with value creation. The new guidance discusses how to accurately delineate an entity's capital structure. It also offers further information on applying a functional analysis to financial transactions.[1]

The UN's new chapter on financial transactions focuses on two of the most common intercompany financing transactions: intra-group loans and guarantees. It suggests applying a three-step approach in determining the arm's-length remuneration involving (1) analyzing the economically significant characteristics, (2) accurately delineating the transaction, and (3) selecting and applying the most appropriate transfer pricing method. The updated chapter includes examples, some with more details.[2]

Some of the similarities demonstrated in both documents include recognizing that implicit support can have an effect on an entity's credit rating in the context of a multinational group. In relation to determining a guarantee fee, the documents address various approaches to its calculation including the comparable uncontrolled price (CUP) method. The UN and the OECD both describe the yield approach and cost method while the OECD goes a step further and provides two other approaches: the valuation of expected loss approach and the capital support method. Guarantee fee payments are justified if an economic benefit, for example, a better credit rating or reduced interest, is agreed to by the OECD and the UN. Furthermore, the OECD and the UN recognize that measures such as safe harbors are used by taxpayers for simplification purposes.

A few notable differences are found in the wider scope of the OECD guidance extending beyond just the loans and guarantees in the UN Manual to include topics of cash pooling and captive insurance, to name a few. In relation to intra-group loans, the OECD seems to put equal weighting on the lender's and borrower's perspectives when assessing the options that are realistically available. The UN's view on assessment focuses on the borrower's debt capacity and credit risk and recognizes only the realistically available options for the borrower. Both the OECD and the UN recognize starting at the borrower rating, whereas the OECD also considers the application of the parent company's rating to its subsidiaries. The UN discusses a bottom-up approach (often applied by credit rating agencies) in more detail compared with the OECD. The UN acknowledges an interaction between financing arrangements and other intercompany arrangements whereas the OECD does not explicitly consider this. Furthermore, the UN is more prescriptive on when a financing transaction, for example, a guarantee, should be priced.

Both organizations agree that the preferred transfer pricing method to be used for financial transactions is the CUP method. The UN extends this by stating that the CUP is the most commonly used method and lists various types of information for consideration in its application (third-party syndicated loans, bonds, credit default swaps (CDSs), credit fee letters, insurance types, etc.) depending on the transaction.

1. OECD, Transfer Pricing Guidance on Financial Transactions, Inclusive Framework on BEPS: Actions 4, February 8-10, 2020.
2. Committee of Experts on International Cooperation in Tax Matters, *Update of the United Nations Practical Manual on Transfer Pricing for Developing Countries*, available at https://www.un.org/esa/ffd/wp-content/uploads/2019/04/18STM_CRP1_Update-UN-Practical-Manual-on-Transfer-Pricing.pdf, accessed January 8, 2020.

Overall, these two documents outlining the institutions' approaches on dealing with transfer pricing issues for financial transactions have many similarities with the OECD having a broader scope extending beyond guarantees and intercompany loans. Both have recognized the importance of these transactions on cross-border arrangements and the complexities inherent in attempting to price them appropriately. Therefore, there is a common desire to achieve the same result in tackling the tax issues resulting from financial transactions and trying to achieve a multijurisdictional consensus on how to deal with them.

2 CASE LAW

When considering case law, the authors find three well-publicized cases that highlight some key complexities with financing arrangements. These are the *McKesson Canada Corporation* in 2013, heard by the Canadian tax courts; the *GE Capital Canada* in 2010; and the *Chevron Australia* brought to the Australian federal courts in 2015. These cases considered numerous points of contention, some of which are summarized below.

2.1 *McKesson Canada Corporation v. The Queen (Canada)*

McKesson Canada Corporation (MCC) was the main operating entity of the McKesson group (headquartered in the United States (U.S.)) in Canada as a distributor of over-the-counter and prescription medications. In 2002 (FY 2003), MCC became party to a receivables sales agreement (RSA) and a servicing agreement with a related entity, McKesson International Holdings III S.à.R.L (MIH; based in Luxembourg). This receivables facility meant MIH purchased all MCC's then-current receivables (approximately CAD 460 million) and daily thereafter as they rose for the next five years up to a CAD 900 million cap. The discount applied was 2.206% of face value, calculated to be equivalent to an annual financing rate of about 27%. Furthermore, the RSA contained a provision allowing MIH to sell back the nonperforming receivables to MCC at 75% of face value, which was later adjusted to the amount collected by MCC.

The Canada Revenue Authority (CRA) took the position that the discount rate applied of 2.206% was greater than the arm's-length rate. Under the RSA, the overall discount rate was calculated using three different components. These were the yield rate, a loss discount, and a discount spread. The latter two were challenged by the CRA which reasoned that the arm's-length discount rate would be equal to 1.0127% for FY 2003, resulting in a very different annualized effective rate of 13%. The difference between the two discount rates resulted in a transfer pricing adjustment of CAD 26.6 million.

MCC relied on an analysis undertaken by a third party (a company referred to as TDSI) with experience in securitization of receivables. However, the judge did not agree with some aspects of the analysis from the parties and found issues with critical assumptions and the calculations that were made. Some examples of the judge's differing opinions included the day's sales outstanding input should have been floating rather than fixed. The judge also did not agree with MCC's loss discount which should have been between 0.06% and 0.08% in contrast with MCC's 0.23% rate. Finally, the total factoring discount rate range was estimated to be between 0.959% and 1.17%; whereby the CRA's findings were within this range.

However, MCC's rate was materially above it. The court agreed with MCC's expert report's statement that none of the main four transfer pricing methods were suitable for pricing the receivables, but applying the "other" method as allowed by the guidelines was appropriate. The judge agreed that one possibility was accurately identifying the risks transferred to MIH under the RSA and its impact on pricing as outlined in TDSI's report. Another option was looking at the public bond market discount rates for the Canadian market and adjusting to capture the RSA's unique characteristics.

This case is reminiscent of the availability of the "other" method that is often overlooked and the importance of documentation clearly rationalizing the assumptions taken and the analytical steps undertaken. Furthermore, it highlights the complexities to consider when dealing with adjustments for material differences between comparable data and the intercompany financial arrangements.

2.2 *General Electric Capital Canada Inc. v. The Queen (Canada)*

General Electric Capital Corporation (GE) was the U.S. parent company engaged in the industrial and financial services businesses during the 1996-2000 taxation years (years under dispute). General Electric Capital Canada Inc. (GE Canada) was an indirect wholly owned subsidiary of General Electric Capital Corporation (GECUS) which was, in turn, indirectly wholly owned by GE and one of GE's primary subsidiaries in the financial services business segment.[3]

GE Canada's model was to borrow funds from the capital markets at the lowest cost and lend the funds to other related parties. Debt was issued to the market in the form of commercial paper and secured debentures.[4] GECUS' treasury department managed these issuances and unconditionally guaranteed the payments to third-party creditors with an explicit guarantee, charging a fee to GE Canada of 1% per year.

GE Canada testified that, without the guarantee, they would not have been rated AAA and conceded that, although the GE name was likely to raise the rating of GE Canada, this was unlikely to result in such a high credit rating to allow borrowings at the volumes that GE Canada required.[5] Experts testified that it would be a shock to the markets to allow the subsidiary to default, but it would be due to GE Canada's economic value and not because it was "core" or "strategically important."[6]

The CRA claimed the value of the guarantee should be zero due to the inherent implicit support since GE Canada was not receiving any economic benefit from the

3. CA: Tax Court of Canada, *General Electric Capital Canada Inc. v. Her Majesty The Queen*, [2009] TCC 563, 1, 2.
4. *General Electric Capital Canada Inc. v. Her Majesty The Queen, supra* n. 3, 2.
5. *General Electric Capital Canada Inc. v. Her Majesty The Queen, supra* n. 3, 14.
6. *General Electric Capital Canada Inc. v. Her Majesty The Queen, supra* n. 3, 14.

explicit guarantee.[7] Furthermore, CRA argued that allowing the default would significantly downgrade the parent's credit rating, causing future borrowing to be costlier than supporting the subsidiary.

Ultimately, the court agreed that a parent and subsidiary relationship should be accounted for alongside any resulting implicit support. It was found that the explicit guarantee provided a benefit to GE Canada that was above the benefit obtained from implicit support and thus the fee that was charged 100 base points was reasonable and at arm's length.[8]

2.3 *Chevron Australia Holdings Pty Ltd v. Australian Commissioner of Taxation*

Chevron Corporation is a U.S.-headquartered multinational energy corporation with subsidiaries involved in upstream, midstream, and downstream segments of the oil and gas industry.[9] Chevron Australia Holdings Pty Ltd (CAHPL) borrowed the AUD equivalent of USD 2.5 billion from ChevronTexaco Funding Corporation (CFC), a subsidiary of CAHPL in the U.S. The loan was issued through a five-year credit facility agreement (financial years 2004-2008 inclusive).

The original funds were sourced by CFC issuing USD commercial paper in the open market, which were guaranteed by Chevron Corporation, and thus benefited from a high investment grade credit rating.

CFC then lent the funds to CAHPL with an interest rate of one-month AUD LIBOR plus 4.14% with no guarantee provided by Chevron Corporation. These onerous borrowing terms suggested that the loan would have received a noninvestment grade rating.[10]

The Australian Taxation Office (ATO) denied a portion of the interest deductions claimed by CAHPL by stating the interest rates were not at arm's length.

The case was taken to the Federal Court of Australia where CAHPL argued that there was no legal recognition of implicit support, and taking this into account "requires a preservation of a key aspect of the non-arm's length relationship ... which is contrary to, and incompatible with, the concept of 'independent parties'."[11] CAHPL's expert witnesses conducted two credit rating assessments, considering that parental

7. S. Dhawan, *Transfer Pricing for Inter-Company Transactions Clarified in GE Capital v. The Queen*, CanLII Connects (March 8, 2015), available at https://canliiconnects.org/en/commentaries/36243, accessed June 25, 2019.
8. P. Wilmshurst, *Dealing with Implicit Support in Relation to Intra-Group Debt*, Charles River Associates (2012), available at http://www.crai.co.uk/sites/default/files/publications/Dealing-with-implicit-support-in-relation-to%20intra-group-debt.pdf, accessed July 1, 2019.
9. Bloomberg, *Chevron Corp*, available at https://www.bloomberg.com/profile/company/CVX:US, accessed July 29, 2019.
10. K.B. Flanigan, *Cleaning up after Chevron: A Proposed Cross-Border Pipeline for the Transfer Pricing of Intra-Group Debt Transactions*, Columbia Journal of Transnational Law, 56, 123, 151 (2017).
11. M. Clayson, *The Recognition of the Effect of Passive Association on Controlled Transaction for Transfer Pricing Purposes*, doctoral thesis (Queen Mary University of London, 2016), 135.

support, and determined that it only resulted in a one-notch but still noninvestment grade rating.[12]

The ATO claimed the loan should have been priced by referencing credit rating agency methodologies, and CAHPL's status as a prominent subsidiary within the group meant it would have benefited from implicit support. ATO's witnesses also argued that the implicit support that was provided would have increased CAHPL's credit rating by four to eight notches and put it in the A investment grade category.

The trial judge stated that, when evaluating a potential borrower, the correct perspective is that of a commercial lender which is different from a credit rating agency's perspective.[13] Though he broadly agreed with the ATO,[14] "There was no legislative warrant for ignoring affiliation between a hypothesised party to a transaction and other members of that party's group of companies," he did not accept the ATO's expert significant notching up of CAHPL's credit rating to A and concluded that,[15] "in the absence of a legally binding parental agreement, implicit credit support had very little, if any, impact on pricing by a lender in the real world."

2.4 Takeaways from Case Law

The foregoing cases highlight how transfer pricing issues of financial transactions are highly contentious, particularly due to the complexity of the issues and financial arrangements that are implemented and often with a high commercial value at stake.

Chevron and *GE* verified that the role of implicit support between related parties should be considered, which was reiterated in the OECD's *Guidance on Financial Transactions* and the UN's update to its *Manual*. The notion of implicit support as a transfer pricing concept is not new, however, as it was already acknowledged in the OECD *Transfer Pricing Guidelines*, Chapter 7, referencing the "incidental benefit" of being part of a wider group. The cases described here merely brought the importance of implicit support to the forefront. The cases furthermore highlighted the subjectivity when assessing implicit support and the difficulties in achieving agreement among stakeholders on the implications of implicit support on financing transactions.

McKesson, on the other hand, highlighted the gaps in information and guidance that were available to taxpayers and tax authorities at the time to appropriately price related party financing transactions. The judge discussed his concerns that neither party had provided the level of evidence that was expected. The case also emphasized the importance of correctly accounting for any material differences in the tested transaction and the terms and conditions expected in an arm's-length arrangement. It also reminded stakeholders that there are times when neither of the main transfer pricing methods may be suitable and an "other" method may need to be employed.

12. AU: Federal Court of Australia, *Chevron Australia Holdings Pty Ltd v. Commissioner of Taxation (no. 4)*, [2015] FCA 1092, 42.
13. *Chevron Australia Holdings Pty Ltd v. Commissioner of Taxation (no. 4)*, *supra* n. 12, 167.
14. *Chevron Australia Holdings Pty Ltd v. Commissioner of Taxation (no. 4)*, *supra* n. 12, 199.
15. *Chevron Australia Holdings Pty Ltd v. Commissioner of Taxation (no. 4)*, *supra* n. 12, 199.

These findings may have been another push for the OECD (and afterward, the UN) to work toward minimizing these information gaps with the latest released guidance. It also highlighted that, although it is commonly asserted that CUP is the preferred method, it may not always be possible to apply it. In these situations, a different or "other" method as provided in the guidelines may be the most appropriate.

3 CHANGES IN THE FINANCIAL SERVICES LANDSCAPE

The financial services sector is an integral part of the global economy and critical for the growth of many nations. The global financial crisis of 2008-2009 has led to intense scrutiny on regulatory standards of various financial institutions (particularly banks) to ensure the severity of the crisis would not be repeated. A host of new regulations was sanctioned to manage liquidity levels and risk management by introducing best practices as seen in Basel III and the recognition of systemically important financial institutions, to name a few.[16] Banks working on the arduous task of meeting their new regulatory requirements also had to conduct extensive reviews of operating practices. These reviews affected not only the terms but also the extent of funding that can be provided by banks. Furthermore, these reviews eased the barriers to entry for more boutique funding providers, such as hedge funds, and other alternative investment lenders to fill the funding gap.

The global crisis also reminded everyone of the great complexity of the industry's inner workings, the (sometimes unimaginable) funds at stake, and competing stakeholders' interests. With these difficulties, it was only evitable that something as broad, nonconsensual, and non-legally binding as the currently available transfer pricing guidelines would create opposing opinions. This was witnessed in numerous circumstances in a wide range of jurisdictions and is reflected in the increasing trend of global disputes between taxpayers and tax authorities.

In addition to this trend, many jurisdictions also noticed an increase in Mutual Agreement Procedure (MAP) cases from 2016, as seen in Figure 7.1. This includes countries such as Germany, the U.S., France, India, Italy, the United Kingdom, and Spain. Furthermore, the authors note that resolving transfer pricing MAP cases take more than twice as long as non-transfer pricing MAP cases (on average, it took thirty-three months to finalize a transfer pricing MAP versus fourteen for non–transfer pricing MAPs). This can be attributed to the complexity of issues requiring consideration in transfer pricing MAPs including financing arrangements when generally compared to other areas of tax.[17]

16. Reserve Bank of Australia's Submission to the Financial System Inquiry, *The Regulatory Response to the Global Financial Crisis* (2014), available at https://www.rba.gov.au/publications/submissions/financial-sector/financial-system-inquiry-2014-03/regulatory-response-to-the-global-financial-crisis.html, accessed January 10, 2020.
17. OECD, *Mutual Agreement Procedure Statistics 2018 per jurisdiction—inventory*, available at https://www.oecd.org/tax/dispute/mutual-agreement-procedure-statistics-2018-per-jurisdiction-inventory.htm, accessed January 10, 2020.

Figure 7.1 Number of Transfer Pricing MAP Cases, 2016-2018

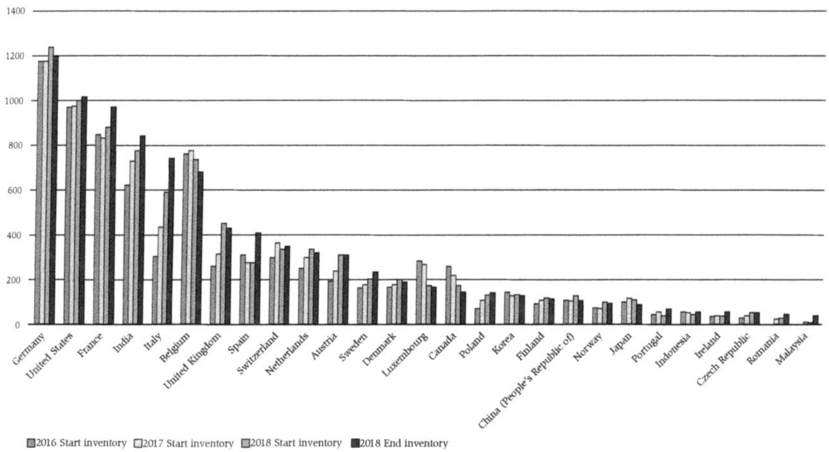

Source: OECD, Mutual Agreement Procedure Statistics 2018 per jurisdiction—inventory, available at https://www.oecd.org/tax/dispute/mutual-agreement-procedure-statistics-2018-per-jurisdiction-inventory.htm (accessed January 10, 2020).

The growth in dispute resolution mechanisms in the transfer pricing world along with the ever-increasing global interest and advancements in the financial transactions' subset of transfer pricing regulations show the importance of addressing the difficulties in pricing these transactions.

Next, the authors outline an analytical framework that can be relied on to effectively manage some of the complexities of financing transactions when determining the arm's-length pricing in an increasingly contentious environment.

4 ANALYTICAL FRAMEWORK TO PRICING FINANCING ARRANGEMENTS

4.1 Establishing the Role of Financing Within a Multinational Group Context

A firm's decision on the type and level of funding and, more broadly, how to manage funding within a group is driven by what is deemed to be an appropriate capital structure for commercial purposes. This appropriation varies depending on the industry in which the firm operates; firm and product life cycles; business strategies and flexibility required; and transactions costs involved, to name just a few considerations. A firm will typically assess the trade-offs between the costs and benefits from a given form of funding vis-à-vis the alternative options that are realistically available.[18]

18. A. Damodaran, *Corporate Finance: Theory and Practice*, Second Edition Chapter 18, pp. 537-541.

Assessing the arm's-length nature of any form of financing arrangement (including its impact on leverage ratios) is very much rooted in the economic environment in which a firm finds itself and should be addressed through the effective application of paragraph 1 of Article 9 of the Model Tax Convention: the arm's-length principle. This is true for all types of financing related issues including loans, cash pooling, guarantees, and thin capitalization assessments. In this context, the most important step in addressing questions relating to financing is to analyze and understand what drives value in the group, the role that financing plays in this process, and how the respective group members that are involved fit into the transaction.

Furthermore, it is important to understand the activities performed by the various group members, the risks assumed, and their ownership of assets (including intangible and tangible assets). The financial transaction would effectively be delineated based on this information that is gathered, as also described in the OECD guidance issued on financial transactions.[19] Such an analysis will improve clarity on the financial and commercial relations between the transacting parties and offer further insight on the strategic and operational importance of a related party to the group's holistic value contribution (a key component when evaluating, say, implicit support).[20]

In addition, the industry and the regulatory environment in which a related party and/or the multinational enterprise operate should be considered. Different industries have different capital needs; for example, trading businesses may rely on large-volume short-term funding and may be highly leveraged. More basic service companies that are less capital-intensive may rely on significantly lower levels of financial leverage. Certain regulatory guidelines may also affect a borrower's preferences for certain types and levels of funding, thereby influencing the potential options that a borrower may realistically consider.

The OECD's Guidance on Financial Transactions lists the above as important considerations as well as the previously mentioned factors of economic, firm and product life cycle, in addition to the availability of other financing opportunities at the time of the transaction.[21]

Moreover, the objective of the above-mentioned analyses is to obtain the necessary insights to understand (1) the commercial reasons for the business financing need, (2) the appropriate structure of the financing and realistically available options to the borrower and the lender, (3) the relational dynamics of the various entities and the influences of any implicit support, (4) the potential factors that may influence default risk in the context of the transaction, and (5) the consequential covenants that would be expected in the transaction.

Only once the "factual" analysis has been completed should the contractual terms of the intercompany financial transactions themselves be looked at including the

19. OECD, Transfer Pricing Guidance on Financial Transactions, Inclusive Framework on BEPS: Actions 4, 8-10, February 2020, paragraph 10.17.
20. *See* section 4.3.
21. OECD, Transfer Pricing Guidance on Financial Transactions, Inclusive Framework on BEPS: Actions 4, 8-10, February 2020, paragraph 10.15.

types of loans, the repayment dates, and interest payment intervals and not the other way around.

4.2 Analysis of the Terms of the Transaction

Companies have several avenues for securing financing. There are also several types of financial instruments with varying terms and conditions linked to them. For specific companies at certain times, only some instruments or terms may be realistically available. The OECD's guidance notes that a transaction is only entered into if it is the most appropriate and attractive option to meet its financial needs when compared to the other options that are realistically available.[22] It also notes that a critical step of the analysis involves the accurate delineation of the transaction to appropriate whether the transaction is to be categorized as a loan before undertaking further transfer pricing analyses on intra-group loans.[23]

To assess those options, several factors need to be considered including the level of funding, the timing surrounding the funding, other funding already in place, and the purpose of the funding. The authors discuss a few of these items below although numerous factors could potentially influence the terms associated with the transaction. Furthermore, the economically relevant characteristics should be considered in line with the perspectives of all of the parties involved (i.e., both the lender(s) and the borrower(s)).[24]

4.2.1 Level of Funding

The level of funding that a lender is willing to extend and the terms associated with that funding are partly (if not largely) driven by the lender's willingness to take on risk. To determine the maximum level of funding, a lender would provide or an entity may be able to carry, the benefits and costs associated with carrying financing instruments should be analyzed considering the full mix of potential financing instruments that a borrower may have available across the whole lending market and the conditions of that market. For example, in some situations, financing such as subordinated debt or hybrid debt may be available to the borrower in addition to senior debt and should be considered. A reasonable level of debt should be determined based on the facts and circumstances of each individual case considering the alternatives that are realistically available to the lender and the borrower.[25]

22. OECD, Transfer Pricing Guidance on Financial Transactions, Inclusive Framework on BEPS: Actions 4, 8-10, February 2020, paragraph 10.19.
23. OECD, Transfer Pricing Guidance on Financial Transactions, Inclusive Framework on BEPS: Actions 4, 8-10, February 2020, paragraph 10.50.
24. OECD, Transfer Pricing Guidance on Financial Transactions, Inclusive Framework on BEPS: Actions 4, 8-10, February 2020, paragraph 10.51.
25. *See also*: A. Damodaran, *Corporate Finance: Theory and Practice*, Second Edition, Chapter 18, p. 542.

4.2.2 *Timing of the Transaction*

Another important consideration is the timing of the financing transaction. This will affect the type of funding available in the open market and the rate at which the funding is available. The significant implication of timing on the price and types of instruments is evident especially during times of economic hardship, such as during the global financial crisis. Estimates showed that loans made to large corporations/borrowers dropped by 47% in the last quarter of 2008 (often synonymous with the peak of the crisis) in relation to the previous quarter.

Also evident was the substantial reduction in all types of loans made available. This could be hypothesized with two broad reasons: one being that corporations themselves were seeking lower levels of funding as they scaled back their requirements (the demand-side factor). On the supply side, after seeing the failure of some major financial institutions (notably Lehman Brothers), the combination of possible bank runs on short-term debt and fear of being the next victim if liquidity was not properly handled led financial institutions to be a lot more stringent on who they would lend to and often deciding to not lend to corporations with which there was no existing relationship. Borrowers had fewer options to switch lenders and even less ability to "shop around" in such constrained conditions.[26] This restricted small to medium enterprises even more, often turning to alternate sources of funding. Due to the bank lending constraints, enterprises that had previous credit applications rejected were more likely to turn to trade credit. There was also an increase in demand for other alternative finance forms such as informal loans, loans from other types of alternative financing companies, or shareholder loans. This highlighted the need for diverse forms of funding in difficult economic times.[27]

Furthermore, timing will affect the interest rate that is available to potential borrowers. For example, during periods of difficulty, the demand and supply of financing becomes more skewed. This stems from the increase in banks' cautiousness and subsequent tightening of funding policies and availability, leading to an increase in the average loan spread. During such periods of difficulty, typical financing institutions will attempt to obtain as much security and certainty as possible.[28] Figure 7.2 indicates the changes in credit spreads for two different credit ratings, an AA-rated EUR bond instruments and A-rated EUR bond instruments over the period of January 2009-January 2020.

26. V. Ivashina and D. Scharfstein, *Bank Lending During the Financial Crisis of 2008*, Journal of Financial Economics, 97, 3 (2010).
27. E. Casey and C. O'Toole, *Bank Lending Constraints, Trade Credit and Alternative Financing During the Financial Crisis Evidence from European SMEs*, Journal of Corporate Finance, 27 (2014).
28. S. Kwan, *Financial Crisis and Bank Lending*, Federal Reserve Bank of San Francisco Working Paper Series (2010).

Figure 7.2 Credit Risk Spreads, January 2009-January 2020

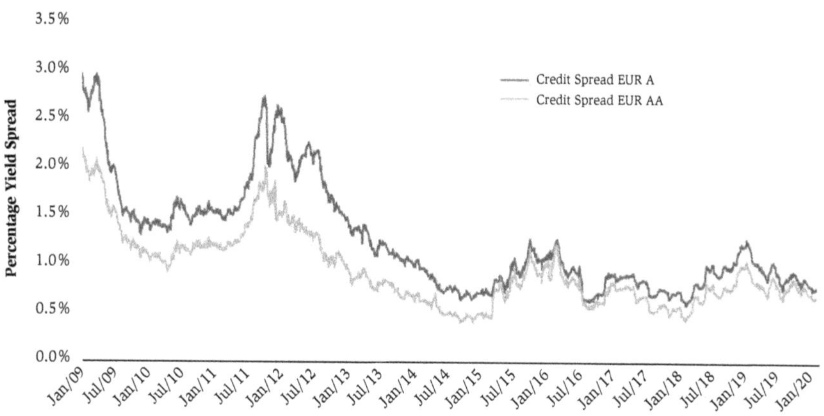

Data source: Bloomberg LP.

4.2.3 Existing Funding in Place and Conditions

In making financing decisions and applications, borrowers also need to consider their current debt scenario and how this will affect their ability to take on more financing. Financial constraints (external, internal, or a combination of both) can arise for various reasons. For example, existing debt burdens can have a material impact on available future debt funding[29] and may lead to internal constraints imposed by the firm. Upon application for extra financing, the issue of asymmetric information on repayment capability between the lender and the borrower may create more external constraints on the borrower.

Such constraints then affect the seniority of funding that a borrower can assume. The greater the existing debt burden that the company exhibits, the riskier they will be viewed by lenders who may query the borrower's repayment ability in light of competing interest payments and, in turn, additional conditions may be imposed if funds are lent. This deemed riskiness is linked to the borrower's credit quality, creating a catch-22 effect whereby firms with lower credit ratings are forced to use a multitiered approach to their debt structure to incorporate secured and subordinated debt variations that, in turn, may further reduce their credit quality.[30] Furthermore, if an entity already has senior/secured debt financing in place, potentially only unsecured debt will be offered and, once unsecured debt is in place, only subordinated debt may be offered, which comes with higher prices in line with the higher level of risk for the lender, causing the firm to reassess if they can afford this more expensive debt.

29. G. Hoberg and V. Maksimovic, *Redefining Financial Constraints: A Text-Based Analysis* (2014).
30. R. Small, *Capital Structure and Debt Structure*, HLS Forum on Corporate Governance and Financial Regulation (2010).

More generally, companies consider their leverage ratio (determined by current funding structures) to decide the cost-benefit analysis in taking on further debt or looking for alternative sources such as equity.[31]

4.2.4 Conditions Associated with Financing

Other factors that may affect the available financing options and their characteristics include reasons for the financing and the business phase.

Lending entities will consider the reason for the funds and weigh up the risks of achieving the desired return which, in turn, affects the conditions of the financing that is provided. One such case is when project financing is needed. This may involve one or more sponsors creating a legally separate entity to conduct the intended business and operations, often with delayed anticipated cash flows. The sponsors provide equity and issue debt on a nonrecourse basis. Due to the separation of cash flows from the sponsors' businesses, creditors can only lay claim to the funds within the project financing entity, often with huge uncertainty, thereby making it riskier than conventional financing. In turn, evidence shows that project financing is often higher leveraged and has a greater value, and thus a higher interest rate is paid when compared with regular financing.[32] Furthermore, it may be seen that project finance, especially in cases when there is uncertainty of cash flows but potential for significant benefits, may be subject to features of a more hybrid nature compared with, for example, day-to-day working capital finance that is more simplistic.

Funding options for start-up businesses would be different from those of an already established and mature business. A robust banking relationship is not yet established for start-up businesses, and this may hinder their options in which lending institutions they could approach. Furthermore, the likely lack of assets and/or collateral could affect their securitization options in obtaining much-needed funding for business growth. It has been shown that the larger the start-up, the greater portion of debt they would have in their capital structure, larger amounts of long-term debt, and the greater access they have to a wider variety of funding (outside financing and bank financing).[33] A combination of these factors may mean that more conditions or legal caveats are imposed on the external financing because of the increased risk compared to an established borrower with a history with financial institutions.

---

31. *See also*: A. Damodaran, *Corporate Finance: Theory and Practice*, Second Edition, Chapter 18, p. 550.
32. S. Shah and A. Thakor, *Optimal Capital Structure and Project Financing*, Journal of Economic Theory, 42 (1987).
33. G. Cassar, *The Financing of Business Start-Ups*, Journal of Business Venturing, 19 (2004).

4.3 Determining the Credit Risk Associated with the Transaction

4.3.1 Stand-Alone Credit Rating Assessment

In addition to the risk framework outlined in the OECD guidelines, section D, Chapter 1, default risk and the entity that bears this risk are important factors to consider when dealing with most types of financing arrangements. Default risk is typically determined by means of performing a credit rating analysis.

Often, a stand-alone credit rating is needed for each entity taking part in the transaction. For this purpose, public credit ratings (if available) can be a reliable source, or they can be estimated using credit models (shadow credit ratings).

The shadow credit rating provides an assessment of an entity's ability to meet its financial obligations in full and on time (issuer rating) or concerns an individual debt issue (issue rating). Furthermore, it affords an indication of the entity's capacity to meet its financial obligations; however, it also provides an assessment on the likelihood of obtaining financing from the market and, if so, to what extent (quantum effect).

The rating of a subsidiary can be lower, the same, or higher than the group rating. A group rating is ultimately an overall average considering both weak entities and stronger entities that form part of the group.

An important consideration when doing credit rating analyses for subsidiaries as also outlined in the OECD guidance is that all related party transactions influencing the financial standing of a related party are priced at arm's length.[34] It is, therefore, necessary to assess the arm's-length nature of all related party transactions that form part of the financial accounts of the subsidiary prior to performing a shadow credit rating assessment. The rating that is derived through performing a shadow credit rating assessment is the issuer rating without considering any implications of group affiliation.

4.3.1.1 Relationship Between the Issuer Rating and the Issue Rating

If the characteristics of the transaction warrant it (e.g., when it is necessary to account for subordination), a specific financial instrument issued by a member of the multinational enterprise can have a different credit rating from the issuer rating derived for said member.[35] This is because the probability of default on a financial instrument is linked to its own features, not just the risk profile of the borrower. Thus, when performing a transfer pricing assessment on a financing transaction, the issue rating should be relied upon rather than the issuer rating for the company, although the issuer rating is, in fact, the starting point for determining the instrument's issue rating.

34. OECD, Transfer Pricing Guidance on Financial Transactions, Inclusive Framework on BEPS: Actions 4, 8-10, February 2020, paragraph 10.75.
35. OECD, Transfer Pricing Guidance on Financial Transactions, Inclusive Framework on BEPS: Actions 4, 8-10, February 2020, paragraph 10.70.

4.3.2 *Measuring the Implicitness*

A subsidiary could potentially get funding at a lower cost than that corresponding to its stand-alone credit rating because of its membership with its group without any binding guarantee agreement.[36] For instance, a Baa1-rated subsidiary may be able to borrow in the market at a cost of debt corresponding to an A1 rating because of its link with the group. Thus, from an economic perspective, the arm's-length pricing should be performed considering the viewpoint of a third party lender on the perceived credit risk of the entity given its affiliation with the group (implicit support).

After assessing the stand-alone credit rating of the transacting parties, the level of implicit support provided by the parent, and thus the adjustment needed to the entity's stand-alone rating is determined. Although it is generally accepted that there may exist some degree of implicit support between a parent and one of its subsidiaries, the degree of this support and its implications for pricing are often qualitative rather than quantitative. Credit rating agencies consider various criteria to assess whether such implicit support is expected and, if it is, the degree to which it will influence the group entity's credit rating. In this respect, it is essential, as also pointed by the OECD guidance, to understand the economic, operational, and strategic links among the different entities of a group.[37] The rating agencies provide reliable frameworks when assessing an adjustment for implicit support. These are briefly discussed as follows.

4.3.2.1 *Moody's Investor Services*

According to Moody's, the likelihood of providing support is based on both the willingness and the ability to do so.[38] Within those two headings, Moody's analyzes several distinct aspects and acknowledges that parents might not always be willing to support financially distressed subsidiaries.

Willingness to Provide Support

The aspects considered by Moody's include the reputation and confidence sensitivity (i.e., the financial implications of any adverse reputation consequences for the parent of not supporting); strategy (i.e., the importance of the operation for the long-term strategy of the group); the operational integration (i.e., whether a subsidiary is fundamental for the survival of the group); marginal return on required investment (discusses the question of whether the parent would be willing to provide further rounds of funding if a subsidiary is in financial distress or was to experience a

36. OECD, Transfer Pricing Guidance on Financial Transactions, Inclusive Framework on BEPS: Actions 4, 8-10, February 2020, paragraph 10.78.
37. OECD, Transfer Pricing Guidance on Financial Transactions, Inclusive Framework on BEPS: Actions 4, 8-10, February 2020, paragraph 10.79.
38. P. Stumpp and W. Rottino, et al., *Rating Non-guaranteed Subsidiaries: Credit Considerations in Assigning Subsidiary Ratings in the Absence of Legally Binding Parent Support*, Moody's Investors Service (December 2003), accessed June 18, 2019.

significant liability impacting the shareholder return); and the role of financial regulators.

In the OECD's Guidance for Financial Transactions, a group member's willingness to provide support to other members in times of hardship was reiterated as an important consideration for assessing the level of implicit support.[39]

Ability to Provide Support

The ability to provide support considers the parent credit rating, the correlation of business risk (between the borrowing entity and its parent—*see* below), and the relative magnitude and timing of all such expected investments. Although this last factor is potentially less important when analyzing implicit support, it is nonetheless a key factor for pricing financing transactions, such as guarantees, since a parent's financial ability to provide support in times of subsidiary financial distress is a key driver of the economic benefit achieved from the guarantee.

A high correlation might occur if both the parent and subsidiary are exposed to the same economic shocks resulting in a parent under financial distress being unable to provide financial support when its subsidiary might urgently need it. This thereby renders a guarantee potentially worthless from an economic benefit perspective even if a rating differential between the parent and the entity being guaranteed can be observed. Moody's methodology highlights the relevance of business correlation between the parent and the subsidiary when the subsidiary has been identified as being strategic.[40] This correlation of default is an important component of the joint probability of default that, in turn, can be translated into a "new" rating for the subsidiary, reflecting implicit support and financial ability of the parent to support in a default scenario. In general, Moody's estimates a rating "lift" of one or two notches to be the norm for nonfinancial corporations.[41]

The criteria provided by the other two agencies are less quantitative and are discussed below.

4.3.2.2 Standard & Poor's

Standard & Poor's (S&P) states that a weak subsidiary owned by a strong parent will usually, but not always, enjoy a stronger rating.[42] This support is contingent on the fact that the parent has the ability to support the subsidiary during a period of financial stress.

39. OECD, Transfer Pricing Guidance on Financial Transactions, Inclusive Framework on BEPS: Actions 4, 8-10, February 2020, paragraphs 10.64 and 10.78.
40. J.S. Fons and R. Cantor, *The Incorporation of Joint-Default Analysis into Moody's Corporate, Financial and Government Rating Methodologies*, Moody's Investors Service (February 2005), 2, available at http://www.fonsrisksolutions.com/Documents/Joint-Default%20SC.pdf, accessed August 20, 2019.
41. Stumpp and Rottino et al., *supra* n. 38, 6.
42. Standard & Poor's, *Corporate Ratings Criteria* (2001), 100, available at http://regulationbodyofknowledge.org/wp-content/uploads/2013/03/StandardAndPoors_Corporate_Ratings_Criteria.pdf, accessed June 18, 2019.

The impact of support on a rating equalization between the subsidiary and the group rating in a total absence of help depends on the evidence of support analyzed (among other factors) through the economic incentive of the parent to provide support. S&P, therefore, stipulates that the gap between the subsidiary's stand-alone rating and that of its parent is a function of their perceived relationship: "the greater the integration, the greater the potential for parent or sponsor support,"[43] and this relationship can narrow the gap between the rating level of the parent and the subsidiary.

S&P states that there is no single factor determining the relationship, but several are considered together. These factors are comparable to those used by the other rating agencies and include factors such as the strategic importance, whether the subsidiary operates under the same name as the parent (reputational risks), the financial capacity to provide support, or whether the parent firm has a track record of supporting subsidiaries in distressed financial situations.[44]

By the nature of these factors, an assessment will always be subjective. Considering all of these factors together will provide a picture that leads to some assessment of the degree to which implicit support can be assumed. Depending on the assumed degree of implicit support, the borrowing entity's rating, therefore, may be raised to a better rating (notching), typically by one or two incremental steps.[45]

4.3.2.3 Fitch

To assess the degree of linkage between the parent company and its subsidiary, Fitch undertakes an analysis of legal ties (e.g., the existence of guarantees, restrictions to provide an intercompany loan, or guarantee of factors affecting the enforceability of legal arrangements), operational ties (this takes into account the degree of parent management control, whether a centralized treasury exists, and if the subsidiary's operations are operationally integral to the core business of the group), and strategic ties (i.e., strategic importance of the subsidiary and proven tangible support for the subsidiary).[46] Jointly, these factors would lead to a notching adjustment to the stand-alone rating.

43. Standard & Poor's, *supra* n. 42, 101.
44. For S&P and Fitch, as opposed to Moody's, "strategic importance" refers to linked lines of business (i.e., supply chains).
45. Amongst the three major rating agencies, S&P assumes that the rating of the borrowing entity cannot be better than the one of the entire group or the parent company, respectively. Fitch and Moody's do not apply that restriction. *See* Stumpp and Rottino et al., *supra* n. 38; Fitch Ratings, *Parent and Subsidiary Rating Linkage*, accessed June 20, 2019 and Standard & Poor's Rating Services, *General Criteria, Group Rating Methodology*, McGraw-Hill Financial (November 19, 2013).
46. Fitch Ratings, *Parent and Subsidiary Rating Linkage—Fitch's Approach to Rating Entities Within a Corporate Group Structure*, 2 (July 16, 2019).

4.3.2.4 *Financial Markets Viewpoint*

The preceding approaches are not the only ones in existence. Most large banks and other financial institutions have developed their own models to assess potential implicit support. These also rely on statistical relationships between a variety of factors and their influence on credit deterioration.

Because of the lack of transparency in the approaches used by financial institutions, it is difficult to assess exactly how they integrate the notion of implicit support and how it could affect the pricing of financial instruments they extend to subsidiaries of a group.

In assessing the return that should compensate investors or lenders for assuming risk on a subsidiary company, some financial markets participants will only consider explicit guarantees when providing financing. This approach can arguably be put down to two key reasons. First, should the borrower default, lenders do not have to wait to see if their assumptions of implicit support materialize as an explicit guarantee can be activated without waiting for the parent company to decide whether to support its subsidiary. This is also the case as lenders often do not have cross-jurisdictional claims on assets in other locations without an explicit guarantee. Second, an explicit guarantee decreases the time to when the lenders will be made whole; their claim is clearly ranked among other claims and can be processed in short order. Other financial institutions do assess and, when relevant, integrate implicit support by notching up or down, directly affecting pricing.[47]

When following the rating agencies for which an upward lift in the subsidiary's rating will result in a lower interest rate, the implications of implicit support on interest rates are less clear when assessed by financial institutions. This is partly because of a lack of transparency in rating assessments of financial institutions[48] and the seemingly different approaches used across the sector, as described above.

These models (whether from credit rating agencies or financial institutions) are at least in part subjective and based on a number of qualitative assumptions. Nonetheless, they provide an indication of what the credit rating of the subsidiary should be when adjusted for implicit support.

After assessing the impact of a potential implicit support between a parent and its subsidiary, the arm's-length price for the relevant financial transaction that is being considered can be determined.

47. The authors are also aware of at least one case in which the approaches to assess and integrate implicit support differ from country to country and between various departments in the same financial institution.
48. Their methodologies are not described in published papers as is the case for credit rating agencies.

4.4 Pricing Methodologies

Credit risk and yields are negatively correlated, as shown in Figure 7.3 (based on bond yields). Credit ratings incorporate credit risk that includes estimations of the probability of default of corporate entities and their expected loss rate once default has occurred (loss given default), which directly affects the price of a financing transaction.

Figure 7.3 Bond Yields per Credit Rating, December 2018-December 2019

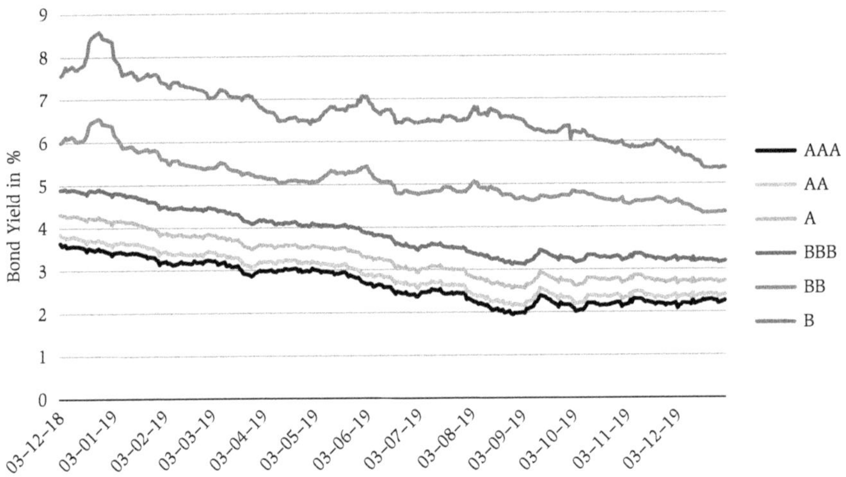

Data source: Factset. *Daily yields to maturity of US industrial financial indices based on iBoxx indices of 7-10Y maturities*, Factset database (March 5, 2020).

When pricing a financial instrument, a major driver to select the CUP approach versus "other" is data availability. In this section, the authors describe some methods and data options when pricing financing arrangements and highlight some key considerations when relying on various sources. Although the focus is on two broad methodologies that can be relied upon when evaluating financing transactions, the OECD Guidance does outline some additional methods as well that the authors do not discuss further.

4.4.1 *Comparable Uncontrolled Price Method (CUP Method)*

As previously mentioned, both the OECD Guidance and the UN Manual consider that, given the availability of information, it may be easier to apply the CUP method when evaluating financing arrangements compared to other transactions.[49,50]

When considering this type of data, economic and financial theory indicates that the interest rate charged for a loan is a combination of (a) a risk-free rate;[51] (b) expected inflation;[52] and (c) the premiums associated with default,[53] liquidity,[54] and maturity.[55] These components of interest rates compensate a lender for the risk it takes when providing capital over a specified time, including its cost of funds.

In the case of banks and other financial intermediaries, the interest rate also includes some element of functional compensation that is typically relied on to cover a bank's operational expenses or payment and liquidity management. Furthermore, some of the lenders' compensations or returns are captured by other fees that are separate from the interest rate or coupon that is charged. When selecting a data source, it is necessary to fully understand and analyze what adjustments may be needed and differences between the tested transaction and the comparables.

Internal CUP transactions, such as the average borrowing rate of a firm, can mask a wide range of factors that influence interest rates. These can include currency, maturity, size, position in the capital structure, the entity borrowing, and default risk. Unless both identified transactions—the tested transaction and the transactions relied on to apply an "internal comparable uncontrolled price"—are very similar (same currency, same maturity, same credit risk, timing, etc.), the interest rate on external

49. OECD, Transfer Pricing Guidance on Financial Transactions, Inclusive Framework on BEPS: Actions 4, 8-10, February 2020, paragraph 10.90.
50. Committee of Experts on International Cooperation in Tax Matters, *Update of the United Nations Practical Manual on Transfer Pricing for Developing Countries*, Chapter B.9 on Intra-group Financial Transactions, paragraph 3.2.5.
51. Hypothetical rate typically reflecting the time value of money. As described in the OECD Guidance, the risk-free rate aims to capture a potential zero risk investment that may often be based on government issued securities but can also be in reference to interest rate swap rates or interbank rates, to name a few. *See* OECD Guidance on Financial Transactions section F.1.
52. The market has expectations of price increases (or declines); inflation expectations, therefore, are factored into interest rates.
53. A higher probability of default increases risk and hence increases the price necessary to bear such a risk (through higher interest rates). This default risk is estimated by considering potential losses of capital (expected loss) given the default of the borrower.
54. Liquidity is defined as the ability to sell an asset on short notice at a price that reflects the level at which the market as a whole values that asset at that time (efficient market). The inability to do so (or the partial ability to do so) might force a seller to concede to a discount when offloading that asset. Holding everything else constant, the holder of a less liquid security must be compensated for that potential scenario and hence receive a higher interest rate than would have been prevalent had the security been fully negotiable at any time.
55. In general, investors need to be compensated for the fact of investing money for longer periods of time. This is true for "normal" environments where the interest rate curve is upward sloping—that is, where long-term rates are higher than shorter-term ones. In case of an interest rate curve inversion, the opposite is true.

debt should not necessarily be considered as a viable comparable unless appropriate adjustments can be performed to achieve reliable valuations.[56]

The availability of reliable external CUP data depends on the facts and circumstances of each individual case. There is typically a vast array of different data sources than can be potentially be relied on, a few of which are discussed below.

4.4.1.1 Yield Data

Typical data that is available include yield data from bonds, private loan data, and syndicated loan data. First, yield data can be obtained through bond indices or a portfolio of individual bonds. The data needs to be of similar credit rating, maturity, currency, timing, and so on. Should these differ, proper adjustments should be performed to equate the external CUPs to the transaction under study, including potential adjustments for floating to fixed coupons and payment frequency. In general, the fewer adjustments required, the more relevant the external CUPs.

A second source of data for external CUPs is private loan data or syndicated loan data from sources such as Thomson Reuters Loan Connector or S&P's LCD. Their main disadvantage is that those transactions are not as numerous as publicly traded bonds and thus might not have similar characteristics as the transaction under review. Furthermore, these types of private instruments are typically subject to numerous different fees that may reduce the listed coupon. An internal rate of return should be estimated considering all of the fees rather than looking at the reported interest rates or coupons in isolation.[57] Here also, a series of adjustments might have to be performed, potentially pertaining to credit rating, maturity, currency, coupon type, and/or coupon frequency, among others.

4.4.1.2 Credit Default Swaps

Another source of yield data is to be found in the CDS market. According to the International Swaps and Derivatives Association, a CDS[58] "is a bilateral agreement designed explicitly to shift credit risk between two parties. In a CDS, one party (protection buyer) pays a periodic fee to another party (protection seller) in return for compensation for default (or similar credit event) by a reference entity." In short, the protection buyer receives a payment from the protection seller only if the reference entity defaults (occurrence of a credit event).

Given the features of CDS contracts, they can be considered as functionally similar to guarantee agreements but can also be used in the context of loan transactions. When relying on this type of data, the definition of the credit event (e.g.,

56. OECD, Transfer Pricing Guidance on Financial Transactions, Inclusive Framework on BEPS: Actions 4, 8-10, February 2020, paragraph 10.95.
57. OECD, Transfer Pricing Guidance on Financial Transactions, Inclusive Framework on BEPS: Actions 4, 8-10, February 2020, section C.1.2.2, paragraph 10.96.
58. International Swaps and Derivatives Association, *Weekly Traded Notional and Trade Count*, available at http://www.isdacdsmarketplace.com/about_cds_market, accessed July 7, 2019.

bankruptcy, failure to pay, restructuring) is key in the comparability between the tested transaction and the CDS agreement.

In theory, CDS spreads should include the same information as bond yields (i.e., credit risk premium). In practice, using bond yield spreads and CDS spreads can yield very different results, as illustrated by Figure 7.4. In this example, the authors used Petrobras' CDS spread[59] and bond yields for comparison. These differences (CDS-bond basis) can be influenced by a series of factors, among others, the definition of a "credit event" in a CDS contract—as described already—and the potential default of the bonds as well as differences in size and liquidity of their respective bond and CDS markets.

Figure 7.4 Petrobras CDS Levels Versus Bond Yields, December 1, 2018-December 31, 2019

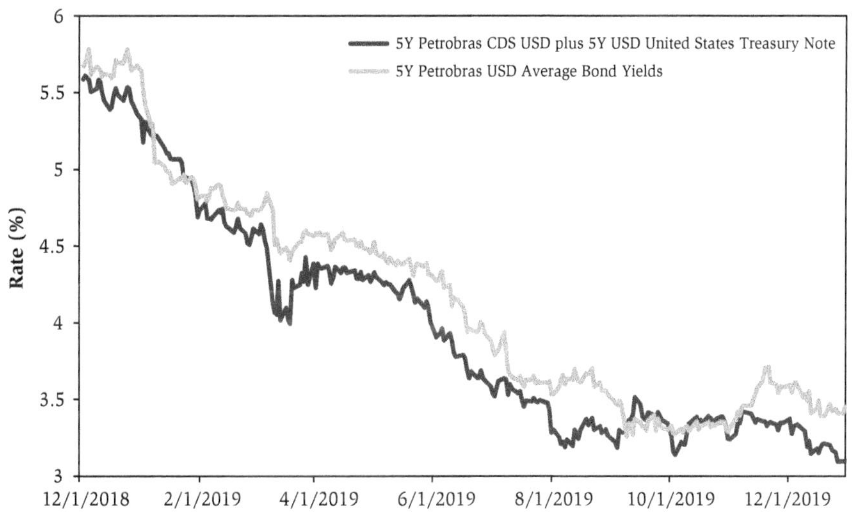

Data source: Bloomberg LP. *5 Year Petrobras bond yields and 5Y US Treasury Note yields*, obtained from Bloomberg database (accessed July 3, 2019).

Other caveats apply when it comes to CDS data, such as manufactured defaults[60] and situations of imbalances in supply and demand of CDS contracts due to exogenous

59. To which the authors have added the corresponding risk-free rate.
60. In the recent past, the CDS market has seen situations of "artificial" credit events in which a lender bought protection via CDSs of a certain issuer. The lender discussed extending new favorable loans to that issuer under the condition that the issuer took steps that constituted an event of default under the International Swaps and Derivatives Association swap definitions (a consequence of which was a windfall for the lender on its CDS positions) on existing debt. One recent case, in early 2018, involved Hovnanian Enterprises Inc. (a home builder). This case illustrates that this event of default (and hence the level of credit default spreads) did not reflect the true financial state of the issuer. In such circumstances, CDS spreads should not be included in any arm's length analysis.

factors.[61] These are just two instances for which CDS spreads might not be appropriate for assessing arm's-length rates on an intercompany financing arrangement since the pricing of CDS spreads can reflect other considerations not directly linked to the default risk of the reference entity (issuer).

4.4.2 *Other Methods*

In some cases, the CUP method cannot be relied on. This is especially the case for some guarantee transactions, factoring, captive insurance type transactions, and lower-rated European debt instruments. It is not because this particular type of financing is not available in the market but that European disclosure laws do not require companies to provide full disclosure on financing and the terms and conditions thereof. In these cases, other methods such as the actuarial approach (loss given default approach) can be relied on.

4.4.2.1 The Actuarial Approach: Overview

The actuarial approach typically assesses the losses associated with a default (loss given default) given the credit risk associated with the relevant party. Although various models can be identified, two can be used to estimate the expected and unexpected losses: the default model and the mark-to-market model.[62] The terms and especially the definition of a credit event would typically determine which model is most appropriate. The key difference between them is that the default model is suitable for situations when there is an estimation of the default loss as derived at issuance of the instrument. In contrast, the mark-to-market model is suitable for transactions in which the pricing is marked to market as and when the credit profile changes. Hence, the latter model would consider the credit migration of an entity while the former would not. More commonly, the default model is applied when it comes to intercompany financing arrangements.

4.4.2.2 The Actuarial Approach: Unexpected Losses and Impact on Pricing

In addition to the expected loss, unexpected losses in a transaction should typically be considered. This is especially relevant for guarantee or insurance-based transactions. The default model and the mark-to-market model assess the unexpected losses in the same way. These can be estimated by the difference between a value-at-risk (VaR) and the expected losses. The VaR represents the losses over a given time period at a given level of confidence. This will determine the amount of capital to be set aside by the

61. One such example is in the context of Basel III/CRD IV (in Europe) on which additional capital requirements on banks have been imposed. These requirements include additional capital requirements linked to potential credit exposure to over-the-counter transactions contracted by the banks with their corporate clients.
62. A. Saunders and L. Allen, *Credit Risk Measurement: New Approaches to Value at Risk and Other Paradigms*, Second Edition Wiley Finance, 2002, pp. 84-106.

financial institution, lender, or guarantor in order to be prepared for such situations. Because this capital could have been deployed to other ends, the price of the funding includes the cost of setting aside this capital to face unexpected losses should they arise. For this reason, "opportunity cost" is referenced when describing unexpected losses.

Once the expected and unexpected losses are computed based on one of the methods above, the price of the instrument can be estimated as the sum of the expected losses and unexpected losses (or the opportunity cost associated with the transaction).[63]

4.4.2.3 *The Actuarial Approach: Accounting for Marginal Benefit Achieved*

Unlike other methods, the actuarial approach can be easily adjusted to determine the marginal benefit from transactions such as guarantees or factoring. The aim is to estimate the added protection received by the creditors of the subsidiary from, for example, the additional guarantee of the parent company. This added protection, which corresponds to the economic value of the guarantee, protects lenders in scenarios in which the guaranteed entity faces bankruptcy without bringing the parent into extreme financial difficulties (co-joint bankruptcies). This method is even more useful if a guarantor has the same rating as that of its subsidiary.

Under the actuarial approach, the probability that the parent does not default following the subsidiary's default is estimated by calculating the joint probability of default of both entities. This hinges on the correlation of their default, that is, the interconnectedness of their respective default probability. This approach ties into measuring the ability to provide support as described by Moody's.

Correlation estimations for this purpose can be based on an analysis of price returns. These can be returns of interest-bearing securities from both entities or, if not available, of comparable companies. Moreover, correlation estimation may rely on equity price returns from both entities or, if not available, of comparable entities. Equity data is, at times, the only data source available.[64]

4.4.3 *Summary of Pricing Approaches*

The CUP and "other method" approaches, such as the capital approach, in the context of guarantees or variations on the actuarial model, cannot be relied on in all cases. Thus, the methodology used to price a particular transaction very much depends on the underlying characteristics and data viability for that market.

When using the CUP method, finding the right data may be difficult because the data needs to be sufficiently comparable to the transaction, or the required adjustments

63. The capital asset pricing model can be relied on to proxy the cost of capital associated to the unexpected losses.
64. Correlation can also be estimated with structural models, such as the one developed by J. Hull and A. White, *Valuing Credit Default Swaps II: Modelling Default Correlations*, 8 NYU Working Paper (2000).

can be performed which might not always be possible. Furthermore, when considering bank opinions, the OECD Guidance on Financial Transactions highlights that such "bankability" opinions are not actual market transactions and, therefore, cannot generally be considered to be evidence of an arm's-length pricing.[65]

On the other hand, although an approach such as the actuarial approach can be relied on in most circumstances, it is rather academic (i.e., technical) and might be difficult to apply for market participants in practice. Being based on historical (default) probability and recovery rate data, comparability to current market conditions might prove to be problematic for which adjustments may have to be performed.

5 CONCLUSIONS

The authors have reviewed some of the main issues surrounding intercompany financing transactions in the transfer pricing world. Alongside the significant increase in attention to the matter from various tax authorities around the world, the authors have also seen key organizations (including the OECD and UN) provide their versions of guidance for financing transactions. The court systems have been testing financing structures and transactions and have provided food for thought for nearly all taxpayers and tax authorities and reminding us of their complexity and contentiousness. Furthermore, the financial landscape has changed, leading to an increase in dispute resolutions including audits and MAPs being used by tax authorities.

In this climate, it is critical to have a robust analytical framework that considers the important role that financing plays in the business with many external and internal factors affecting the capital structure and the funding decisions available and decisions made. Overall, the financial sector is an incredibly multifaceted and ever-evolving industry that has received much scrutiny over recent years as institutions and stakeholders attempt to reach consensus on dealing with its complexities.

In an ever-evolving industry, it is even more important that the arm's-length principle should be applied consistently when pricing intercompany financing. In this context, endeavoring to produce simplified guidance as that attempted by the OECD or the UN is unlikely to capture the full essence of the financial transactions at stake and could lead to some manipulation and abuse in application. It remains to be seen whether, in the future, the OECD and the UN released guidance may better enable tax authorities and taxpayers to deal with intercompany financing and the complexities of the environment that are faced.

65. OECD, Transfer Pricing Guidance on Financial Transactions, Inclusive Framework on BEPS: Actions 4, 8-10, February 2020, section C.1.2.6, paragraphs 10.107 and 10.108.

CHAPTER 8

Recent Developments on the Use of New Technologies for Transfer Pricing*

*Sam Sim, Markus Baur & Sid Paruthi***

* The views expressed in this article are solely those of the authors and do not constitute tax advice nor reflect the views of their employers or organizations.

** The authors wish to thank Prof. Dr. Robert Risse and his team at Henkel, Dr. Torben Petersen, Marek Kobol, Dr. Holger Richter, and Mr. Ram Vadakke for their assistance and comments. Any errors, of course, remain that of the authors.

This chapter follows the acclaimed tax notes article "Going the Way of the Polaroid: Digital Taxation and the End of the Arm's-length Principle?"

In this chapter, the authors examine recent developments in the Transfer Pricing (TP) world and how the use of new technologies for transfer pricing analysis can potentially help both taxpayers and tax administrations.

This use of technology is informed by several macro-trends that are impacting the transfer pricing post-BEPS (Base Erosion and Profit Shifting) such as the increase in the volume of documentation with the three tiers introduced by BEPS Action 13, growing local reporting requirements (such as SAF-T and TP disclosure forms), and global transparency in the form of exchange of information. Furthermore, the need for tax departments to "become digital" and thus enhance their internal control frameworks as well as cost efficiency imperatives are driving this agenda.

The market has reacted to this development, and both tax advisory firms as well as technology providers are offering a suite of tools and solutions aiming to support companies in moving toward digitalized TP compliance, documentation, and operational transfer pricing.

While companies clearly want to leverage automatization, this increase in TP data and compliance may not always be amenable to technology solutions. Doubts and concerns may exist whether such solutions can deliver on their promise to simplify TP documentation, work seamlessly with the companies' enterprise resource planning (ERP) systems, and whether tax departments possess the skills required for the future. The authors survey the field, including solution providers, and draw from their experience with a selection of multinational enterprises (MNEs) of different sizes and business sectors to understand the approach taken by these companies.

The questions companies pose in relation to new technologies and the desire to apply technology to improve tax compliance can be complex, but the conclusion to these questions is often rather simple—it all depends on the facts and circumstances of each taxpayer and jurisdiction. There is no one-size-fits-all solution or approach to using technology for transfer pricing. However, one thing is also clear, no company or tax authority should neglect the developments in technology.

The authors make a contribution to the ongoing discourse in this area by drawing out the key principles, fleshing out real life experiences by surveying MNEs, reviewing TP tools available in the market,[1] and identifying new technologies such as robotic process automation (RPA), data wrangling, artificial intelligence (AI), and blockchain that are rapidly advancing and promise to reshape transfer pricing in the years to come.

1 THE CHANGING GLOBAL TRANSFER PRICING LANDSCAPE

The global transfer pricing landscape has, in recent years, been transformed by the G20-OECD (Organisation for Economic Co-operation and Development) Base Erosion and Profit Shifting Project.[2] In the drive toward reforming the international tax system to target nowhere income and to align taxation to where value is created, transfer pricing has played a central role. This role can be described as follows:

(1) The TP rules permit the articulation of (and, some would say, adjusted to counteract avoidance) where value is created. This is a matter of policy.
(2) The information required to map and understand the global transactions and structure of MNEs beyond the entity level view provided by tax returns is achieved by vastly expanding TP reporting requirements under Action 13 to encompass the country-by-country report (CbCR), the master file, and local file.[3] In particular, the master file now emphasizes mapping out the entire value chain across the group and key elements such as intangibles, financing, and competent authority rulings and agreements.[4]

To the above can add the proliferation of:

(a) Extensive local related party transaction reporting forms that form part of the income tax returns, a recent example of which is Thailand's new form.

1. The market for TP tools and solutions is very wide and constantly changing. The selection of tools mentioned in this chapter, therefore, can only represent a snapshot and sampling of what is available today and should not be understood as a full overview of all available products. The authors also want to clarify that the mentioning of a particular product should not be understood as an endorsement for it.
2. OECD (2013), *Addressing Base Erosion and Profit Shifting*, OECD Publishing, Paris, available at https://doi.org/10.1787/9789264192744-en, accessed August 28, 2020.
3. OECD (2017), *BEPS Action 13 on Country-by-Country Reporting- Peer Review Documents, OECD/G20 Base Erosion and Profit Shifting Project*, OECD, Paris.
4. OECD (2017), *OECD Transfer Pricing Guidelines for Multinational Enterprises and Tax Administrations 2017*, OECD Publishing, Paris, available at https://doi.org/10.1787/tpg-2017-en, accessed August 28, 2020.

(b) The OECD SAF-T (Standard Audit File for Tax)[5] is an international standard for electronic exchange of reliable accounting data from organizations to a national tax authority or external auditors. More and more tax administrations are implementing e-audits of a business's financial records and systems, including adopting tools that can interrogate these records on the basis that they must support the SAF-T methodology. These range from Norway, Austria, Luxembourg, and Singapore to Portugal, with SAF-T generally applying first to large businesses. Farther down the road, the European Commission is looking to develop a European Union SAF-T with the aim of facilitating ongoing compliance by taxpayers and allowing tax administrations to carry out tax audits that are more effective.

(c) In the same vein as SAF-T, jurisdictions such as Germany adopt their own electronic tax balance sheet or define their own e-audit file standards like Sweden and the Netherlands, and still others including Brazil and China, with their Thousand Enterprise Initiative, require businesses to hand over all of their electronic financial records down to transactional level data.

2 IMPACT ON MNE's TAX AND TP DEPARTMENTS

The result of the above trends is a massive increase in the compliance workload of tax departments, including TP teams, which typically runs contrary to the spirit of the OECD TP Guidelines which state that they should ideally not pose unnecessary burden on the taxpayers while complying with them.

The most significant new burden is that of preparing and vetting the CbCRs.[6] Resources will often have to be drawn not only from finance but also from other business areas within the company to perform the task, and TP teams will have to perform a review and analysis in anticipation of more queries arising from the automatic exchange of CbCRs.[7]

Even if the TP function is not directly involved in the preparation of the forms, they have to be familiar with the trend toward requiring the use of standardized value-added tax codes, standardized chart of accounts, detailed invoice information, source documents, assets, and inventories and be able to reconcile (a) between jurisdictions that have implemented SAF-T and those who have not in implementing TP and (b) their TP computations with the specific formats required by the local country.

5. OECD (2010), *Forum on Tax Administration Guidance Note: Guidance for the Standard Audit File, Tax Version 2.0*, April 2010, OECD, Paris, available at http://www.oecd.org/ctp/administration/45045602.pdf, accessed August 28, 2020.
6. Guidance on Country-by-Country Reporting: BEPS Action 13, available at https://www.oecd.org/tax/beps/guidance-on-country-by-country-reporting-beps-action-13.htm, accessed August 28, 2020.
7. *See* the list of countries that have signed up to automatic exchange of country-by-country reports available at https://www.oecd.org/ctp/exchange-of-tax-information/CbC-MCAA-Signatories.pdf, accessed August 28, 2020.

This workload increase is exacerbated by the deluge of tax information arising from tax transparency and widespread exchange of information, especially TP data between authorities, be it in the form of CbCRs or rulings and unilateral Advance Pricing Agreements. Furthermore, the trend toward cooperative compliance and joint audits by one or more tax authorities require TP data to be integrated and presented in a coherent and consistent manner.

On a more positive note:

(a) the preparation of a CbCR and a master file anchored on value chain analysis has meant that there is a need to centralize the TP function at the headquarter levels;
(b) the drive toward formats that are more standardized and XML based reporting has meant cleaning up and harmonizing data when it previously may have been a lone endeavor by the TP team to extract manually, unstructured data from multiple databases or ERP sources.

This need for centralized control and resourcing is further driven by the need for proper tax control frameworks including TP compliance to qualify for cooperative compliance regimes (horizontal monitoring and ICAP)[8] and the universal trend toward greater tax transparency with more exchange of information and joint audits that require integrated, consistent data in order to tell a "consistent story" across several different jurisdictions.

The higher attention to TP can mean more management attention and, in an ideal case, more resources, including a budget to digitalize or automate in order to cope with the increased workload. Second, the standardization of formats across a sprawling conglomerate and being compelled to clean up data means such data become much more amenable to big data analytics and application of AI techniques to yield insights.

Lastly, more emphasis on standardization also helps companies to have the SOX/internal audit control procedures aligned with the business realities.

3 OPTIONS AND TECHNOLOGY SOLUTIONS AVAILABLE

3.1 A General Approach Is a Mix of In-House and Outsourced Solutions

(a) Keeping It In-house: In many cases, especially in larger MNEs, a dedicated member of the tax/finance team or even an entire team responsible for looking after the TP matters of the company can be found. Their responsibilities can span from setting prices for intercompany transactions in accordance to the arm's length standard to full operational TP including monitoring and

8. OECD (2019), *International Compliance Assurance Programme Pilot Handbook 2.0*, OECD, Paris, www.oecd.org/www.oecd.org/tax/forum-on-tax-administration/publications-and-products/international-compliance-assurance-programme-pilot-handbook-2.0.htm, accessed August 28, 2020.

planning of results to the TP documentation processing.[9] An in-house TP team will make sense for companies that want to keep key functions within their organization and thus actively manage how much they spend on advisor fees by relying less on external services providers.

On the other hand, many corporations are under cost and headcount pressure and, therefore, having a dedicated in-house TP team or department might not be optimal for them.

In either case, the company will need to ensure that its staff who have responsibility over TP are constantly educated and will need to consider how to ensure their "upskilling" to keep up with new technologies.

(b) Outsourcing of key TP functions to external tax advisers might offer a lot of advantages for corporations who cannot or do not want to maintain their own TP department. From a technology perspective, this option might be even more attractive to corporations as the burden of the selection, deploying, and maintenance of the most suitable technology tools and upskilling of employees is transferred to the service provider. Furthermore, outsourcing can also be helpful if the advisors have in-house experience. Having advisors with in-house experience helps in receiving practical and pragmatic advice which lowers the cost to the company. Some large- and medium-sized audit and accounting firms have the resources such as teams of programmers or have consulting teams that can come up with systems and solutions for which a relatively small tax department cannot afford to invest. Some, such as *PricewaterhouseCoopers* with their takeover of the GE tax compliance team, claim to offer an advantageous model by offering to take on wholesale outsourcing of the transfer pricing function. However, caution must be taken as to whether outsourcing will work for each company's circumstance. Outsourcing often can mean loss of institutional knowledge and control of key TP processes. External consultants might require substantial time and effort to understand the company, its data, and ERP infrastructure and could lack access to the internal stakeholders to be able to effect change. The cost savings that were intended may not materialize as reliance on external advisors can lead to escalating costs year after year.

(c) Hybrid approach: Frequently, companies will use a mix of in-house and external resources to manage the TP processes. This can span from outsourcing, e.g., benchmarking to the full TP documentation process, to selectively purchasing tools or solutions and integrating them into existing systems. An MNE, for example, purchases Alteryx for use on data extracted from its existing Hyperion system with Microsoft BI software used to visualize the data. In such instances, systems integration aspects need to be considered, for example, how well the tools installed in-house interact with tools used by the

9. Whereby also here variations are possible from the preparation of the master and/or local file to the full end-to-end documentation including benchmarking studies and, wherever relevant, CbCR.

external service provider. There is also a need for clear roles and responsibilities as these systems and tools cross functional lines between the different finance, tax, and IT teams.

3.2 Critical Assessment of the Types of Technology Solutions Available

No company can avoid considering and adapting its IT and technology strategy to the constant changes in the market place and industry. Recent surveys[10] confirm that technology is very high up on the agenda of tax/TP departments.

While most of these decisions will focus on the core business segments, the tax/TP function should also start to examine their processes and consider how to leverage technology to get ready for the future. Increasing efficiency by using state-of-the-art tools and automatization have become top priority agenda items for any head of tax.

According to WTS Global, a tax specialist, a fully integrated digital end-to-end process (E2E) (from the initial price setting, involving individual transaction data, to the final transfer pricing documentation report) consists of the following parts:

1	Determine price mechanisms, assessment of individual facts	Price Setting
2	Define attributable KPIs (e.g., profit margins) per transaction type	
3	Extract separate financial numbers from differently adapted ERP and non-ERP systems	Operational TP
4	Correction of out-of-range prices or dynamic adjustments in an automated IT environment	
5	Identify and extract intercompany transactions after the end of the financial year	TP Documentation
6	Query of master data and qualitative information via tool-supported standardized forms	
7	Automated creation of TP documentation reports	

So what solutions are there currently on the market, and how will they be developing in the near future?

3.2.1 Leveraging Existing ERP Systems

Standardized reports generated from the leading ERP systems such as SAP are used for common TP tasks including monitoring operating margins of entities in a group. These

10. *See*, for example, https://www.arkksolutions.com/tax-survey-results/, accessed August 28, 2020.

reports can be extracted or generated by the users in the finance, accounting, or TP teams into a spreadsheet format which then allows further manipulation and analysis. The clear advantage of such a solution is the ease of creating and extracting the relevant reports as well as the very little extra cost and limited effort in implementing such a solution as, in most cases, this functionality is already available in standard ERP installations.

A downside is that users still need to pro-actively extract the data and then perform their analysis using the created spreadsheet, which can be very time consuming. Moreover, Excel spreadsheets are inherently limited in their functionality and, importantly, the amount of data they can handle. For example, an earlier version of Excel could only handle 64,000 lines of data. More recent versions can handle 1,048,576 rows or 16,384 columns. Beyond that, the source file has to be opened in a text editor such as Microsoft Word, saved as several smaller files that conform to this row and column limit, and then open the smaller files in Excel. If the source data cannot be opened in a text editor, the alternative is to import the data into Microsoft Access and then exporting subsets of the data from Access to Excel.

Manipulating large amounts of data, calculating, and then making profit allocations across the group can also pose risks from data entry errors and transposition mistakes to lack of controls or review of significant amounts entered into the financial books, resulting, in the worst case, in errors that jeopardize the true and fair nature of financial entries.

3.2.2 Benchmarking Tools

It is popular for MNEs to consider in-sourcing benchmarking searches and preparing studies in-house. In this area, there are numerous service providers on the market who offer a variety of solutions.[11]

The scope of these tools/solutions vary from providing the ability to search very specific types of data, such as interest rates, to tools that enable searches in the more commonly used databases such as royalty rates and corporate financial data. What is common across these tools is that they offer user friendly interfaces to structure the search for comparables and thus enable users without extensive training to run the database searches.[12] Some of the solutions on the market also offer the option to create a fully analyzed report including a profit level indicator (PLI) computation and screening criteria from the database searches which can then be incorporated as part of the TP documentation of the company. Others have value-added functionalities such as

11. Zanders, https://inside.zanders.eu/en/transfer-pricing; RoyaltyStat, https://www.royaltystat.com/; Market intelligence, https://www.spglobal.com/marketintelligence/en/; Royalty Range, https://www.royaltyrange.com/; ktMine, https://www.ktmine.com/transfer-pricing-beps/; BVD, https://www.bvdinfo.com/en-gb/our-products/catalyst/tp-catalyst, accessed August 28, 2020.
12. To illustrate what tools were available 20 years ago, reference is made to: M. Cools, International Commercial Databases for Transfer Pricing Studies, Int'l Transfer Pricing J. September/October 1999, IBFD (accessed March 3, 2020), available at https://research.ibfd.org/collections/itpj/pdf/itpj059901.pdf, accessed August 28, 2020.

saving search strategies or collaborative tools that allow different account IDs to review each other's work. The latter is particularly useful when MNEs have geographically dispersed teams and offshore shared services centers.

An additional value-added service offered by some solution providers includes support from their team of trained economists for the clients' search and analysis. They help in fine-tuning and validating the results of the benchmarking studies created by the clients with their technical tools. Nevertheless, it is the authors' experience that it is sometimes not optimal to outsource the element of benchmarking that requires precise understanding of the tested parties and close analysis of the comparables such as close scrutiny of agreements where the Comparable Uncontrolled Method is used.

One of these tools calculates the arm's length pricing for a financial transaction in relatively simple steps starting with uploading the financial data of the tested companies and then determining the credit rating of the borrower based on quantitative and qualitative information such as implicit group support.[13] Based on the data of the tested companies, the tool will look up the relevant interest or bond market rates for the relevant transaction and then generate a full report that includes all input data, search and screening criteria, description of the methods used, and the transfer pricing results.

The benefit of subscribing to such benchmarking tools lies in the flexibility they offer to companies to run searches or alternative scenarios for planning purposes whenever they are needed without having to wait to scope a project and for an external service provider to deliver a report.

While the installation of such tools as stand-alone applications is not complicated, the need to invest in the training of the in-house users from the TP or finance department should not be underestimated to ensure good quality outputs. This often involves subjective qualitative judgment such as the TP staff handling the report having to run a qualitative screening (e.g., website check of the selected comparable companies) and manually exclude search results that are not reliable as comparables.[14] Finally, as part of translating the search results into policy that can be operationalized and tracked, there are additional steps involved in loading the search results into any further analytical or tracking reports, be it simple spreadsheets or a more complex tool.

3.2.3 "Total" TP Documentation Solutions

Compiling information for multiple business units and entities across many jurisdictions in order to draft TP documentation can be a very challenging task.

13. Importance of credit rating is discussed in A. Sulejmani, Pricing Intercompany Financial Transactions: Loans, Guarantees and Cash-Pooling Arrangements, 26 Intl. Transfer Pricing J. 6 (2019), Journal Articles & Papers IBFD (accessed March 2, 2020), available at https://research.ibfd.org/#/doc?url=/collections/itpj/html/itpj_2019_06_int_3.html, accessed August 28, 2020.
14. E. Muyaa, Transfer Pricing Comparability Adjustments: The Pursuit of "Exact" Comparables, 21 Intl. Transfer Pricing J. 5 (2014), Journals IBFD (accessed March 2, 2020), available at https://research.ibfd.org/#/doc?url=/collections/itpj/html/itpj_2014_05_int_3.html, accessed August 28, 2020.

The technology solutions on offer purport to help TP departments better manage their workflows and control the content of their TP documentation. There are a variety of solutions on the market offering a wide range of functionalities.[15]

The common value proposition that these documentation solutions offer to companies is a structured approach to managing the workflow and facilitating collaboration between the different stakeholders, including teams across different geographies, in the TP documentation process. The programs permit assignment of roles to individuals across the team—TP specialists would be responsible for compiling the report, those supplying information (mainly finance, accounting, business units) would be designated and informed, and the more senior tax management and local tax managers would serve as reviewers for consistency with the intended global position and adherence to local rules and circumstances.

A second feature is that the solution enables tracking of the entities and jurisdictions for which the TP documentation needs to be prepared. Deadlines can be set with an alert function in some of the tools.

A third feature is that these solutions often take a modular approach toward creating the relevant write-up for TP documentation, be it the master file or local file. The authors/editors are able to pick from a menu of standardized modules for individual transactions. These modular text blocks will contain the functional analysis and the underlying TP method applied for the transactions. The TP documentation is then assembled from the various relevant modules with an overview of the legal entity, its financial results, and the benchmarking/economic analysis. For the latter, some tools integrate the comparability database search function in order to come up with the entire TP report while others adopt more of an open architecture where benchmarking reports created by tools from other external sources may be integrated. The content for the individual modules range from clients documenting the functions, assets, and risks as well as other company facts based on functional interviews and an analysis to more generic standard text such as language around method selection and the OECD arm's length principle, which can be used as is or adapted as required.

Fourth, the solutions these days tend to offer Cloud hosting as it permits scalability and the ability to offer access from multiple locations across the MNE's footprint. However, owing to cybersecurity requirements and data privacy concerns, some providers continue to offer their MNE clients the option to run the solution on the MNEs' own IT infrastructure.

Some solutions go further to offer a feature that allows the user to upload and store the main intercompany agreements. Such a feature is both a convenient way of sharing and storing data especially across dispersed teams, e.g., between the TP department in the group's HQ and the local tax teams in the different countries and are increasingly becoming a necessity as more and more TP legislations around the world

15. Otico www.otico-software.com and TPCa BVD, https://www.bvdinfo.com/en-gb/our-products/catalyst/tp-catalyst; Reptun, https://www.reptune.net/#features; Intercompany Software, https://www.intercompany-software.com/solutions.html#close; Aibidia, https://www.aibidia.com/; Thomson Reuters, https://tax.thomsonreuters.com/en/corporation-solutions/transfer-pricing; exa AG, https://www.exa-ag.com/products/operational-transfer-pricing-otp/ also the larger advisers offer such tools, all links accessed August 28, 2020.

specify intercompany agreements as part of the mandatory documentation requirements.

In all, the main difference between the different solutions on the market is the scope offered within the tool, the ease of integration with other existing applications of the MNEs, and also the flexibility of the manner in which data is uploaded into the TP drafting tool.

MNEs need to weigh the pros and cons of implementing such as the TP documentation tool before committing to the journey. One advantage is the possibility for an MNE to effectively centralize and steer the TP documentation process by allowing users across the organization to prepare and upload content, review and sign-off documents, and receive streamlined TP documentation for their local compliance needs. Such a centralized approach can lead to improved collaboration within the TP/tax/finance functions and thus positively improve TP risk management. Companies can implement their review process within the tool and utilize the workflow management option built into most solutions to monitor and also document the different stages of the preparation of their TP documentation. The modular construction offers the ability to scale and ensures consistency via a template approach to fit institutions of various sizes and needs and input customized content to cover the different dimensions of documentation—from a business unit (divisional), territorial (legal entity), or product line perspective.

Notwithstanding the attractiveness of such solutions, MNEs need to understand the potential downsides. The most common criticism of these solutions is that the pre-written modules in some tools might not capture the true nature of the business or the tested transaction. The rigidity of the input modules, which is unavoidably designed to be used across the whole spectrum of companies and industries, suffer from the same challenge as the country-by-country one-size-fits-all template in that it may fail to present a full picture by not capturing certain areas while overemphasizing others. This disadvantage is amplified when a taxpayer is under audit and the tax authorities typically use an in-house economist to run the searches and come up with different economic reasons for using one PLI over another. This disadvantage could be overcome by MNEs not relying on the off-the-shelf templates but rather redesigning their own to fit their circumstances (e.g., more extensive write-ups on risks for financial services) and crafting their own descriptions or reasoning (such as rejecting certain TP methods) instead of relying on the standard offerings. While such an approach would enhance the content and quality of the TP documentation, it also means additional work to adapt to the modular format and templates of the solution, which some MNEs may find not worth the trouble when compared to staying with their pre-existing house style of drafting TP documentation.

3.2.4 CbCR Solutions

The BEPS Project Inclusive Framework's minimum standards introduced a new challenge for MNEs in the form of preparing the third tier of the OECD TP documentation—the CbCR, alongside a more extensive value chain disclosure of the master file and the "traditional" details previously required in the local files.[16] The CbCR requirements pose a heavy compliance burden for MNCs in terms of gathering all of the relevant information, sorting and validating, and reporting the data in the required format. For companies with sizeable foreign operations in multiple jurisdictions, this will require a significant time commitment from resources across the organization. The data that is required resides in the systems of the finance, accounting, and human resources departments. As a consequence, the tax function will need their cooperation as the CbCR is a recurring compliance requirement.

MNEs dealing with a CbCR for the first time might believe that compiling it is a mere spreadsheet exercise using available data from the various departments thus mistakenly assigning this as a standardized routine task to junior tax staff or other junior finance/accounting staff.

However, such an assumption can lead to major issues for the MNE in the following years because the CbCR should rightly be considered as a strategic overview or snapshot of the TP profile of the entire group which can form a basis for the tax authorities to develop an audit roadmap for the MNE. The overall picture provided in the CbCR needs to be aligned to the narrative in the master file, the group's TP policies, and local files. Therefore, it is the authors' view that MNEs should devote the due attention, including at the senior levels, to the preparation, review, and analysis of the CbCR as this report is and will be used to a great extent by tax authorities around the world to gain an understanding of the groups' major centers of activities and the actual results by jurisdiction. The analytical nature of this work means that it is not possible nor desirable to automate the entire CbCR process. Instead, technology can be leveraged to reduce the workload in the preparation of a CbCR and in recurring analyses.

Several providers offer software solutions designed specifically for the creation of CbCR reports.[17] These tools offer the creation of OECD BEPS Action 13 compliant CbCRs including Table 1 (Overview of allocation of income, taxes, and business activities) and Table 2 (list of all constituent entities of the MNE group included in each aggregation per tax jurisdiction) based on the data provided by the MNE in a relatively straightforward manner.

The main difference between the different solutions on offer is how the company's data is imported into each tool. Some applications allow upload via common data formats such as CSV files, tab-separated text files, XML, DBF, and a FileMaker Pro file or support upload from standard ERP or accounting tools. Other CBCR solutions rely on specific application program interface (API) which is a set of routines, protocols, and tools for building software applications. Basically, an API specifies how software components should interact, in this case, how the companies' accounting systems should interact with the CbCR tool.

16. *OECD TP Guidelines supra*, C.3 p. 235.
17. Intercompany Software, available at https://www.intercompany-software.com/solutions.html#close Aibidia, https://www.aibidia.com/ Crossborder Solutions, https://www.crossborder.ai/person/fiona/, accessed August 28, 2020.

Once the information is uploaded, the tools offer analytics of the results that can be presented in graphical form to show the global TP profile of the MNE and highlight any outliers such as locations with high income, low headcount, and low taxes that suggest lack of substance or tend to attract greater scrutiny. Such an analysis should support the senior tax management to better understand the group's risk profile from a base erosion and profit shifting perspective.

As mentioned above, the tools can help speed up the task of preparing and performing repetitive analyses of the CbCR such as computing ratios of revenue or taxes to the number of employees. However, technology is no substitute for the subsequent human analysis, judgment, and intervention to address any risks that emerge.

First, Table 3 of the CbCR is a free-form field where companies can provide a substantial amount of additional information to supplement the profile conveyed by Tables 1 and 2. Such further information and explanations crucially help to clarify any ostensible mismatches that Tables 1 and 2 appear to suggest and can go a long way to facilitate a more appropriate appreciation of the global profile of the MNE. For example, it is the norm for the insurance and funds industry to operate out of Bermuda and other island jurisdictions. Qualitative descriptions are needed to provide the context. The process of providing such descriptions beyond the financial numbers cannot be automated.

Second, the CbCR does not require the use of consolidated financials and can be reported using aggregated numbers at an entity level. It is sound practice, therefore, for companies to reconcile the aggregated data from the CbCR with the consolidated financial statements. The latter is the starting point for most local country audits and, naturally, any mismatches between the CbCR and local statutory financial numbers could be the point for queries. The tools presently available do not support such reconciliations, in part, because the accounting conventions differ from country to country and certain adjustments entail judgment calls. This task will remain manual for the foreseeable future.

Finally, even if there are mismatches, the judgment of senior tax leaders and further inputs by others is required to assess the implications and determine the course of action. Such factors include taking into account the audit history in a particular jurisdiction and the trade-off of disrupting or creating exceptions to otherwise uniform global modes of conducting business.

3.2.5 Robotic Process Automation

RPA builds on predetermined rules and algorithms, implements them to the regular and routine workflows, and does not require any human involvement. RPA can help MNEs centrally manage the workflow of transfer pricing via facilitating data collection, analysis, operational transfer pricing, and reporting.[18]

18. Available at https://www.africataxjournal.com/wp-content/uploads/2018/05/Blockchain-Benefits-of-Robotic-Process-Automation-in-Transfer-Pricing.pdf, accessed August 28, 2020.

RPA can help with data collection and analysis as part of implementing transfer pricing. Bots can collect and store the intercompany transactions on a periodic basis (e.g., quarterly) and facilitate earlier and more frequent analyses of the TP related data that is extracted from the ERP system.

RPA are appropriate where TP policies can be distilled into clear rules and repetitive TP computation. Examples of these instances include computation of margins or costs, which can be codified with clear distinct and sequential steps. RPA can assist in automating computational steps that are repeated in volume with minimal errors. RPA is generally better suited to structured, digitalized data that can be combined with tools like Xceptor as an enabler to capture and transform data for onward transmission to an RPA robot.

The potential of RPA to help reduce a repetitive manual workload is receiving increasing attention. For TP tasks, this is applicable to situations in which companies rely heavily on Excel spreadsheets for their key TP operations. RPA can be thought of as a gateway—a way to introduce automation and gain business efficiencies at low cost and with minimal risk or disruption since it simply automates what would otherwise be manual processes. The concept is simple. A software "robot" replicates routine human-computer interaction, automating what would otherwise be tedious, repetitive tasks. RPA thus bridges the gap between repeated manual processing and full automation.

RPA can span over multiple platforms and tools and can thus be implemented quite efficiently within reasonable timeframes. RPA will perform activities such as repetitive click-by-click actions and will thus mimic human actions.

Automating repetitive tasks by using these "bots" can save time and money. RPA bots can help the company expand the value of an automation platform by completing tasks faster, allowing employees to perform higher-value work. Other benefits include reduction of human errors compared to manual work when data is copied over multiple times from one data source into another.

Deploying RPA software is not equivalent to building fully automated processes and platforms from the ground up; the process is simpler and, therefore, less disruptive to the TP and IT functions that are involved. With stand-alone RPA, a software robot literally does what a human would do: tasks such as data retrieval and entry, button clicks, file uploads and downloads, or invoice processing. As applied to TP, this could be accessing reports from the ERP or other sources such as benchmark studies or other databases containing TP relevant data.

Such bots can be rolled out in relatively short time frames. The creation, testing, and deployment of such automation schemes can happen within hours or days. This can significantly increase the throughput related to this specific task very quickly and generate saving valuable time of highly skilled employees who then can concentrate on more high value adding work.

RPA is particularly appealing when IT resources and budgets are limited or for working with back-end applications that lack good APIs[19] and would thus be difficult to automate without significant change. However, to deploy RPA wisely, companies need to understand the technology's benefits and limitations—and the ways in which it can be leveraged to expand their capability and the value it brings.

Nonetheless, RPA is not without its limitations. One of the limitations with using RPA is that processes need to be well defined and well designed in the first place. RPA does not make a bad process better; in fact, it may exacerbate existing issues with poor processes. Changes in upstream systems or applications need to be carefully monitored to ensure that "bots" do not pick up incorrect data. In many organizations, it is viewed as an end user computing tool and carries with it the need to monitor and manage related risks with appropriate controls.

3.2.6 Data Wrangling

A next logical step after automation by using bots is implementation of the so-called data wrangling tools.

Data wrangling is the process of converting and mapping data from its *raw* form to another format with the purpose of making it more valuable and appropriate for advance tasks such as data analytics and machine learning.

In the context of financial data that is relevant for TP, this means transforming data from different sources within one single tool so as to offer a friendly user interface that allows connection to different source systems. Such a tool would allow data that was previously retrieved by bots to be reconciled and consolidated in one standardized repeatable workflow based on a defined set of rules. The advantage of such a solution would be to get precise and actionable data to business analysts in a timely matter.

Both RPA and data wrangling tools make sense for companies with complex intercompany transactions that are still using mainly spreadsheet-driven processes as an effective first step into adopting new technologies. It paves the way for further next steps such as implementing TP specific applications or tools.

The ability of these tools to enable the efficient and frequent computation of margins (even down to the stock keeping unit level), true-ups or customs impact helps in the monitoring of the proper implementation of TP and, more importantly, permits anticipation or earlier reaction if there is a deviation from the intended arm's length range or if there are ancillary implications such as customs liabilities arising from the TP adjustments. The ability to process data quickly also helps in the generation of tax/TP reports providing an overview of the status/state of TP across the MNE.

19. API refers to application program interface, a set of routines, protocols, and tools for building software applications. An API specifies how software components should interact thereby allowing the creation of applications that access the features or data of an operating system, application, or other service.

3.2.7 *Artificial Intelligence*

Once an MNE moves beyond "plug and play" solutions and is comfortable with RPAs and data wrangling, the new field of AI offers interesting new possibilities and tools in TP digitalization. Relatively few providers have begun to integrate AI capabilities into their TP solutions as AI is still an emerging field.

A common use of AI is in pattern recognition. Patterns are recognized with the help of algorithms used in machine learning. Recognizing patterns is the process of classifying the data based on the model that is created by training data which then detects patterns and characteristics from the patterns. Pattern recognition is the process that can detect different categories and get information about particular data.[20] Here, AI is particularly suited to large standardized data sets. It has already been used for detecting anomalies in customs reporting[21] and thereby enabling corrective action to be taken to optimize customs compliance. Such pattern recognition capability can be deployed for analyzing patterns in intercompany accruals and entries across an MNE group.

One of the successful approaches involves adapting techniques that have been developed elsewhere to taxation. For example, AI used in word searches in West Law, a legal database, have been deployed to make searches more accurate and intuitive in Checkpoint, a search tool for tax, with the accuracy of the search improved by applying machine learning techniques to the millions of search history generated by subscribers. AI has also been used to improve the efficiency of checking and reconciling tax accounting data from the general ledger to those in the tax returns with a high degree of accuracy before a human makes the final judgment as to whether the two fields are correctly matched.[22]

More specific to TP, a tool available in the market integrates TP documentation and CbCR software and combines them with AI capabilities, which allows the tool to not only utilize currently existing information but also touts the ability to learn new information incrementally as soon as such information becomes available.[23] The prospect of a tool being able to tap into all of the existing TP information that is published, being able to understand the information and, from this information, provide the necessary requirements for TP documentation and/or benchmarking for each country in the world is indeed exciting. The provider of this technology expects that, with these enhanced capabilities, they will be able to offer to their users localized documentation that should meet all of the expectations of the local tax authorities. The advantage of such a localized approach would mean reduced exposure to penalties due to non-compliance to specific local rules and fewer disputes. An example of how the AI

20. Available at https://medium.com/edureka/pattern-recognition-5e2d30ab68b9, accessed August 28, 2020.
21. *See* for example, available at https://wts.com/wts.com/insights/uploads/wtsai_flyer.pdf, accessed August 28, 2020.
22. *See* https://tax.thomsonreuters.com/blog/the-impact-of-artificial-intelligence-on-the-tax-and-accounting-profession/, accessed August 28, 2020.
23. Crossborder Solutions, available at https://www.crossborder.ai/person/fiona/, accessed August 28, 2020.

functionality purports to mitigate local risks is the AI algorithm learning what a local tax authority might expect in a benchmarking study, be it a one-year or three-year interquartile range and then conducting the search accordingly. The provider claims that the ability of the AI to learn, adapt, and interface in an interactive manner with the users, enables support and guidance to the companies that is more accurate, and thus is a decisive edge for their tool.

Another dimension that AI can bring is to perform predictive analytics. This can help TP departments gain better control of their operational transfer pricing. For example, if the AI spots certain trends at the transactional level which suggests that the pricing or margins will overshoot or undershoot the intended range, it can trigger an alert so that corrective actions (e.g., change in pricing or true-ups) can be taken earlier.

The implementation considerations are similar to the other documentation and CbCR tools and, consequently, the same considerations outlined above such as whether there is a genuine business case and return on investment and the need to train the staff in using the tool apply as well.

3.2.8 Blockchain

Blockchain is yet another emerging technology with great promise. China has already announced that blockchain is a key technology[24] and, in a recent conference in Hangzhou that WU has organized with the Chinese State Administration for Taxation, various provincial and city tax bureaus are eagerly embracing blockchain with Shenzhen Province leading the way.[25]

In the intercompany context, blockchain, or the trust protocol as it is called, addresses the lack of trust across three aspects that results in the need to engage intermediaries who broker trust by checking, auditing, and verifying the entries made by the company. It is frequently done on a centralized basis and is a great expense for companies.

First, to overcome any concerns of management of shareholder in the diligence of their staff there is the need for an internal audit function that is independent and that reports to the board of directors. Second, there is a lack of trust that books, records, and financial entries are properly and correctly made. This results in the creation of the financial controller role and systems to check and ensure that the financial books are properly kept. That the books are true and fair is policed by an external auditor via annual year-end book closing audits. Third, there is a lack of trust from the tax authorities that transfer pricing is not abused in order to avoid taxes, the outcome of which are risk assessments and audits by the tax inspectors on a regular basis.

24. Available at https://www.cnbc.com/2019/12/16/china-looks-to-become-blockchain-world-leader-with-xi-jinping-backing.html, accessed August 28, 2020.
25. Available at https://www.ledgerinsights.com/china-shenzhen-blockchain-tax-invoices/, accessed August 28, 2020.

Figure 8.1 Loss of Data Resolution and Linkage in Process, Causing Problems When Being Audited

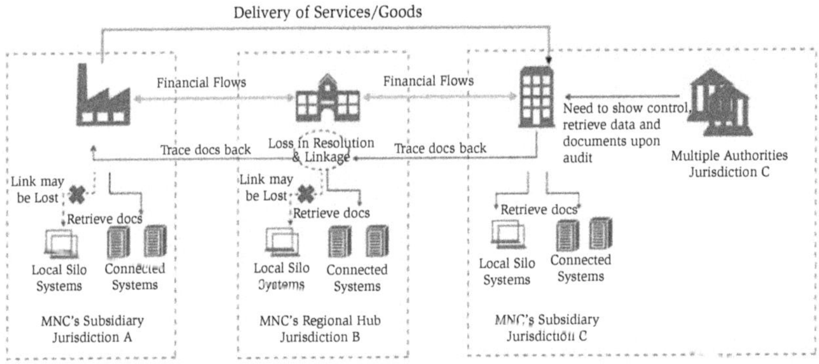

Source: IBM Corporation—IBM research White Paper.

Blockchain offers a solution to address this lack of trust by way of an immutable, distributed ledger. A blockchain is, briefly, a time-stamped series of immutable records of data that are managed by a cluster of computers not owned by any single entity. Each of these blocks of data (i.e., block) is secured and bound to each other using cryptographic codes (i.e., chain).[26]

Blockchain establishes a secure, shared source of truth:

- Data is stored in a ledger with records of every transaction, even errors.
- Participants in the chain exchange information so that each participant has an individual, identical copy of the chain.
- The ledger is updated with the participant's agreement, and information cannot be altered or deleted without the knowledge of the whole network.
- Due to its distributed nature, it does not have a single point of failure unless data that is stored in a central server or processes that rely on and run via a centralized server location.

At this point, there must be a clear distinction between public blockchain and private or permissioned blockchains. Participants can access public blockchains such as Bitcoin or Ethereum and download the data stored on the blockchain. The ledger on these public blockchains is supported and verified without the need for a trusted intermediary through proof-of-work consensus validation. Clearly, intercompany transactions and data are confidential. Therefore, for transfer pricing purposes, private blockchains are used as they permit only known parties to participate (hence "permissioned"). Only such permissioned participants get a copy of the immutable records.

26. IBM Corporation (2017) IBM Research White Paper: Blockchain/DLT: A game-changer in managing MNCs intercompany transactions, New York, available at https://mlaus.org/wp-content/uploads/bp-attachments/7057/IBM_Research_MNC_ICA_Whitepaper16456.pdf, accessed August 28, 2020.

The members can be entities within the same MNE group or even a consortium of different firms as long as they agree on the access rights and the parameters of the blockchain entries.

The key advantage of blockchain over a traditional ERP solution to operational transfer pricing is that it can overcome or mitigate the lack of trust by allowing permissioned access to the chain to external parties such as auditors, tax inspectors, etc. who need to be assured as to the truth. Cryptography, in essence, enables recording of intercompany transactions that are immutable to fraud and establishes a shared truth. The trust that this creates in knowing that records are not falsified or altered subsequently allows such auditors or inspectors to focus on verifying that the process of making intercompany entries is correct rather than spending time in auditing a sample selection of entries as is the usual practice. Auditing intercompany transactions then becomes an exercise in a systems/process audit rather than the conventional sample testing. Audits can become more efficient, and the time and resources saved can be deployed elsewhere both on the part of the taxpayer and the auditor.

A further use of blockchain is for it to link data across various databases and systems. This is particularly advantageous for MNEs with transfer pricing computations that draw from multiple ERP, HR, and other systems across the MNE and consortium type situations in which the systems are not integrated. This linkage also permits the tracing of transactions back to the source. For example, if entity A provides a service that is received by entity B but is billed via entity C, for entity B to trace the transaction back to A in order to, for example, understand the nature of the transaction in order to claim expense deduction, it has to enquire with B. Information may get lost, or the staff handling the recharge in B may no longer be around to verify the data. The records on a blockchain down to each transaction overcome this difficulty.

Figure 8.2 Envision a Future of Connected Networks of Enterprises' Blockchains

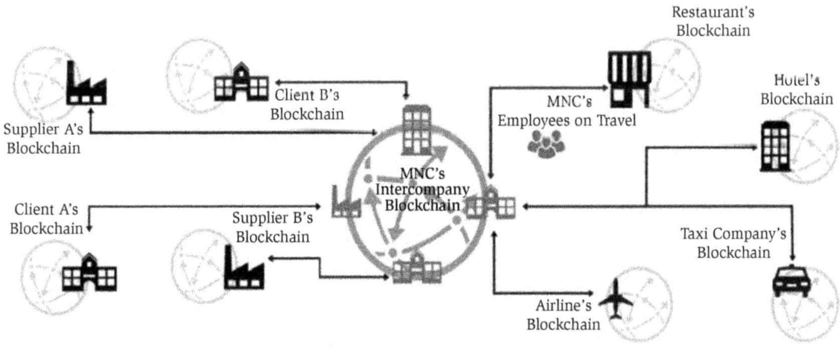

Source: IBM Corporation—IBM research White Paper.

However, there are several caveats to implementing this blockchain solution:

(i) It does not solve the basic issue of incomplete or erroneous data being entered. There still needs to be a robust process and controls to secure off chain transactions and ensure that what is written onto the blockchain is not erroneous in the first place.
(ii) Unfortunately, the immutable nature of the technology cuts both ways; once written, errors are also captured indelibly.
(iii) Blockchain is still an emerging technology and, although there are efforts underway to harmonize standards and platforms, compatibility between different initiatives remains unclear.
(iv) The investment in introducing a whole different type of technology, onboarding and educating users are not trivial, and the return on investment can be long-dated and not always as compelling as, for instance, the alternative of offshoring and outsourcing the work to a cheaper location or provider.
(v) Finally, there are some who predict that quantum computing will be able to break the cryptography, although this is some way off into the future.

For large global corporations, transfer pricing processes are as important as their policies. Processes can be complex, involve multiple functions, and are generally not very automated. Getting the processing of transfer pricing correct is not only an area of focus for tax authorities but also boards of group companies and regulators; it is also an important aspect of the governance agenda. As transfer pricing gets more complex, automation will be a key area of focus but, along with automation, the accuracy, timeliness, and governance around the transfer pricing process become equally important. The use of blockchains can help with transaction booking, verification including audit controls, automation of allocations of expenses across group entities, etc. Equally, solutions that leverage blockchain technology such as digital currencies (private blockchains) may be used to settle transactions instantaneously between group companies once such transactions are verified.

However, blockchain is an emerging technology and, while being more widely explored for a number of areas such as trade settlement by financial institutions, it is likely that it will take some time before it is commonplace in transfer pricing. It may not be effective for companies to implement blockchain solutions for transfer pricing in isolation of other areas of operation, and it needs to be considered as part of the overall technology solution for financial reporting.

4 RESPONSES OF THE SURVEYED COMPANIES

The authors interviewed several heads of tax and TP in companies of different sizes and from different sectors. All interviewees recognized the fact that tax/TP functions need a clear focus and vision on technology, mainly for the simple reason of not being left behind. However, other motivations differ company by company. From the interviewees, the authors find most interest among the small and the very large taxpayer groups in being open to implementing TP technology.

Some taxpayers see the smart use of technology and automatization as a mere survival strategy as the growing reporting and also audit demands mean that the workload would become too much to cope with for the existing resources. This is particularly so for smaller companies that have opted for not outsourcing core TP work. They are attracted not only by the time savings but also by overall process improvement enabled by specific TP tools. In contrast, larger groups are very keen on not only cost savings generated by the tools but also the need to enhance the internal collaboration among their very often geographically and functionally dispersed teams.

Therefore, most of the small and very large companies have embarked on the journey of implementing TP solutions. In most cases, their starting point has been implementing tools related to in-housing benchmarking studies. This area is seen as the ideal testing ground for new tools that could be implemented in a short time frame with relatively low risk of disruption to the TP functions' core processes.

From the interviews, the majority of mid-size companies appear to rely more on currently available solutions and standardized reporting capabilities within the ERP/accounting systems. However this does not mean that these companies are not focused on advancing in technology, but they more often team up with the larger finance/accounting functions in their organizations to actively seek improvements of currently deployed systems and tools.

4.1 Desired Outcomes Versus Limitations and Constraints

Companies considering moving forward with the implementation of TP tools and technology will need to reflect and weigh the desired outcomes and advantages versus eventual constraints and related disadvantages.

4.1.1 Enhance Risk Management: Better Control and Oversight (Dashboards) and Ability to React Quicker (Planning, E.g., Margin Control)

It is a dream of TP professionals to have all of the TP relevant data available at their "finger-tips" in real time from anywhere in the world. Most of the tools that are available on the market aim to bring this dream closer to reality. Tools provide tailored reports and can highlight areas that require special attention via dashboards. This enables the TP department to react in real time and make relevant adjustments to the TP of the company. These include adjusting the pricing to land at the targeted profit margins for a certain business units or transactions.[27] The condensed and simplified data presentation in dashboard views can help tax management make better, educated decisions. The structured workflows embedded in most applications allow assigning tasks to relevant stakeholders and tracking those tasks. An example of this is in monitoring input suppliers and reviewers and tracking due dates thereby helping to enhance the overall risk posture of the company. Such improvements could help to

27. F. Schoeneborn, Price Setting: Why Proactive Intercompany Margin Management Is "Behaving at Arm's Length" and the Preferred Option for Multinational Enterprises, 22 Intl. Transfer Pricing J. 4 (2015), Journals IBFD (accessed March 2, 2020), available at https://research.ibfd.org/#/doc?url=/collections/itpj/html/itpj_2015_04_int_1.html#d17e24, accessed August 28, 2020.

reduce risks on the side of operational transfer pricing and thus strengthen the risk control framework of the company.[28]

4.1.2 *Increase Efficiency and Thus Realize Cost Savings, Automate Routine Activities, and Free Up Resources for Work That Adds More Value*

Automatization of routine tasks by using new technologies can free up resources to concentrate on tasks and analyses, which add higher value. Tools can also be used to generate cost savings and avoid heavy reliance on external tax advisers, such as in the case of in-housing benchmark studies.

However, any productivity improvements and resulting cost savings need to be put into relation to the implementation, recurring license, and maintenance charges.

4.1.3 *Qualitative Constraints to Automation and Skill Constraints*

Transfer pricing is part qualitative and partly quantitative. The economic analysis may appear to be numbers and logic driven and amenable to digitalization. However, there are many variations in the facts, judgment, and ambiguity in the functional analysis, identifying value drivers of the business and choice of methods. In this regard, the template approach seen in some documentation solutions entails the risk of over-simplifying the value-chain Development, Enhancement, Maintenance, Protection, Exploitation analysis.

Some question the ability of off-the-shelf solutions to be able to plug seamlessly into pre-existing ERP systems, with the latter having unique interfaces or proprietary ways of inputting, processing, and presenting data. Finally, there are issues of the appropriate skill sets to look out for when hiring and building a tax team that is digitally capable beyond possessing conventional tax skills and the need for governance, cybersecurity, and data privacy, which further adds to the burden of the chief tax officer.

A potential hurdle in the way to digitalization of a TP department could be the staff itself.[29] New digital tools will require new skills (such as programming bots) but also require an open growth mindset that will allow the team to easily cope with change and adopt new ways of working. Digital upskilling is currently the buzzword, and tax professionals around the world are facing new challenges but equally exciting new opportunities with tax departments going "digital." Management, therefore, is well advised to actively demystify digital workforce transformation and encourage employees to understand the new digital working world including all of the

---

28. C. Plesner Rossing, T.C. Pearson & A. Nesimi, Strategic Control of Transfer Pricing in a BEPS Context, 23 Intl. Transfer Pricing J. 3 (2016), Journals IBFD (accessed March 2, 2020), available at https://research.ibfd.org/#/doc?url=/collections/itpj/html/itpj_2016_03_int_3.html, accessed August 28, 2020.
29. For further aspects of knowledge management for transfer pricing, also *see* C. Plesner Rossing & T.C. Pearson, Transfer Pricing Knowledge Management Systems, 21 Intl. Transfer Pricing J. 4 (2014), Journals IBFD (accessed March 3, 2020), available at https://research.ibfd.org/#/doc?url=/document/itpj_2014_04_int_2, accessed August 28, 2020.

expectations to the new skills that employees should adopt but equally also promote the chances connected to this new way of working.

4.1.4 *Benchmarking Tools: Availability of Data, Necessity for Trained Resources to Operate the Tool and to Validate Results*

Companies considering using benchmarking tools in-house should not underestimate that their staff using the tools will need to have the relevant skills and knowledge to operate them to get meaningful reports. Even though most of the tools have very intuitive user interfaces and guide the users through the steps of the search process, the users still need to have basic understanding of benchmarking searches in order to validate the results provided by the tool.

Most providers, however, offer either intensive training when companies implement their tools or even provide support by their own economists to support the company later on in the case of specific questions or problems.

4.1.5 *Documentation Tools: Functional Analysis, Template Approach Risks Missing Out the Texture and Context When Describing Value Chain*

As mentioned earlier, companies need to pay special attention to the write-up/modules they use for their TP documentation. Simply using out-of-the-box write-up on generic transactions that are not adapted to the companies' actual business entails the risk of misrepresentation and thus putting the TP documentation out of context and making it no longer useable. This is where a need for a seasoned practitioner will be very helpful.

4.1.6 *Implementation Concerns: Stakeholder Buy in, Ease of First Time Set-Up and Compatibility with Existing Systems and Processes (Accounting, ERP)*

At a companywide level, as transformation takes hold and technology evolves in other adjacent functions such as finance or accounting, the tax and TP functions should ideally be part of such change to ensure their requirements are considered and that any specific tax or TP tools are compatible to the overall company's IT environment. However, the reality is that tax is a part of finance and the other priorities of finance such as automating customer or business support tend to rank ahead of those of tax. It is then difficult for tax to get a substantial allocation of budget for its projects. Consequently, the first order of things in any successful digitalization project is to convince and involve the relevant stakeholders. This often means going beyond an individual's comfort zone of taxation and articulating the benefits of the change to senior finance and operations stakeholders such as the CFO, financial controller, and COO. It is even more advantageous if the project can be crafted so as to meet the needs of such stakeholders. For example, the use of blockchain will enhance the assurance of control across the finance processes impacted by TP while the ability to visualize intercompany flows in aggregate using dashboards can yield insights in terms of burn or run rate of expenses that may in turn affect budgeting decisions.

Implementation of TP tools can prove to be tricky especially in the case of lack of attention to the existing system environment. Both the IT provider as well the company implementing a tool should already be closely cooperating in the selection phase to ensure the new tool fits into the existing IT and system infrastructure and that the current accounting systems can be successfully linked up to the new TP tools to ensure that the relevant data can be uploaded. Only if all data is made available to the tools will they be able to play out all of their functionalities. However, such benefits of linking data from different sources into a common pool (what some would term as a "data lake" approach) and interrogating the data with analytics can run into issues of data privacy. This issue involves both comingling individual data such as salaries with other data (salaries are often used as an allocation key in TP) and cross-border transmission of sensitive data (such as where a shared services center performs the analytics). It is imperative that proper controls be instituted to ensure information security.

4.1.6.1 Business or Investment Case

At the end of the day, MNEs need to justify the exercise of digitalization of their TP with cost savings. The hurdle of ensuring a proper return on investment before resources are invested in implementing a tool or solution is good discipline. TP is rarely (perhaps unfortunately) time sensitive or mission critical. Audits will take place years later, and the incremental time and manpower savings from introducing new tools and processes may not be justified if the risks are low or if there are readily available alternatives such as working with existing ERP interfaces/reports or readily available tools such as Microsoft Power BI instead of subscribing to expensive bespoke solutions.

As a result, automation and digitalization projects tend to be successful only when they are backed by the CFO or finance function. The investment case to be made by tax for investing in a digital tool is often further complicated for large companies that have the option of offshoring the work, albeit manually, to a cheaper offshore location—a team of diligent associates wielding Excel in a shared service center location may yet prove to be a more attractive cost proposition than engaging a team of expensive data analysts at headquarters.

5 HOW TAX AUTHORITIES ARE USING TECHNOLOGY

5.1 Building Own Databases Down to Transactional Levels

Tax administrations have several advantages when it comes to digitalization.

First, they have superior access to information both domestically (with the power to requisition information from other government departments and the private sector) and overseas in the form of exchange of information.

Second, by setting the standards and format for e-filing and compliance such as SAF-T or XML, they have the advantage of compelling accounting and tax data to be reported in a manner that is most compatible with the software they are using for analysis.

Third, with a centralized budget, they may be better resourced than any tax department to invest in technology and over a longer term horizon. The Korean Tax Authorities, for example, are into the advanced stages of their "e-Home Tax" system which has evolved for the past decade or two into a formidable integrated system that aims to shift from the conventional returns and post-filing audits to a pre-filing population of returns and pre-screening for avoidance. Information from various sources including financial statements from banks to point of sales information is consolidated and analytics are applied to the data. The result is that the post-filing audit via sampling of data is being replaced. A further instance is where the Australian taxation office has invested in building up its AI and data analytics capability and has applied their machine learning algorithms to over one hundred models based on taxpayer data.

5.2 Using Big Data Analytics to Gain Insights with AI and Pattern Recognition

It is not surprising, then, that a number of tax authorities have already started using data analytics to support the case selection for audits, e.g., the Belgian Tax Authorities run a system that scans the tax returns and, based on certain criteria embedded in it, the tool will then make a first risk assessment of the taxpayer/company. In the case of predefined red flags, the case will then automatically be forwarded to the tax audit division with the request to conduct a field audit. In regard to AI, the same capabilities of AI to recognize patterns may be used by tax auditors to spot irregularities.

The exact criteria defined as red flags are, of course, not published and, therefore, confidential, but it can quite easily be guessed that continuous losses, fluctuating profits, or high royalty payments to a related party could be such indicators that lead to a high-risk classification.

In the Far East, China has been requisitioning data directly from taxpayers, sometimes even accessing taxpayers' accounting systems directly, and building their own database of financial information down to the transactional level and using it to perform their risk analysis and audit target selection. This effort is separate from the CbCR regime.

So far, most of the interviewed companies have not experienced any major challenges from tax authorities based on the CbCR reports filed with their local home country tax authorities. However, there are emerging reports of tax auditors using the information from CbCRs that they obtained via a competent authority's exchange of information. This information combined with data often at the industry level (including secret comparables learnt from other audits), they are constructing an overall perception of the company using the same tools described above to suss out avoidance and raise audits. However, this is not in accordance with OECD recommendation—the

OECD recommends that the CbCR only be used for risk assessment and not as a basis for audit adjustments.[30]

In the future, the trend of increasing use of more data analytics by tax authorities around the world not only for case selection but also for their field audit work is palpable. A close linkage can be expected between different areas of taxation such as indirect taxes, withholding taxes, or even customs for which a lot of data is available to tax authorities. Tax filings or automatic reporting obligations will be used by tax auditors to get a better understanding of the taxpayer transactions. They will be able to piece together a picture of the taxpayer beyond what is represented in the TP documentation and reported tax return results.

6 CONCLUSION AND WHAT THE FUTURE MIGHT BRING

In this age of disruption and digitalization, no company can avoid considering and adapting its IT and technology strategy to the constant changes in the market place and industry. While most of these decisions will focus on the core business segments, the tax/TP functions should also start their tough process about how to get ready for the future and leverage technology.

Increasing efficiency by using state-of-the art tools and automatization has become a top priority agenda item for any head of tax. As technology evolves in other functions such as finance or accounting, the tax and TP functions, in a sense, have no choice but to embrace change. It is also in the TP function's own interest to ensure that their requirements are considered and that any specific tax or TP tools are compatible with the overall company's IT environment.

In line with the increasing focus on operational aspects of taxes—apart from the traditional division of responsibilities by geography and by business lines, an increasing number of MNEs have created senior director or even VP level leadership positions to drive tax automation and transformation in recognition of IT and process competence becoming an essential competence within the tax department. These people would typically work with either the internal IT or external vendors to tailor the systems to provide relevant information needed for TP purposes. TP, being process intensive and extensive in its impact on the financial books by nature, is one of the areas of priority in chief tax officers' digitalization plans. The trend toward centralization after the advent of CbCRs and group-wide value chain analyses after BEPS Action 13 also encourages standardization of data which then facilitates the application of analytics.

30. OECD (2017), *OECD Transfer Pricing Guidelines for Multinational Enterprises and Tax Administrations 2017*, OECD Publishing, Paris, available at https://doi.org/10.1787/tpg-2017-en. C.3 5.25 M. Lagarden, Behavioural Transfer Pricing: Towards Enhanced Transparency and Compliance?!, 26 Intl. Transfer Pricing J. 3 (2019), Journals IBFD (accessed March 3, 2020), available at https://research.ibfd.org/#/doc?url=/document/itpj_2019_03_int_3 S.B. Huibregtse, P. Ottoni & S.C. Muñoz Rodríguez, How Technology Is Changing Taxation in Latin America, 73 Bull. Intl. Taxn. 3 (2019), Journals IBFD (accessed March 2, 2020), available at https://research.ibfd.org/#/doc?url=/collections/bit/html/bit_2019_03_o2_2.html#d17e205, accessed August 28, 2020.

Our survey shows that there is no one-size-fits-all approach or solution to digitalization of the TP function. The approach varies by company and their unique circumstances, needs, and resources. While technology can potentially be adapted, companies need to carefully consider their approach and then act accordingly. Implementation of technology tools appears to be easier and most efficient for rather small tax departments with a limited scope of countries that need to be supported. They seem to gain the most in terms of efficiency, control, and cost management. They are driven to automation by the sheer necessity to cope with their vastly increased daily compliance and operational TP workload.

Large MNEs, on the other hand, are also eager to adopt digital solutions. For them, the compelling proposition is often better control over a complex web of TP processes and entries across many entities around the globe. They possibly have larger budgets, a longer term horizon to invest, and better access to solution providers who are keen to market to them, often even offering pilot projects as proof that their solutions work with well-known global taxpayers. However, the size of global MNEs also increases the complexities of implementation, particularly when reporting lines cross and when ERP systems are not linked to one another.

For the companies "in between," the small enterprises and the large ones, however, the picture is not as clear. While the benefits of deploying technology appears attractive, for many, more synergies can be achieved through improvement of existing tools and closer cooperation with accounting and finance functions to ensure TP requirements are addressed in the IT agenda of these functions rather than embarking on separate TP projects. Furthermore, the dilemma for such companies increases if they are looking for an exit strategy by getting acquired. The motivation to go "all in" on technology for TP is lesser in such companies.

Regardless of the size of companies, however, the most successful digital transformation projects are commonly those that are supported by the CFO and finance and those that invest in training and education in order to realize the full benefits of the technologies that are deployed.

Just as the tax departments of MNEs are embracing or perhaps being swept along by the strong current of digitalization, tax authorities are also rapidly building up their own data analytics capabilities leveraging of the flood of new information through the exchange of CbCRs and other TP information as well as joint audits with other jurisdictions.

As AI becomes more widely used in audit selection or even to raise assessments, a whole new dimension arises as to the ethical use of AI. Digitalization offers vast new opportunities to capture, store, process, and extract insights from data using AI and big data techniques. The challenge in this new era of cross-linking multiple data sources, exchange of information across borders, and ever great transparency means taxpayers' rights, data privacy, security, and other issues come to the fore as challenges facing tax administrators. Further, does the audit target selection require human judgment to be made so that there is proper due process as a purely machine determined audit may be open to challenge under administrative law?

The Holy Grail in the future perhaps lies in technology enabling the combination of TP, indirect tax, and customs along with treasury and capital/exchange control compliance in a way that is verifiable and that increases trust.[31] Technology will then really advance the concept of cooperative compliance wherein the trust is in the system's architecture and tools to execute intercompany entries accurately. The role of the TP team and auditor then becomes one of designing the correct algorithmic programs and rules and verifying systems with the former explaining how the technology works rather than the traditional adversarial audit relationship in which auditors are suspicious that information is hidden from them and perform random sampling and raids.

31. Idea first discussed in "Blockchain, Transfer Pricing, Customs Valuations, and Indirect Taxes: Transforming the Global Tax Environment" by Sam Sim, Jeffrey Owens, Raffaele Petruzzi, Romero J.S. Tavares, and Clement Migai, Bloomberg BNA Transfer Pricing Report 2017.

APPENDIX: THREE CASE STUDIES

Case Study 1—Central Automation of Operational Transfer Pricing

A multinational group with more than EUR 20 billion in turnover and presence in more than one hundred countries had a very manual process of making transfer pricing year-end adjustments. It had over six hundred adjustments including true-ups for its subsidiaries worldwide to make in a typical year-end and was dealing with drawing data from multiple ERP systems across the group. The result was not only a high-pressure rush to complete passing all of the entries before the books closed but there were material "misses" that resulted in entries not passed and transfer prices/margins not being at arm's length. Worse still, for smaller subsidiaries in the group, if such transfer pricing adjustments are material, it can affect the true and fair nature of their statutory accounts.

The headquarters team conducted a structured selection process of service providers and eventually settled upon a solution provider that did not just sell off-the-shelf software tools but also had transfer pricing trained personnel who could work together with the group to implement the systems changes.

The consulting team started by first agreeing with the client the desired outcome and spending time understanding the ERP, the data, and transfer pricing accounting process. Together with the client, they identified areas of risk and improvements. Some were process deficiencies that required a process streamlining rather than a technological fix.

When it came to implementation, they first attacked the data by centralizing and automating, where possible, the collection and validation of system and non-system sourced data to enable fast and detailed access to transfer pricing information. Next, the combined team looked into the possibilities of leveraging off the existing ERP system and found that the pre-existing functionalities could create automated reports using a flexible set of data rules that enabled ongoing review and analyses of intercompany entries. What was required was a change in the current finance processes. This obviated the need to procure and install new systems though it meant that not all of the desired functionalities when the project first started could be achieved using the current ERP system.

Although the project took a year to implement, it took the new processes some time to stabilize, cost the group a significant amount of consulting fees, and the benefits were significant. These included less volatility in effective tax rates, lesser risks from a finance controls perspective, and fewer unanticipated year-end adjustments.

Lessons Learnt:

The efficiency promises, i.e., valuable tax staff spending less time on manual tasks and more time on value-added activities, did not materialize at least in the first two years of the project. In fact, it required more man-hours to keep both the current process going and transition and continued commitment to train stakeholders in the new system and processes.

Going Forward:

The group is considering robotics process automation in which tasks are repetitive and also to deal with the issues of high turnover in their shared services center staff.

Case Study 2—Experience of a Small Enterprise

P group is a small MNE operating in eight countries. It is below the country-by-country threshold as it has a turnover of less than EUR 750 million. There is one manager in charge of transfer pricing. This limits the ability of this manager to implement complex processes or systems. The manager's main focus is on compliance and planning.

P group chose to use a new solution from a mid-sized TP solutions provider. The tool claims to offer AI capabilities and is hosted on the Cloud, making it scalable. The tool further enables integration of benchmarking search and modules for TP documentation. The tool also does benchmarking which is then reviewed by experts at the solution provider. P needs to upload the existing benchmarking, in particular, the screening criteria, and then also the related entities' list and their profiles. The tool then automatically starts the searches. The tool can pull the public results of the company and then perform real-time analytics against the benchmarking results.

Considerations:

P group has a limited budget; however, the annual cost of the tool per country makes it affordable and flexible. The motivation for adopting the tool was to save costs and increase flexibility compared to the previous practice of outsourcing the benchmarking to advisers. The tool permits more searches to be run on an ad hoc, on demand basis without additional costs.

For a one-person TP function, the tool usefully provides a dashboard view and facilitates workflow and documentation retention. Time savings is expected from the tool as less time is spent on coordination with external advisers. There are further time savings from reducing the time spent on reviewing of comparables.

Implementation:

The expected time for full integration of the new tool is around three months. The first two months involve intensive onboarding, setting up company profiles, and uploading existing TP documentation and benchmark studies. Thus far, the project scope is limited to TP documentation. There is no integration planned for indirect tax systems. In the future, P group expects to continue to work with the accounting functions to improve accounting systems and also to introduce TP requirements there.

Case Study 3—Mid-Sized MNEs

Q group having revenue of between EUR 3 and EUR 4 billion is thus subject to CbCR and a headcount of between 10,000 and 20,000 persons with operations in fifty countries.

The tax team is small between four to eight persons, and one person is dedicated to transfer pricing.

Benchmarking is outsourced to one of the Big4 due to concerns around quality and acceptance by tax authorities. Local studies are performed in certain jurisdictions such as BRIC countries. In general, due to cost pressures, investments in systems and tools are challenging. Moreover, the headcount constraints do not permit time and resources to do training or onboard new tools.

SAP is the main ERP system. The tax function is a key stakeholder in SAP Hana implementation, which is owned by the financial controller function. Standard SAP reports are generated that allow continuous control of margins and managing the actual versus target margins of the sales subsidiaries. The expectation is that the greater functionality of SAP Hana will provide better availability of data and, therefore, allow better control of margins on a more real-time basis.

TP documentation preparation remains largely manual and is done in-house using a standard Microsoft software supported by a shared services team in an emerging market jurisdiction.

Considerations

Q group examined various TP offerings and solutions on the market but decided against adopting them. The issue was that the significant efforts needed to implement and maintain these solutions appeared to outweigh the perceived benefits. There were also security concerns around how and where data is hosted in the Cloud. There is also ongoing investment needed to first clean up data, including historical ones, before uploading it into any new tool and ensuring that the data in accounting systems and any such TP tool is reconciled or reconcilable. The approach for now is to leverage pre-existing SAP functionalities or "off-the-shelf" software such as Microsoft PowerBI[32] for visualizing data rather than adopt a potentially more complex bespoke TP solution.

32. Power BI is a business analytics service by Microsoft. It aims to provide interactive visualizations and business intelligence capabilities with an interface simple enough for end users to create their own reports and dashboards.

Index

www.ingramcontent.com/pod-product-compliance
Ingram Content Group UK Ltd.
Pitfield, Milton Keynes, MK11 3LW, UK
UKHW020805290926
15470UKWH00003B/973

9 789403 523927